two meatballs
in the italian kitchen

two meatballs
in the italian kitchen

PINO LUONGO AND
MARK STRAUSMAN

ARTISAN

Published by Artisan
A Division of Workman Publishing Company, Inc.
225 Varick Street
New York, NY 10014-4381
www.artisanbooks.com
_____
Library of Congress Cataloging-in-Publication Data
Luongo, Pino.
Two meatballs in the Italian kitchen/Pino Luongo and
Mark Strausman
p. cm.
Includes index.
ISBN-13: 978-1-57965-345-3
1. Cookery, Italian. I. Strausman, Mark. II. Title
TX723.L833 2007
641.5945—dc22
2006102501
_____
Design by Jan Derevjanik
Printed in China
First printing, September 2007
10 9 8 7 6 5 4 3 2

To my mother. What I learned from you as a young teenager counted more than the many years of school and university. I am ashamed for having realized this only now that I am an adult. *"Mamma, più tempo passa e più mi rendo conto di essere stato un figlio fortunato ad avere te come madre." Grazie.*

—P.L.

To my mother. Your sacrifice and hard work after Dad passed away enabled me to be the chef I am today.

—M.S.

contents

Introduction 8

1 · Stand-Alone Soups 15

2 · The Great Meatball Debate 35

3 · Dried Pasta and the Unification of the Two Meatballs 63

4 · Fresh Pasta Like Mama Used to Make: Essential Techniques
and Well-Matched Sauces 87

5 · Risotto and Farrotto 131

6 · Two Meatballs Go Fishing 149

7 · Meat and Poultry: Rustic Oven Cooking 181

8 · Cucina al Fresco: Grilling Italian-Style 201

9 · The Twenty-First Region of Italy: Italian-American Cooking 221

10 · Sunday Means Dinner 243

11 · The Two Meatballs Go Veggie 263

12 · Dessert at Last 287

The Pantry 302
Resources 306
Acknowledgments 309
Index 310

introduction

Who are the two meatballs? One of us is a native New Yorker, a nice boy from Queens with a culinary school degree and years of experience in some of Europe's best hotel restaurants. The other is an Italian immigrant, a former actor who learned to cook by watching and helping his mother in a typical Tuscan home kitchen in the 1950s. Our backgrounds and training could not be more different. One of us likes to play with rustic Italian dishes such as pumpkin ravioli, filling the pasta with pureed baby carrots for a dish with the same vibrant color and a fresh new flavor, and to rethink Italian-American favorites like lobster fra diavolo by way of bouillabaisse and sauce américaine. The other is so grounded in Tuscan traditions that he finds it inconceivable to cook with cilantro.

Putting the two of us together in the kitchen may sound like a recipe for disaster. And it is true that during the twenty-plus years we've known each other and worked together, we've argued constantly about the right way to make everything from pot roast to eggplant parmigiana to meatballs, of course. But through it all, we've actually grown closer, bonded by our shared philosophy that the simplest food is the best, and our shared desire to please our families, friends, and loyal customers with food that will make them happy.

Our unusual friendship, with all of its conflict, is the basis for this book. By setting down our best recipes for simple dishes, along with our arguments for why we think they're the best, we defend our often divergent styles. We'll never agree on the best method for making risotto, the best chicken broth to put into bean soups, the merits of fresh versus canned tuna, or whether meatballs should be fried in olive oil or simmered in tomato sauce. But our shared passion for unpretentious food that is timelessly pleasing always unites us in the end.

We are two guys who love to go to the market, take in the possibilities, make our choices, and then go home and cook dinner. This book isn't for armchair cooks, but for people like us, people who find comfort and pleasure in shopping for and preparing food. Our story often splits into separate voices. Take our two points of view, and use them in ways that make sense in your own kitchen.

the history of the two meatballs

pino I arrived in New York in October of 1980. I came here so I couldn't be forced to serve in the military while my lawyers argued in court for my status as a conscientious objector. I thought I'd be staying for less than six months. To support myself while I was living with an American girlfriend I'd met in Rome, I went out looking for a job. Possibilities were limited, since I spoke little English, but finally I was hired as a busboy at an Italian restaurant.

It was a lonely time for me. I had been an actor in Italy, and a real talker. Now I had so much trouble communicating with people in this new language. Food became the medium through which I could approach people and connect with them. It was my salvation, really, knowing something about Italian cooking. The restaurant was a filmmakers' hangout, and I got to meet some of my idols—Robert DeNiro, John Cassavetes, Michael Cimino—and, after two months, I was managing the restaurant.

Six months turned into two years as my case dragged on in Italy. Meanwhile, my English improved and I started to have ideas about opening a restaurant of my own, where I could offer my food and style of cooking at last.

When my lawyers finally called to say my case had been dismissed and I could come home, I didn't know what to do. I walked from Greenwich Village to my apartment on the Upper East Side. The ground floor of my building was occupied by a Ray Bari's Pizza, and the entire building was painted the colors of the Italian flag. I lived upstairs, in the red stripe. I finally felt at home in New York. I decided to stay. Less than two months later, I opened Il Cantinori, the city's first Tuscan restaurant, where I was the chef/restaurateur.

mark I grew up in a working-class neighborhood in Queens of Eastern European and Italian immigrants. The Jewish specialties my mother and grandmother made, the matzo ball soup, the brisket, the latkes, I took those for granted. But I really became curious about cooking when I saw what the neighbors were making: baked ziti from the lady down the hall, fried calamari at Angelo's Restaurant on Queens Boulevard, sausage and peppers at an Italian street fair in the summer.

While you were busing tables in New York, I graduated from the New York City Hotel and Restaurant School in Brooklyn and then headed to an internship at the Hotel Hessicher Hof in Frankfurt, Germany. I too got sidetracked. I was supposed to be there for three months but wound up spending the next two years there and at hotel kitchens in Amsterdam and Montreux. The chefs were incredibly skilled and meticulous. I learned all of the important classical techniques for making sauces and stocks and for preparing all kinds of meat and vegetables. In Switzerland, I wound up hanging out with a lot of Italian cooks, and that's where I got interested in the more casual kind of cooking they did for the staff and in their off hours, the pasta with tomato sauce, maybe a little leftover ham or stewed rabbit or sausage, a handful of herbs. They weren't quite the same dishes I had eaten in Flushing, but the clean, simple flavors reminded me of home and why I had gone to cooking school in the first place. When I got back to New York, I was tired of formality, and I wanted to make the kind of food that I really liked to eat, the pastas my Italian friends were making, and the grilled meats and wonderful vegetables that I had eaten in trattorias on many weekend trips across the Alps.

pino But there were no trattorias in New York. When I opened Il Cantinori in 1983, there were only two types of Italian restaurants here. There were the places with the red-checkered tablecloths that served spaghetti and meatballs and veal piccata and there were the very fancy fine-dining establishments, like Giambelli, Roma di Notte, and a string of others on East 58th Street, the Italian Restaurant Row. They served continental dishes you could get at hotels in Rome catering to American tourists—veal scaloppine, pasta primavera, veal chops. At Il Cantinori, in contrast, I was serving food that you could find at homes and trattorias throughout Tuscany—ribollita, pasta with chicken livers, bistecca fiorentina. It was my mother's food, but to New Yorkers it was exotic.

mark We were introduced by the butcher Mark Sarazin, who was a matchmaker for chefs and restaurateurs in 1988. When you wanted a job, you'd go see him. He told me there was this guy, Pino Luongo, an Italian. He was kind of difficult, but was doing something unusual downtown. . . .

pino It's hard to believe now, but Americans were so unfamiliar with regional Italian cooking that a lot of them would come into Il Cantinori, having misread "Tuscan" as "Tucson," and think that it was a Southwestern restaurant!

Italian chefs working in New York at the time were not open to the concept of simple, authentic Tuscan food. They were stuck in this old-fashioned idea of fine dining. So I thought maybe a young European-trained American chef would be a better fit. Someone forward-thinking, who was willing to work hard, harder than any Italian, to re-create the food I remembered from home.

mark The timing was right. Nouvelle cuisine, with its fussy presentation, was on its way out. Our first big project together was Sapore di Mare, a seafood restaurant in the Hamptons with a menu of simply prepared Mediterranean-style dishes: fresh fish with olive oil, lemon, herbs, tomatoes. Sophisticated diners immediately embraced what was very simple, country food served in a stylish setting.

I had always preferred rustic food. I'm not a formal guy. So I loved working on that menu, using all of my experience to cook to my personal taste. I had cooked fish in parchment in Switzerland, it's a classical technique, but at Sapore di Mare I was able to use the Italian ingredients I loved and present the dish to the customers in an informal but elegant way.

pino You learned a few new things in that kitchen—how to make fresh pasta like a true Italian, for one.

mark From an unlikely teacher—a seventy-year-old Italian grandmother you had hired to help out in the kitchen, Maria Fillabozzi. But it was great. When I stop learning, that's when I'll stop cooking.

pino The idea with all of my restaurants was to make food that a real Italian *mamma* would make. So I thought, why not hire real Italian mothers? You can't get more authentic than that. But it was a little *too* authentic for you!

mark Tuscan food isn't what I was brought up with, and I wanted to cook a broader menu based on my own background. I opened my restaurant, Campagna, so I could reinterpret the country cooking I had loved in Italy, unbound by region or inhibition. And I wanted to reinterpret some of the classic Italian-American dishes I had as a kid in Queens, informed by my training in Europe. At Campagna, I developed my recipes for lasagne, *frutti di mare,* spaghetti and meatballs, and the rest.

pino Then you brought those recipes with you when you rejoined me at Coco Pazzo. At Coco Pazzo, you continue with your uninhibited Italian country cooking. A few blocks away at Centolire, I rule the menu with my Tuscan sense of restraint. And everybody's happy.

two meatballs: the book

Early in our collaboration, we were ahead of so many trends. Il Cantinori was the first authentic regional Italian restaurant in New York, Coco Pazzo served food family-style at communal tables before anyone else, Campagna's lasagne and spaghetti with meatballs predated the craze for old-fashioned Italian-American dishes. Now, among the newer restaurants in the city serving every kind of fusion cuisine, we are old-timers. But for us, it was never about being trendy. We continue to do what we do, secure because the philosophy behind our food—shop wisely, cook simply—will always be relevant.

A lot of people want to eat this way. We know, because they come to our restaurants every night. But our customers also tell us that they want to eat our food at home. And the fact is, our food is easier to prepare at home than most restaurant food, because it is based on principles of good home cooking. A few years ago, we each decided to write a book that would help Americans cook simple Italian food, and we immediately began to argue about whose book would be better.

pino My recipes represent hundreds of years of inherited tradition and knowledge. Everything my mother taught me and everything I absorbed growing up in Tuscany and traveling throughout the country as a young man can be found in my food. When you cook my food, you are cooking the real thing.

mark I'm an American who cooks Italian food, and I don't think authenticity is necessarily what Americans want. They want to know

the rules, sure, but then they want to know they can break them. That's what I offer. Pino, you only use two herbs on fish—rosemary and sage. But I like to put thyme or oregano on my fillets sometimes.

pino But that won't taste as good! Certain herbs are meant to be used in certain ways.

mark According to Tuscans. But millions of people living in France and Greece and a lot of other places would disagree. I have adopted the Italian style of straightforward cooking, but I'm not afraid to put lobster together with tomato sauce, like you are. I've done it, and the world has not come to an end.

pino You talk as though I can't deviate from the recipes my mother made, but that is not true. I am constantly challenging my palate, coming up with new dishes. But these new dishes are elaborations on a theme, and perfectly in balance, and that's why they work. Take the classic dish of spaghetti with garlic, oil, and hot red pepper flakes. One summer at Sapore di Mare, I wanted to make this dish, but with a touch of acidity, which is nice in warm weather, so I added just a splash of chopped fresh tomato. This is something you wouldn't see in Italy, but it is Italian because it remains true to Italian principles. The tomato was cut small enough so it made sense with the long, thin pasta shape. I didn't put so much tomato in that it became spaghetti and tomato sauce. The dish was still essentially *aglio e olio,* but with some color and a bright new flavor.

mark The changes I make are also informed by my knowledge and experience. I make a "Tuscan" pot roast, but instead of using eye round, as you do, I use brisket, which is the cut I grew up with and prefer for its flavor and tenderness. Brisket braised with tomatoes and rosemary acknowledges who I am—a Jewish boy from Queens who fell in love with Italian food. I'm not awkwardly trying to fuse two different cuisines. It is utterly natural, because I understand what the Eastern European peasant cooking of my grandparents has in common with Italian home cooking, and why I'm attracted to both styles.

Finally, instead of competing, we decided to write a book together, and call it *Two Meatballs in the Italian Kitchen* after ourselves. In it you'll see how an Italian cooks in America, and how an American cooks Italian, and you can decide for yourself who knows meatballs (and soup, pasta, risotto, fish, and everything else) best.

how to use this book

This book was not designed for the coffee table or nightstand. Use it in the kitchen to feed your family every day of the week. Choose recipes from several different chapters and make them in rotation. There's nothing wrong with eating chicken every Tuesday and pasta every Wednesday. Our mothers both cooked according to this kind of schedule, and it was an anchor for us as we grew up. Children develop a sense of security and even anticipation when they know what they'll be eating on a certain night of the week. (Remember "Wednesday Is Prince Spaghetti Day"?) There are other advantages. Shopping is easier, because you don't have to come up with a dinner idea as you pull into the supermarket parking lot at 5:30 on your way home from work. Cooking this way also allows you to develop your skills with a particular dish or ingredient. The first time you make gnocchi it may take you a while and your dumplings might not be uniformly shaped, but make them every Monday for a year and you will become an expert. This is the way Italian cooks learn, not in a classroom, but at home, through practice.

This isn't to say that you should cook the same seven dishes all year round. One of the wonderful things about Italian home cooking is how it changes with the seasons. If you make soup every Sunday, that may mean Worker's Farmhouse Soup in the fall, Lentil and Sausage Soup in February, and Carrot-Orange Soup in the spring. There is an elemental pleasure to eating this way. Once you begin cooking with the seasons, you will be satisfying cravings that you may not even have been aware of before. There are health benefits to eating this way as well. Thinking about the seasons as you shop will naturally lead to eating a greater variety of vegetables and fruits as they become available throughout the year.

In Italy, where frugality is often a spur to the creative cook, making something new and delicious from leftovers has been elevated almost to an art. Restaurant cooks, concerned with the bottom line, likewise think about ways to use leftovers in an appealing way instead of tossing them in the trash. Throughout this book, we show you how we use leftovers creatively, filling ravioli with yesterday's ribollita or making pasta sauce with yesterday's pot roast. Use your imagination to make sandwiches, omelets, risotto, and other dishes with the good food from the night before, and you will experience the satisfaction that comes from stretching one meal into two.

There is nothing we like better than to spend time in the kitchen with friends and family, so we have also included some of our favorite recipes for weekend cooking and special occasions. One of us may serve Braised Lamb and Artichokes with Oven-Roasted New Potatoes and Spring Onions for Easter while the other chooses Braised Lamb Shoulder for Passover, but the message is the same. These seasonal dishes, cooked with care, are a show of hospitality and a celebration of our good fortune in sitting down at the table with people we love.

1

stand~alone soups

There's an American tradition, now dying but well remembered by diners of a certain age, of soup as an appetizer. If you've ever heard a waiter ask, "Would you like soup or salad with that?" you know what we mean. But to both of us, a native Italian and a chef trained in Europe, soup is much more than an accompaniment or a freebie that you get when you order a steak. We take it seriously and, to prove it, we often make soup the center of a meal.

This chapter gathers together our favorite recipes for stand-alone soups, one-pot meals that satisfy the stomach and feed the soul. In most cases they're kind to the pocketbook, made with inexpensive ingredients like vegetables, dried beans, and even stale bread. Just because they're economical, though, doesn't mean they're not impressive. Serve them every day, but don't hesitate to make them for special occasions. A big pot of soup brought from the stove to the table makes a wonderful centerpiece for an informal dinner party or family gathering. With good bread and wine and these memorable soups, everyone will be satisfied.

pino So many times during my childhood, I'd try to refuse my mother's soup. I'd much rather be eating pasta. But there's an old expression she'd use, *"Mangia la minestra, o salta la finestra* (Eat the soup, or jump out the window)," so I'd have to eat it before she'd let me eat anything else. My mother made phenomenal soup, but I didn't know it then.

I'm a great believer in taste memory. Although I thought I wasn't enjoying her cooking, I had filed away memories of her soups that I rediscovered years later when I was on my own in Rome, broke, and believed all I could afford was a cappuccino and a roll. But when I started to wander around the food markets, I found that for the same price I could buy a few vegetables. I brought them home, added water and herbs, and those memories came flooding back. I was only a beginner, but my soups were good enough for me to remember the greatness of my mother's cooking. And from then on, I strove to create soups as nourishing and soul-satisfying as hers.

mark When I worked in Europe, I was mostly in the north, and the weather was cold and wet. Everyone ate soup. The chef I worked with in Germany had the greatest respect for soup. It was almost a religious experience for him. The ingredients were chosen so carefully—you didn't just throw things into a pot of water. "The soup pot is not a garbage can," he would say. The vegetables had to be fresh, the flavors harmonious. When I do a soup, I don't want anyone asking me what it is. If I make asparagus soup, it has to taste like asparagus. Because of my training, no "mystery" soup comes out of my kitchen.

That chef in Germany taught me that stock is the basis of any good soup. My chicken soup is so rich because I cook the chicken bones for the stock for four to six hours. And I use that same stock in almost all of my soups, to give them the same rich base. Then I build from there. The main-dish soups in this chapter all begin with stock, but it is also one of the building blocks for every other kind of soup, from the most refined consommés, cream soups, and pureed vegetable soups to the chunkiest, meatiest peasant-style soups. That's my training. In the five-star hotel kitchens I worked in, there would be eight or nine soups on the menu every day, all different but all beginning with the same high-quality stock.

pino Of course, for the Jewish boy from Queens, every soup is chicken soup. Tuscans, on the other hand, prefer to use water so the flavors of the beans that we love, along with our fresh vegetables, come through. The only soup I would even consider using chicken stock in is one that contains meat—like Neapolitan Marriage Soup.

mark Only a Tuscan would say something so ridiculous. You just can't get a soup with body and flavor if you don't start with stock. Sure, it takes some time, but it couldn't be easier. Basically, you put a couple of chickens in a pot, fill it with water, and cook for a few hours. And if you are in a hurry, College Inn and other companies make organic chicken broth that will help you achieve a complexity in your soup that water won't give you.

pino For me, the starch from bread stirred into ribollita, for example, adds enough body. And beans give soups a wonderful body without heaviness. In Tuscany, there are more varieties of beans than there are people. There's an economical simplicity to Tuscan soups. If I added chicken stock, I would only be able to taste the chicken.

mark I don't know, Pino, eating so many beans, and sticking so close to one style of cooking, has closed your mind.

pino I like what I grew up with, and I'm not going to apologize for it. Why would I look farther afield? There are so many wonderful Tuscan choices for every season. Soup is the most seasonal dish there is. That's why ribollita is an

October dish—that's when the fall vegetables are at the market. After that come the beans. . . .

mark People tend to forget about soup in the spring and summer, and that's too bad. Just because cold-weather soups were the first ones I learned doesn't mean I serve them year round. My Carrot-Orange Soup is vibrant, great in the spring when you want something on the lighter side. And hearty soups can be just as good in summer as in winter—Worker's Farmhouse Soup is a chunky chicken soup made with vegetables harvested in the late summer and early fall: zucchini, broccoli, cauliflower, Swiss chard. You could shop for almost all of the ingredients at the farm stand.

pino Finally, a point of agreement. Here or in Italy, I love to shop for soup ingredients at a farmers' market.

mark That reminds me of one last thing—these soups, both yours and mine, are healthy main dishes. Full of vegetables, beans, and just a little meat. There's not a cream soup in sight. They're traditional recipes, but they are in sync with my taste for wholesome, lower-fat foods.

The recipes in this chapter are a sampling of some of the most interesting Tuscan soups we have encountered—a Farro and Bean Soup that is a delicious variation on pasta fagioli; Mushroom Soup from Maremma that is transformed into a one-dish meal when poured over a slice of toasted bread and a farm-fresh egg yolk; a soup from Garfagnana that weds Tuscany's beloved beans with another product of the fall harvest, apples. But we go well beyond Tuscany in search of satisfying soups. There is a recipe here for an Italian version of pot-au-feu (Worker's Farmhouse Soup) and one from New York City (Estelle's Chicken Soup) that are also satisfying enough to stand alone.

farro and bean soup lucca-style

FARRO E FAGIOLI ALLA LUCCHESE

mark · In 1988, I worked as a chef at Sapore di Mare in East Hampton, where I first met Pino. East Hampton is a summer resort, which meant we workers vacationed in the colder months, so my fiancée and I planned a winter wedding followed by a six-week honeymoon in Italy. We spent most of it in Tuscany, where the winter can be damp and chilly, perfect soup weather. Passing through the northern Tuscan town of Lucca, we feasted on this hearty soup, a Tuscan version of pasta fagioli. In this region, they use farro, a type of wheat, instead of pasta to thicken bean soups. And it does a much better job—pasta doesn't release starch into the soup the way farro does. I also like farro's whole-grain flavor and texture, which contrast nicely with the creamy beans. · MAKES ABOUT 5½ QUARTS (5 LITERS)

2 pounds (908 grams) fresh cranberry beans, shelled, or 1 pound (3 cups/454 grams) dried navy beans, picked over

2 tablespoons (30 ml) extra-virgin olive oil

3 slices smoked bacon, minced, or 4 ounces (114 grams) pancetta or guanciale, minced

1 large red onion, diced

2 garlic cloves, thinly sliced

½ cup farro (100 grams)

2 large fresh rosemary sprigs, leaves chopped (2 tablespoons)

1 bay leaf

4 quarts (3.8 liters) Chicken Stock (page 29) or 3 quarts (2.8 liters) canned low-sodium organic chicken broth plus 4 cups (960 ml) water

2 cups (480 ml) canned crushed Italian plum tomatoes, preferably San Marzano

1 teaspoon crushed red pepper flakes

Kosher salt

¼ cup (1 ounce/28 grams) freshly grated Parmigiano-Reggiano cheese

Tuscan extra-virgin olive oil, for drizzling

IF USING DRIED BEANS, place them in a large pot and cover with water. Let soak at room temperature for at least 3 hours, or up to 12 hours. Drain and rinse well. Set aside.

Place a heavy-bottomed 6- to 8-quart stockpot over medium heat, and when it is hot, add the olive oil. Add the bacon and cook until it is just beginning to crisp and has rendered all its fat, about 5 minutes. Add the onion and garlic and sauté until soft and golden, 5 to 7 minutes. Add the farro and beans and, using a wooden spoon, stir until they are well combined with the onion, about 1 minute. Add the rosemary, bay leaf, chicken stock, and tomatoes and bring to a gentle boil. Reduce the heat to low and simmer until the beans are very soft and have split open, 1¼ hours for fresh, about 2½ hours for dried. Add the red pepper flakes and salt to taste.

To serve, ladle into bowls, sprinkle with the grated Parmigiano-Reggiano, and drizzle with extra-virgin olive oil.

tip: When fresh cranberry beans are in season in the fall, I use them, because they add thickness and flavor that is lost in the drying process. A timesaving bonus: You don't have to soak them.

wine: I like a Merlot here, or any lighter style of red wine that won't overpower the soup.

jerusalem artichoke soup with cumin

MINESTRA DI TOPINAMBUR CON IL CUMINO

pino • Jerusalem artichokes, also known as sunchokes, are not artichokes at all, but tubers. They have the yellowish color of the Yukon Gold potato, but a sweeter, nuttier flavor than a potato. Sage leaves cooked along with the artichokes bring a floral note to the soup, and cumin imparts an aromatic earthiness.

The farmers at the weekly produce markets in the small villages around the Tuscan countryside used to advertise them as poor man's artichokes, *carciofi poveri*. Their low price appealed to my mother, who bought them whenever they were available, from the late summer all the way into the winter, to make this surprisingly rich-tasting soup. I remember that she could never remember or pronounce *topinambur*, so she would call them *topini* (little mice). Whenever I make this soup, I think of how my brother and sister and I would giggle about that as we ate our dinner. • MAKES ABOUT 8 CUPS (1.9 LITERS)

2 tablespoons (30 ml) extra-virgin olive oil, plus more for drizzling

1 tablespoon (28 grams) unsalted butter

4 medium scallions, white and green parts, finely chopped

2 pounds (908 grams) sunchokes, peeled and cut into ¼-inch-thick (0.6-cm) slices

2 cups (480 ml) vegetable stock or broth made from Knorr powdered bouillon, warmed

¼ teaspoon ground cumin

10 fresh sage leaves

Kosher salt and freshly ground black pepper

1 cup (240 ml) whole milk

¼ cup (30 grams) diced pancetta or bacon, sautéed until crisp and drained (optional)

PLACE A 5- TO 6-QUART POT over medium heat, and when it is hot, add the olive oil and butter. Add the scallions and cook until softened and translucent, 3 to 4 minutes. Add the sunchokes and cook, stirring to coat them in the oil and butter, about 1 minute.

Add the stock, cumin, sage leaves, and salt and pepper to taste and bring to a simmer. Reduce the heat and cook at a bare simmer until the sunchokes are tender, about 1 hour.

Stir in the milk and simmer, stirring occasionally, until the sunchokes are very soft, another 30 minutes.

Puree the soup, in batches if necessary, in a food processor or blender, and return to the pot to reheat. Ladle into soup bowls, sprinkle each portion with some pancetta or bacon, and drizzle with a little olive oil. Serve immediately.

wine: A gentle and unassuming wine is best with this delicately flavored soup. My choice: a clean, bright, citrusy Vermentino from the Cinque Terre.

mushroom soup from maremma

ACQUACOTTA ALLA MAREMMANA

pino • The name "acquacotta," which translates literally as "cooked water," indicates a simple, poor-man's soup. I have tasted acquacottas all over Tuscany. Every village, even if it only has a few houses and four chickens, has its own recipe, each one with a little twist. This one, from Maremma in southwest Tuscany, is my favorite. Maremma is a sparsely populated area, a former swamp that was dried out and richly fertilized for planting at the turn of the last century. From the roadside you see fields of red soil that produce crops all year round, from tomatoes to corn to artichokes. The acquacotta from Maremma is improbably rich, considering the dish's name. It uses meaty porcini mushrooms grown in the area. If you can't find fresh porcini, use dried porcini. Or use button or cremini mushrooms. The soup won't have the same perfume, but it will still have an earthy goodness. Giving the soup even more substance is a slice of toasted bread topped with an egg yolk placed in the bottom of each bowl. (Reserve the whites for another purpose or discard—they would only add unappetizing strings to the soup.) Leave the egg yolk out if you are not a fan of this sort of thing, but I love it. When the hot soup is poured into the bowl, it soft-cooks the egg. Delicious. • MAKES ABOUT 2½ QUARTS (2.4 LITERS)

1 pound (454 grams) fresh porcini mushrooms or 4 ounces (114 grams) dried porcini mushrooms

1 cup (240 ml) cold water, if using dried porcini

3 garlic cloves, minced

3 carrots, finely chopped

5 celery stalks, finely chopped

1 large red onion, finely chopped

1 small Italian chili pepper or other chili pepper (1 inch/2.5 cm long)

1½ teaspoons kosher salt

6 cups (1.4 liters) water

2 tablespoons (30 ml) extra-virgin olive oil

2 tablespoons chopped fresh Italian parsley

6 slices crusty peasant bread, toasted

6 large egg yolks

Freshly ground black pepper (optional)

2 tablespoons (14 grams) freshly grated Parmigiano-Reggiano cheese

IF USING DRIED MUSHROOMS, place the mushrooms and cold water in a bowl and set aside to rehydrate for 15 minutes. Lift the mushrooms from the liquid and transfer to a cutting board, squeezing out any excess water. Coarsely chop them, and set aside. Strain the soaking liquid through a cheesecloth-lined sieve or a coffee filter; save the liquid.

If using fresh mushrooms, cut them into small strips. Add the garlic to the plumped dried mushrooms or to the fresh mushrooms, mix well, and set aside.

Place the carrots, celery, onion, chili pepper, salt, and the 6 cups water in a 6- to 8-quart stockpot and bring to a slow boil over medium heat. Add the porcini water, if using, reduce the heat slightly, and simmer for 30 minutes to allow the vegetables to release their flavors into the liquid.

Place the olive oil, 1 tablespoon of the parsley, and the reserved porcini mixture in a 2- to 3-quart saucepan over medium-low heat and sauté, stirring, until the mushrooms are supple and the garlic is softened, 4 to 5 minutes.

Place 1 slice of toasted bread in the middle of each of six large shallow soup bowls, and top each with an egg yolk. Add the porcini to the broth and mix well. Season with salt and pepper if necessary. Gently ladle the soup over the egg yolks. Sprinkle with the remaining 1 tablespoon parsley and Parmigiano-Reggiano, and serve immediately.

wine: This southern Tuscan soup loves local wines. An ideal choice would be Morellino di Scansano, a great little gem similar to Chianti but from the Maremma region. It's a wine best enjoyed young. My favorite is made by Fattoria delle Pupille.

carrot-orange soup

ZUPPA DI ARANCIA E CAROTE

mark • I used to own Campagna Home, a take-out shop across from Campagna, my former restaurant in New York City. It was like an Italian *alimentari,* a type of deli common in Italy where you can buy prepared foods. Every day one of my cooks made this soup. When I took it off the menu to make room for something new, my customers complained vociferously. "Okay, okay," I promised. "It'll be back tomorrow." When I saw how popular it was, I created a ravioli dish with the same flavors, which I now serve at Coco Pazzo (see page 110). • MAKES 8 CUPS (1.9 LITERS)

6 carrots, cut into 1-inch (2.5-cm) pieces

1 medium yellow onion, cut into 1-inch (2.5-cm) dice

1 leek, white part only, well washed and cut into 1-inch (2.5-cm) pieces

1 medium parsnip, peeled and cut into 1-inch (2.5-cm) dice

1 large potato (8 ounces/228 grams), peeled and cut into 1-inch (2.5-cm) dice

8 cups (1.9 liters) Chicken Stock (page 29) or canned low-sodium organic chicken broth

1/2 teaspoon kosher salt

1/2 cup (120 ml) orange juice

1 bay leaf

1/2 teaspoon ground ginger

Pinch of freshly grated nutmeg

Pinch of ground cinnamon

1 navel orange, washed and halved, seeds removed

1 teaspoon grated orange zest

PLACE ALL THE INGREDIENTS except for the orange zest in a 6- to 8-quart stockpot and bring to a boil over high heat. Reduce the heat and simmer until all the vegetables are very soft, about 25 minutes. Remove and discard the bay leaf and orange halves.

Transfer 4 cups of the solids to a blender or food processor. Process until completely smooth and silky, gradually adding broth from the pot as necessary. Pour the soup into a large bowl or container. Repeat until all the soup has been pureed. If necessary, gently reheat the soup.

Ladle into soup bowls, sprinkle with the orange zest, and serve immediately.

wine: A Pinot Grigio would complement the sweet citrus flavor of this soup. Long Vineyard in Napa Valley makes a fine version of this Italian varietal.

zucchini and ricotta cheese soup

MINESTRA DI ZUCCHINE E RICOTTA

pino • Romolo Valli, one of the most acclaimed actors on the Italian theatrical scene, also happened to be a great gourmet, or *buongustaio,* and as a young actor I spent many nights at the table with him and the rest of our troupe, learning about fine dining at obscure restaurants in the countryside and famous ones in the big cities. Valli was a great lover of soups, especially the more refined purees like this one. He would order zucchini and ricotta soup as a beginning to a lavish meal that included fish and veal dishes, but when I began to make it for myself, I found it rich enough to be a meal on its own, accompanied by bread and salad.

Zucchini has quite a lot of water, which it releases into the pot as it cooks, producing its own vegetable broth. If your zucchini looks dry or starts to stick to the bottom of the pot before it is finished cooking, add a little bit of water, but not too much, to loosen it up. Leave the skin on—it's what gives the soup its pretty pale green color. Fresh ricotta cheese and a little bit of mascarpone, the very buttery and delicate milk cheese, enrich the zucchini puree without weighing it down. If you can't find mascarpone, don't worry, just substitute Philadelphia-brand cream cheese—believe it or not, it's available in Italy, and many Italians use it this way.

• MAKES ABOUT 6 CUPS (1.4 LITERS)

2 tablespoons (30 ml) olive oil

2 tablespoons (28 grams) unsalted butter

4 large zucchini (2 pounds/908 grams), thinly sliced

2 large scallions, white and green parts, finely chopped

1 1/2 cups fresh ricotta cheese

1/4 cup (2 ounces/56 grams) mascarpone or cream cheese

Kosher salt

1 teaspoon freshly ground black pepper

2 tablespoons (14 grams) freshly grated Pecorino Romano cheese

PLACE A HEAVY-BOTTOMED 4- to 5-quart pot over medium heat. When it is hot, add the olive oil and butter, and heat until the butter melts. Add the zucchini and scallions and stir to coat. Cover the pot, turn the heat to low, and cook, stirring occasionally, until the zucchini is tender and falling apart, about 45 minutes. If the mixture is sticking to the bottom of the pot, add a few tablespoons or so of water to loosen it.

Puree the zucchini mixture in a food processor or put through a food mill and return to the pot. Turn the heat to low and add the ricotta and mascarpone. Heat, stirring, until the ingredients are well combined and hot. Season with salt and the pepper.

Ladle the soup into bowls and sprinkle with the Pecorino Romano. Serve immediately.

wine: A rosé, with the flavor it gets from the skin of the grapes, complements the delicate taste of the cheeses in this soup. Reasonably priced Domaine Ott from Provence is my favorite, especially when serving this summertime soup.

lentil and sausage soup

ZUPPA DI LENTICCHIE E SALSICCIA

mark • Working in German kitchens, I developed my love for beans and legumes. At the Hotel Hessicher Hof in Frankfurt, I learned soup basics from a skilled Scotsman named Jock, who taught me, among other things, how the acidity of white wine can extract brilliant flavors from carefully chosen ingredients. He made this wonderful German-style lentil soup with sautéed onions and bacon. To give an Italian twist to his recipe, I use Italian sausage, Parmigiano-Reggiano cheese, and a little *guanciale,* cured pork cheeks. Bacon makes a fine substitute. • MAKES ABOUT 3 QUARTS (2.8 LITERS)

1 tablespoon (15 ml) extra-virgin olive oil, plus additional for drizzling

2 sweet Italian sausages (about 8 ounces/ 226 grams), removed from casings and crumbled

1 slice bacon, chopped

1 onion, finely chopped

1 garlic clove, thinly sliced

1 pound (454 grams) French le Puy lentils, picked over and rinsed

1 cup (240 ml) dry white wine

1 fresh rosemary sprig, leaves chopped (1 tablespoon)

10 cups (2.4 liters) Chicken Stock (page 29) or 8 cups (1.9 liters) canned low-sodium organic chicken broth plus 2 cups (480 ml) water

Kosher salt and freshly ground black pepper

¼ cup (1 ounce/28 grams) freshly grated Parmigiano-Reggiano cheese

PLACE A HEAVY-BOTTOMED 10- to 12-quart stockpot over medium heat, and when it is hot, add the olive oil. Add the sausage and cook, stirring, until it loses its pink color. Add the bacon and cook until it is just beginning to crisp and render its fat, about 3 minutes.

Pour off all but 1 tablespoon fat from the pot. Add the onion and garlic and sauté, stirring occasionally, until soft and golden, 5 to 7 minutes. Add the lentils and stir until they are well coated with oil, about 2 minutes. Add the wine and rosemary and bring to a boil. Turn the heat down and simmer until the wine has reduced by one-third, about 10 minutes.

Add the chicken stock and bring to a gentle boil. Reduce the heat, cover, and simmer until the lentils are very soft, many of them have fallen apart, and the soup is thick, 1 to 1½ hours.

Season the soup to taste with salt and pepper. Ladle into bowls. Drizzle with olive oil and sprinkle with the Parmigiano-Reggiano cheese.

tip: French le Puy lentils hold their shape better than brown lentils and have a more delicate, slightly peppery flavor.

wine: I loved Pinot Noir years before I saw the movie *Sideways*. It's earthier and more complex than Merlot, and great with this meaty lentil soup. Try a Rex Hill Pinot Noir from Oregon, where some of the best American Pinots are made.

garfagnana bean and apple soup

LA ZUPPA DELLA GARFAGNANA

pino • The Garfagnana region is in the northern part of Tuscany, where the Apennines meet the Alps. Its most famous town is Carrara, where Michelangelo's marble was quarried. When I was a young actor touring the more remote parts of Italy, I used to look forward to eating this local specialty. It is traditionally made with fresh cranberry beans, which are in season in September, but you can substitute borlotti (dried cranberry) beans if fresh are unavailable. What makes it interesting is the addition of apples, which are harvested at the same time as the beans. After the beans have simmered until they're soft and plump, diced apples are added to the pot to simmer until they fall apart, giving the soup its unique sweet-tart flavor. Granny Smith apples are the best choice here. They add just the right note of acidity to the mix. • MAKES 3 QUARTS (2.8 LITERS)

2 cups (1 pound/454 grams) shelled fresh or dried cranberry beans

2 tablespoons (30 ml) olive oil

1 small red onion, chopped

6 fresh sage leaves

1/2 teaspoon freshly ground black pepper, or more to taste

2 1/2 quarts (2.4 liters) water

2 Granny Smith apples, peeled, cored, and cubed

Kosher salt

2 tablespoons (30 ml) extra-virgin olive oil

IF USING DRIED BEANS, pick over the beans and place them in a large pot and cover with water. Let soak at room temperature for at least 3 hours, or up to 12 hours. Drain and rinse well. Set aside.

Place a heavy bottomed 6- to 8-quart stockpot over medium heat, and when it is hot, add the olive oil. Add the onion and sauté until soft and translucent, 5 to 7 minutes. Add the beans and cook, stirring occasionally, until they are hot and well coated with oil, 7 to 8 minutes.

Add the sage and pepper and stir well, then add the water. Bring to a boil over high heat, reduce the heat to low, and simmer for 20 minutes if using fresh beans, 45 minutes if using dried.

Add the apples and simmer, stirring occasionally, until they have fallen apart and melted into the beans, about 30 minutes. Add salt to taste.

Ladle into soup bowls, drizzle with the extra-virgin olive oil, and serve.

wine: A good Chianti Classico may be predictable—that's what the locals drink with this soup in Garfagnana—but it's just right. Or choose another lighter style of red, a Merlot perhaps, that won't overpower the delicate apple flavor.

estelle's chicken soup

mark · Some of the most popular items on the menu at Fred's, my restaurant inside Barneys department store, are adaptations of recipes I bring in from home. What's homier than chicken soup, especially in the winter, to ward off flu and colds? This recipe, which I learned from my mother, is named after my grandmother, although I've made some refinements. I wish she had lived to see a version of it printed in *The New York Times*. She would have enjoyed seeing how far I'd gone with her soup!

Making good chicken stock takes a while, but it is essential for achieving a rich and flavorful soup. I make the stock with abundant chicken bones and vegetables and then let it sit overnight in the refrigerator so I can skim off the fat the next day (you can use this recipe as your basic chicken stock and freeze it to use in sauces and soups when you need it). Then, to make the soup, I add more chicken and vegetables to the stock and cook it very slowly, so the broth stays clear. Double-cooking, as it is called, makes for absolutely the richest chicken flavor.

In the restaurant, we use chicken necks and backs to make the stock. They're inexpensive and full of flavor. Ask your butcher for them (he'll have some in the back if they're not in the case), or substitute two chicken fryers, cut up. · MAKES ABOUT 3½ QUARTS (3.4 LITERS)

2½ quarts (2.4 liters) Chicken Stock (recipe follows)

One 3- to 3½-pound chicken (1.4- to 1.6-kilo), cut into 8 pieces

1 carrot, cut into ¼-inch (0.6-cm) dice

1 small onion, cut into ¼-inch (0.6-cm) dice

1 leek, white part only, well washed and cut into ¼-inch (0.6-cm) pieces

1 celery stalk, cut into ¼-inch (0.6-cm) dice

1 turnip, peeled and cut into ¼-inch (0.6-cm) dice

Kosher salt and freshly ground black pepper

2 tablespoons (30 ml) sherry, preferably Tio Pepe (optional)

1 bunch fresh chives, cut into whisper-thin pieces (almost shredded)

COMBINE THE CHICKEN STOCK with the remaining ingredients except the salt and pepper, sherry, and chives in a 6- to 8-quart stockpot and bring to a simmer. Reduce the heat to low and simmer gently for 2½ hours; do not allow the soup to boil. Season with salt and pepper to taste.

Use tongs or two large serving spoons to transfer the chicken to a shallow bowl, and set the pot aside. When the chicken is cool enough to handle, separate the meat from the bones. Discard the bones and shred the meat with your hands. Return the chicken to the soup, cover, and refrigerate for 24 hours.

Remove and discard the solidified fat from the top of the soup, and reheat over medium heat. Ladle into bowls, spoon a little sherry into each bowl, if desired, sprinkle with the chives, and serve.

chicken stock ·

5 pounds (2.3 kilos) chicken necks and
   backs or 1 large or 2 small chickens,
   cut up

2 medium onions, quartered

1 carrot, quartered

2 celery stalks, quartered

2 leeks, white and light green parts,
   well washed and roughly chopped

½ bunch fresh Italian parsley

1 turnip, quartered

6 black peppercorns, smashed

2 bay leaves

3 fresh thyme sprigs

3 fresh rosemary sprigs

PLACE ALL THE INGREDIENTS in a 10- to 12-quart stockpot, cover with cold water, and bring to a gentle boil over high heat. Reduce the heat and simmer, uncovered, for 4 to 6 hours. During the first 2 hours, if the liquid reduces so that it is no longer covering the vegetables and chicken, add more water to cover. Let cool, then cover the pot and refrigerate overnight.

Remove and discard the solidified fat from the top of the stock. Use a slotted spoon to remove and discard the chicken and vegetables. Strain the stock through a fine strainer. The stock can be covered and refrigerated for up to 3 days, or pour into airtight containers and freeze for up to 1 month.

wine: I have no problem pairing a French white wine—Sancerre—with my grandma's soup. Or do what most New Yorkers at lunch do: have a Diet Coke.

neapolitan marriage soup

MINESTRA MARITATA

pino • Mark, take note: here is a traditional dish that uses bite-sized meatballs in a way I approve. Minestra Maritata is a Neapolitan soup that has been served for a hundred years as a first course at wedding celebrations, especially in the southern regions of Abruzzi and Puglia. But I've heard that it's actually called *maritata* because the recipe was passed from mother to daughter upon a girl's marriage. An explanation that I like better is one that has to do with the cooking technique: the tasty meatballs and slightly bitter escarole are "married" during the final stage of cooking. Hearty homemade chicken stock is a flavorful base for the soup, since, unlike Tuscan soups, it contains no beans or bread to give it body. • MAKES 2½ QUARTS (2.4 LITERS)

FOR THE MEATBALLS

⅓ pound (152 grams) ground pork

⅓ pound (152 grams) ground veal

⅓ pound (152 grams) ground beef

1 large egg

½ cup (2 ounces/56 grams) freshly grated Pecorino Romano cheese, plus additional for garnish

2 tablespoons chopped fresh Italian parsley

2 garlic cloves, minced

½ teaspoon kosher salt

¼ teaspoon crushed red pepper flakes

FOR THE SOUP

8 cups (1.9 liters) Chicken Stock (page 29) or chicken broth made from Knorr powdered bouillon

1 bunch escarole (about 1 pound/ 454 grams), trimmed and chopped

¼ cup (1 ounce/28 grams) freshly grated Pecorino Romano cheese

Kosher salt and freshly ground black pepper

PREHEAT THE OVEN to 375 degrees (190°C). Lightly grease a baking sheet.

TO MAKE THE MEATBALLS

Place the meats, egg, cheese, parsley, garlic, salt, and red pepper flakes in a mixing bowl and, using your hands, mix thoroughly until well combined. Take a piece of the meat mixture about the size of a large grape, press your hands together, and gently roll the mixture into a meatball about 1 inch across. Place on the prepared baking sheet and repeat with the remaining meat mixture. Transfer the baking sheet to the oven and bake until the meatballs are crunchy and browned, turning once, 20 to 25 minutes. Set aside.

TO MAKE THE SOUP

Place the chicken stock in a 6- to 8-quart stockpot and bring to a boil over medium-high heat. Add the escarole and cook until tender, about 10 minutes. Using a slotted spoon, gently drop in the meatballs. Reduce the heat to low and cook until they have flavored the broth, about 15 minutes.

Just prior to serving, add the cheese. Add salt and pepper to taste and stir well. Ladle into bowls and serve.

tip • For meatballs that are even crunchier outside, you can panfry them: Cover the bottom of a 10- to 12-inch skillet with extra-virgin olive oil and set over medium-high heat. When the oil is hot, add the meatballs and cook until they are crunchy on the outside, about 2 minutes per side. Drain on a paper-towel-lined plate before adding to the soup.

wine: An Aglianico, a light red from Puglia, would make sense with this southern Italian soup. Similar in style would be a Pinot Noir from Sonoma or Oregon.

ribollita

pino • Originally ribollita was simply leftover minestrone that was boiled again with chunks of bread to extend it for another meal. Now it is much more. It is a classic of Tuscan cooking that is rarely made from leftovers, because it is enjoyed so much for itself. The main ingredient is *cavolo nero,* a curly, dark blue-green kale, which adds an incomparable smoky, rich taste. Then, of course, there is the bread. Tuscans use their famous saltless bread, which soaks up the flavors without competing with the well-seasoned soup. A good-quality baguette or country bread will do the same thing. Don't use a sourdough loaf—its flavor will be too intense. My brother, Riccardo, is probably one of the biggest fans of ribollita. He makes two or three gallons a week and freezes it, then, every single day from the beginning of winter until Easter, goes off to work with his *lasuela* (thermos) of ribollita. If you make this on a cold winter's day, you'll find out what a great meal it can be. • MAKES 4¹⁄₂ QUARTS (4.2 LITERS)

2 cups (1 pound/454 grams) dried cannellini beans, picked over

2 tablespoons (30 ml) olive oil

1 medium red onion, thinly sliced

3 garlic cloves, thinly sliced

1 carrot, chopped

2 celery stalks, chopped

4 ounces (114 grams) pancetta or prosciutto, diced

2 bunches *cavolo nero* (Tuscan kale) or regular kale (about 2 pounds/ 908 grams total), tough stems removed, leaves cut 2 inches (5 cm) in length

¹⁄₂ Savoy cabbage (about 12 ounces/ 342 grams), cut into 2-inch (5-cm)- long strips

1 bunch spinach (about 12 ounces/ 342 grams), cut into 2-inch (5-cm)- long strips

4 quarts (3.8 liters) water, plus more if necessary

One 1-pound (454-gram) loaf crusty bread, cut into ¹⁄₂-inch cubes

Kosher salt and freshly ground black pepper

PLACE THE BEANS in a large pot and cover with water. Let soak at room temperature for at least 3 hours, or up to 12 hours. Drain and rinse well. Set aside.

Place a 6- to 8-quart stockpot over medium heat, and when it is hot, add the olive oil. Add the onion, garlic, carrot, and celery and cook until the vegetables are wilted and softened, about 10 minutes. Add the pancetta and cook, stirring with a wooden spoon, until fragrant and melting, about 3 minutes. Add the beans and cook until the skin just begins to crisp, about 2 minutes. Add the kale, in two batches, and stir until wilted. Add the Savoy cabbage and stir until wilted, 3 to 4 minutes, then add the spinach and cook, stirring, until wilted.

Add the water and bring to a gentle boil. Then reduce the heat to low and simmer, partially covered, for 1 hour, stirring occasionally. Add the bread, mix well, and set aside for 1 hour.

Return the pot to low heat and simmer for 1 hour. Add more water if necessary: the soup should look thick and dense but not dry. Add salt and pepper to taste. Let the soup rest for 15 minutes before serving.

tips: I love to eat this soup with a long sweet scallion in my left hand and take little bites between spoonfuls of soup. Ribollita can be made using leftover Worker's Farmhouse Soup (page 32) as a base. Leftover ribollita is one of my favorite ravioli fillings (see page 116). I also like to make *frittelle* (vegetable fritters) with it: Scoop a couple of tablespoons of cold soup into the palm of one hand and sprinkle some flour on it. Incorporate the flour by shaping the mixture into a small, flattish patty. Dredge the fritters in some more flour, or fresh bread crumbs if you like, and slowly panfry in olive oil, turning once, until crispy. Serve the warm fritters on top of frisée as a light lunch or appetizer salad.

wine: This quintessential Tuscan soup deserves respect. If you're in the mood for spending, drink a Tignanello from Antinori or Campaccio from Terrabianca, both serious super Tuscan wines.

worker's farmhouse soup

ZUPPA DELLA FATTORIA

mark • I've always been fascinated with the Italian *fattoria*—a farmhouse with a massive kitchen and dining room that serves the owners, the hired hands at harvest, and paying guests traveling through the countryside. This hearty and filling one-pot soup made with chicken and vegetables from the farm is a mainstay at the farmhouse table, and just the right dish to serve a hungry crowd. I love the way the pesto, spooned into the center of each bowl just before serving, brightens up the flavors of the vegetables when stirred into the soup. Even if you're not bringing in the harvest or serving a crowd, this soup is perfect for a filling fall lunch. The recipe makes a lot, so you can freeze some of it for later if you like. • MAKES ABOUT 6 QUARTS (5.7 LITERS)

FOR THE SOUP

1 cup (6 ounces/228 grams) dried cannellini beans, picked over

4 quarts (3.8 liters) water

Kosher salt

2 tablespoons (30 ml) extra-virgin olive oil

1 large or 2 small onions, chopped

2 garlic cloves, minced

1 zucchini (8 ounces/228 grams), cut into 1-inch dice

1 head cauliflower (1½ pounds/ 680 grams), core removed, florets chopped

1 head broccoli (1½ pounds/680 grams), stems removed, florets chopped

1 bunch Swiss chard (12 ounces/ 342 grams), trimmed and chopped

1 large carrot, cut into 1-inch dice

2 celery stalks, chopped

8 ounces (228 grams) green beans, trimmed and cut in half

8 ounces (228 grams) fresh or thawed frozen green peas

4 ounces (114 grams) cremini mushrooms

8 ounces (228 grams) potatoes, peeled and cut into 1-inch dice

2 fresh rosemary sprigs, leaves chopped

1 bay leaf

1 large chicken, cut into 8 pieces

1 cup (240 ml) dry white wine

2 cups (480 ml) canned crushed Italian plum tomatoes, preferably San Marzano

4 quarts (3.8 liters) Chicken Stock (page 29) or 3 quarts (2.8 liters) canned low-sodium organic chicken broth plus 4 cups (960 ml) water

Freshly ground black pepper

FOR THE SOUP

Place the beans in a large pot and cover with water. Let soak at room temperature for at least 3 hours, or up to 12 hours. Drain and rinse well.

Place the beans in a 6- to 8-quart stockpot, add the water and 1 teaspoon salt, and bring to a boil. Reduce the heat and cook at a gentle simmer until the beans are tender, 1 to 1¼ hours. Drain and set aside.

Place an 8- to 10-quart stockpot over medium-high heat, and when it is hot, add the olive oil. Add the onions and garlic and sauté until soft and golden, 5 to 7 minutes.

Add the vegetables, herbs, and chicken, and stir well. Add the wine, tomatoes, and chicken stock and bring to a boil. Reduce the heat to low and gently simmer until all the vegetables are soft, about 1 hour. If the liquid evaporates too quickly, add water ½ cup at a time, but do not add any water during the last 30 minutes, or the soup will not be as rich. Season with salt and pepper.

2 tablespoons lightly toasted pine nuts

1 garlic clove

2 bunches fresh basil, leaves only

½ cup (120 ml) extra-virgin olive oil

3 tablespoons (21 grams) freshly grated Parmigiano-Reggiano cheese

2 tablespoons (14 grams) freshly grated Pecorino Romano cheese

Kosher salt

Freshly grated Parmigiano-Reggiano cheese, for serving

Extra-virgin olive oil, for drizzling

WHILE THE SOUP IS SIMMERING, MAKE THE PESTO

Place the pine nuts, garlic, and basil in a food processor and process until well chopped. While the machine is running, drizzle in the oil and process until thick, scraping down the sides of the bowl once or twice as necessary. Add the cheeses and pulse until combined. Transfer to a small bowl and season with salt to taste. Cover with plastic wrap to refrigerate. (The pesto can be made up to 1 day ahead. Bring to room temperature before serving.)

To serve, ladle the soup into bowls, being sure to divide the chicken pieces equally. Place a dollop of pesto in the center of each bowl. Garnish with grated Parmigiano-Reggiano cheese and drizzle with extra-virgin olive oil.

wine: A nice Tocai from the north of Italy works for me because it's more flavorful than your average Pinot Grigio, and you need a white with a little more complexity to compete with the flavors in this soup.

2

the great meatball debate

We are like the two brothers in the film *Big Night*,

partners in a struggling Italian restaurant on the Jersey Shore in

the 1950s. Primo, the artist, insists on cooking only the authentic

Italian dishes like the spectacular *timpano*, a drum-shaped pie

layered with meatballs, eggs, cheese, and vegetables. Secondo,

the entrepreneur, sees nothing wrong with serving meatballs with

spaghetti—the dish is an American invention, but it tastes good,

will make the customers happy, and will bring in some money.

Like the brothers, our differences are cultural and philosophical.

One of us reveres Italian tradition. The other applauds Italian-American

innovation. The brothers' many arguments about food, and ours too,

can be summed up with one question: should meatballs be served

with spaghetti? Everything else follows from this. Do the meatballs

have to be made from beef and pork? What's the proper meat-to-

bread-crumbs ratio? What is the proper size for meatballs? What's

the best way to cook them? We've been debating these questions for

years and still haven't settled them. It's a debate for the ages, because

even if we miraculously come to an agreement on meatballs sometime

in the near future, we will still have to settle our differences on the

subject of meat loaf. . . .

mark I like the sense of abundance you get with a big, juicy meatball. For many of my customers, there's nothing more beautiful than a pile of spaghetti topped with a couple of them.

pino That's exactly my problem with your dish. I know it tastes great—I've eaten it with you. But the proportion is all off. Italians like their food to make sense aesthetically, for the sauce to fit with the pasta. And there's nothing more incongruous than a big meatball and a skinny strand of spaghetti.

mark Is the dish too humble for you? Oh, I forgot, you were born in northern Italy, wearing an ascot.

pino No, I wasn't born wearing an ascot. Quite the opposite—my mother's meatballs were an extremely economical dish. But we Italians, no matter how humble, demand a sense of proportion. I say, serve the spaghetti as a first course and save the meatballs for a second.

mark You realize that you are insulting a dish invented by Italian immigrants and embraced by every single citizen of the United States? Even now, when you can walk into a restaurant in Anchorage, or Cleveland, or Kansas City and order dishes from every part of Italy, spaghetti and meatballs is still the iconic Italian dish. When I make spaghetti and meatballs at my restaurant, I'm part of a tradition that started with Italian restaurateurs here in the 1940s. They were trying to please American customers, and so am I.

pino What you're talking about has no basis in *Italian* tradition. Maybe you could trace it back to the southern Italian dish called *sugo finto,* which means "fake sauce." That's a kind of ragu, where meat is cooked in tomato sauce, and the sauce absorbs the flavor of the meat. Then the meat is removed (that's why the sauce is called *finto,* because it tastes like meat but doesn't have any), and it is served separately as a main course after the pasta.

mark Does every dish have to have a traceable ancestor in order for us to enjoy it? When I think of meatballs, I think of the city housing project in Queens where I grew up in the sixties. Down the hall there was an older Italian woman who lived alone. She loved to cook, but she couldn't possibly eat all the food she made, so she'd always send some to our apartment. Only rarely would my father let me have some of her meatballs. They were incredible, and he guarded them jealously. That's the kind of flavor memory I'm trying to re-create when I make meatballs. I want people to fight over my meatballs!

pino For me, meatballs aren't an invention of Italians who came to America. My mother used to make *polpettine,* tiny fried beef and pork sausage meatballs, every Thursday night. The dish was a testament to her talent as a cook, that she could make something so good out of whatever scraps of meat the butcher would sell cheap at the end of the day. In Italy, meatballs have always been very much an improvised dish. The frugal housewife would buy the butcher's leftovers or use what she had left over from meals of the last few days—little scraps of beef, pork, a little sausage—which she'd chop up and mix with some stale bread to bind everything together.

mark Meatballs are all about the meat. Italian-Americans came to this country with nothing, and as soon as they could afford to buy meat, however inexpensive, they created big, juicy meatballs. I think their happiness and generosity and love of life are symbolized by this dish.

pino Well, I think that the Italian culture of parsimony has produced a better dish than Italian-American prosperity. I was born in 1953, and let me tell you, in 1958 we were still suffering with a terrible postwar economy in Italy. When my mother made meatballs, it was a way to extend the meat. But she turned

this into an art—the dish became more about the flavor of the eggs, cheese, parsley, onions. The most important ingredient wasn't the meat. It was stale bread—the way it absorbed the flavors of the meat and in turn gave the meatballs a tender texture.

mark Bread can add flavor, sure. But too much becomes just filler. I'm with first-generation Italian-Americans on this. There's a reason they're called meatballs. That's because they're meaty.

pino I do enjoy your spaghetti and meatballs. They taste good. But food should appeal to the eye as well as the stomach. Can I make one small suggestion?

mark If I say no, will that stop you?

pino Instead of making big round meatballs the size of golf balls, just take a look at my meatball recipe. I make grape-sized balls, and then I flatten them a little. You'd like them. They look like little hamburgers.

mark Why on earth would I want to make my meatballs flat?

pino This way, when you panfry them, they cook all the way through and get a perfectly crunchy crust without drying out on the inside the way larger round balls would.

mark You've conveniently forgotten that I don't panfry my meatballs. In the great Italian-American tradition, I simmer them in the tomato sauce until they're cooked through.

pino Yes, you put raw balls of meat into tomato sauce and cook them long enough to suck all of the juices out of the meat.

mark You don't know what you are talking about. My meatballs are famous for being plump and juicy. We don't suck out anything. My meatballs are the best. But I *do* like to panfry meatballs that I make with ground turkey. . . .

pino Meatballs made with turkey? Now you've gone too far. Save the pale, tasteless turkey for Thanksgiving.

mark You are so stuck in tradition that you are missing out on some of the best innovations in Italian cooking—all made by Americans. You won't try turkey meatballs, which are a healthier, lower-fat alternative to yours, and happen to taste sensational. You won't eat meatballs with spaghetti, even though this dish has been around so long that it is part of your adopted country's food culture. You live in twenty-first century America, Pino, not in 1950s Rome.

pino I'm searching my brain for some common ground. Okay—I make two traditional dishes where pasta and meatballs are served together: Fresh Pasta with Meatballs and Mushrooms and my father's lasagne. The first one combines fresh pasta with tiny meatballs, mushrooms, and peas. It's the furthest thing from your spaghetti and meatballs, because the meatballs are small enough that they are actually integrated into the dish. You're able to pick up a meatball, a mushroom, and a few strands of pasta on your fork at the same time. It feels natural to eat these components together. The second is a Neapolitan-style lasagne with layers of pasta, eggplant, tomato sauce, hard-boiled eggs, cheese, and tiny meatballs. The ingredients, including the meatballs, become one during baking. When you eat both of these dishes, you can see how they make sense to the eye as well as the palate—the meatballs don't sit on top, separate from the pasta, they are a part of the whole.

mark I'll take mine on top of spaghetti any day. A cook-off is in order. Let the readers decide.

pan-fried meatballs

POLPETTINE IN BIANCO

pino • Home cooks in Italy will tell you that this dish evolved as a way of using scraps of different meats—a little bit of beef, a little bit of pork, some leftover sausage. Frugal house-wives would chop the leftovers themselves and mix the meat with bits of stale bread soaked in milk to extend the leftovers further. In Italy, meatballs are panfried to give them their delicate crunch. They are only occasionally served with tomato sauce (see the variations on page 42), and *never* on the same plate with spaghetti.

When I was growing up, my mother made a specific dish for each night of the week, and this was the Thursday-night special. My job was to soak the stale saltless Tuscan bread we always had around the house in milk and then squeeze out the excess liquid and put the soggy bread into a dry bowl. At the time, I received an allowance of 200 lire a week, about 25 cents, for this and many other chores. Maybe my mother was taking advantage of me. I guess my sisters had it worse, though, because they had to cook and do the dishes too. Anyway, what I didn't earn in money, I earned in experience. I learned from her to add lemon zest to the mixture. The lemony flavor imparts some bite to the meatballs. You may be surprised at the generous amount of bread in the recipe, but this is the way my mother made it. Too much meat and too little bread would make them tough. She also taught me how to flatten the meatballs slightly so that they would cook through quickly without drying out. • MAKES ABOUT 24 SMALL MEATBALLS, SERVING 4 AS A MAIN COURSE

8 ounces (228 grams) soft country-style bread, torn into 1-inch pieces

1½ cups (480 ml) whole milk

1 cup (125 grams) all-purpose flour

1 cup (60 grams) bread crumbs (page 303) or store-bought unseasoned bread crumbs

1 pound (456 grams) ground chuck

8 ounces (228 grams) sweet Italian sausage, removed from casings and crumbled

2 large egg yolks

½ cup (2 ounces/56 grams) freshly grated Parmigiano-Reggiano cheese

1 tablespoon kosher salt

1 teaspoon freshly ground black pepper

Grated zest of ½ well-washed lemon

½ cup (20 grams) chopped fresh Italian parsley

1 cup (240 ml) olive oil

PLACE THE BREAD and 1 cup (320 ml) of the milk in a medium bowl and let soak for 5 minutes.

Place the flour in a large shallow bowl or pie plate. Place the bread crumbs in another large shallow bowl or pie plate. Set aside.

Squeeze the milk out of the bread, discarding the milk and breaking the bread into very small pieces, about the size of small peas, and transfer to a large bowl. Add the beef and sausage and, using your hands, mix until well combined.

Using your fist, create a crater in the middle of the mixture. Add the egg yolks, cheese, salt, pepper, lemon zest, parsley, and the remaining ½ cup milk and mix with your hands until well blended. Once you think it's well combined, continue mixing for another minute or two.

To make the meatballs, take a piece of the meat mixture about the size of a large grape, roll it into a ball between the palms of your hands, and then flatten it slightly into a patty about 1½ inches in diameter. Repeat with the remaining meat. Dredge both sides of each meatball in the flour and shake off any excess. Then roll them in the bread crumbs to coat and place on a baking sheet or large plate.

Line a large shallow plate with paper towels. Set aside.

Heat the oil in a 10- to 12-inch skillet over medium heat. Place only as many meatballs in the pan as you can without crowding them and panfry

until browned and crisp on one side, about 3 minutes. Flip and cook until the other side is browned and crisp, about 2 minutes more. Remove the meatballs from the pan with a spatula and place on the prepared plate to drain. Repeat with the remaining meatballs, and serve immediately.

tips: To test the meat mixture for seasoning, before you shape the meatballs, heat a tablespoon of oil in a small skillet. Pinch off just a small piece of the meat mixture and cook it in the hot oil for a couple of minutes. Then taste to judge whether or not you need more salt and pepper.

You can substitute ground pork for the sausage, as my mother often did. For a more piquant flavor, substitute Pecorino Romano for the Parmigiano-Reggiano cheese.

wine: Something *schietto*, which means straightforward, like a young Chianti.

meatballs in a quick tomato sauce

POLPETTINE IN UMIDO

Maybe Mark will approve of Meatballs in a Quick Tomato Sauce (Polpettine in Umido): Just before preparing the meatballs, make a simple tomato sauce by bringing 1 tablespoon (15 ml) olive oil and 2 cups (480 ml) tomato puree to a low boil in a saucepan. Reduce the heat and simmer slowly for 3 minutes. Sprinkle ¼ teaspoon chopped fresh thyme into the sauce and season with salt and pepper. Keep warm, then pour the tomato sauce over the cooked meatballs and serve immediately.

meatball sandwiches

Leftover polpettine make great sandwiches: Rub the insides of sliced crusty rolls with the pulp of halved very ripe tomatoes until the bread is pink. Slice a few meatballs in half and place them on the rolls. Drizzle with olive oil and sprinkle with a little salt and pepper.

veal meatballs with green apple

POLPETTINE DI CARNE E MELE

pino • This is a recipe that I got from my mother. She used to make it for herself when she was nursing, because she had heard the combination of meat, apples, and wine would help her keep up her strength. I remember these meatballs well because I was the fourth of six children, and I ate a lot of them after my brother and sister were born.

The meatballs are added to a pan of simmering wine, and as they cook, something wonderful happens. The meatballs absorb the wine, which enhances the sweet-tart flavor of the fruit with its own fruitiness. Use only Granny Smith—its acidity is essential to the success of the dish. And use good Chianti or Brunello here, because you will really taste it in the end. • MAKES 12 MEATBALLS, SERVING 4 AS AN APPETIZER OR 3 AS A MAIN COURSE

½ cup (62 grams) all-purpose flour

1 pound (454 grams) ground veal

1 large Granny Smith apple, peeled, cored, and cut into very small dice

2 large egg yolks

2 tablespoons finely chopped fresh Italian parsley

Kosher salt and freshly ground black pepper

4 tablespoons (56 grams) unsalted butter

2 tablespoons (30 ml) extra-virgin olive oil

1¼ cups (180 ml) Chianti or Brunello

1 tablespoon sugar

PLACE THE FLOUR in a large shallow bowl or pie plate. Set aside.

Combine the veal, apple, egg yolks, parsley, and salt and pepper to taste in a large bowl and mix with your hands until well combined. Take a piece of the meat mixture about the size of a large grape, roll the mixture into a ball between the palms of your hands, and then flatten it slightly into a patty about 1½ inches (37 cm) in diameter. Repeat with the remaining meat. Dredge both sides of each meatball in flour, shake off any excess, and place on a baking sheet or large plate.

Heat a 10- to 12-inch skillet over medium heat. When it is hot, add the butter and olive oil. When the butter is melted, add the wine and sugar and bring to a low boil. Add the meatballs and simmer vigorously, turning several times, until all the wine is absorbed. Serve immediately.

wine: Serve these with the Chianti or Brunello you used in the dish.

Mark makes his meatballs (page 47)

meatballs with spaghetti coco pazzo

POLPETTINE CON SPAGHETTI

mark · Spaghetti and meatballs may seem like an odd dish for a fancy restaurant like Coco Pazzo, but my customers are always looking for the tastes they remember from childhood. I don't fry my meatballs, as Pino does. I simmer them in the tomato sauce until they're cooked through. Pino may turn up his nose at this classic Italian-American shortcut, but a lot of fine chefs simmer ground meat this way so that it retains its moisture. When I trained with a chef in Germany, I watched him simmer his sausages before he grilled them. They never shrank or dried out. I thought of those plump sausages when I was working on my meatball recipe in the kitchen of Coco Pazzo and decided to just drop the uncooked meatballs into the tomato sauce, with no breading or sautéing. The result was plump, juicy meatballs. What's more, the sauce was deliciously flavored by the meat.

A lot of home cooks use bland commercial white bread in their meatballs, but it's worth it to seek out bread with some flavor. I like sourdough bread for the slight acidity it lends to the meatballs; it adds another flavor dimension. If you are like Pino and can't bear the idea of meatballs on top of spaghetti (I'd like to know how many of you there are out there!), you can prepare this dish without the spaghetti and simply serve the meatballs in the sauce with lots of crusty artisan bread. · MAKES 16 TO 18 MEATBALLS WITH SAUCE, SERVING 4 TO 6

FOR THE MEATBALLS

1 cup (about 50 grams) day-old sourdough bread cubes (crust removed)

1 cup (240 ml) whole milk

2 tablespoons (30 ml) extra-virgin olive oil

1 medium red onion, finely chopped

8 ounces (228 grams) ground veal

8 ounces (228 grams) ground chuck

8 ounces (228 grams) lean ground pork

8 ounces (228 grams) sweet Italian sausage (about 2), removed from casings and crumbled

3 tablespoons dried oregano, preferably Sicilian

1/2 cup (2 ounces/56 grams) freshly grated Parmigiano-Reggiano cheese

1/2 cup (2 ounces/56 grams) freshly grated Pecorino Romano cheese

2 large eggs

1/4 cup (10 grams) chopped fresh Italian parsley

(INGREDIENTS CONTINUE)

TO MAKE THE MEATBALLS

Place the bread and milk in a medium bowl and let soak for 5 minutes.

Heat a 7- to 8-quart Dutch oven over medium heat, and when it is hot, add the olive oil. Add the onion and cook until soft and golden, 5 to 7 minutes. Remove the pot from the heat and set aside.

Place the veal, beef, pork, and sausage in a large bowl and, using your hands, mix well. Add the oregano, cheeses, eggs, parsley, and bread one at a time, mixing until thoroughly combined after each addition. Add the onion and mix until very well combined. Add the salt and pepper. Set aside.

TO MAKE THE SAUCE

Heat a 10-quart casserole over medium heat, and when it is hot, add the olive oil. Add the onion and garlic and cook until wilted. Add the tomato paste and stir for 1 minute. Add the wine, tomatoes, 1 teaspoon of salt, and red pepper flakes and bring to a boil. Reduce the heat to low and simmer gently for 30 minutes, stirring occasionally. Season with salt and red pepper flakes to taste if necessary.

WHILE THE TOMATO SAUCE IS COOKING, FORM THE MEATBALLS

Take a piece of meat the size of a golf ball and roll it between the palms into a ball. Add it to the sauce, and repeat with the remaining meatballs.

Return the sauce to a simmer and simmer gently until the meatballs are cooked through, about 1 1/2 hours. Be sure to cook the meatballs at a

1 teaspoon kosher salt

½ teaspoon freshly ground
black pepper

FOR THE SAUCE

¼ cup (60 ml) extra-virgin olive oil

½ medium red onion, minced

1 garlic clove, minced

1 tablespoon tomato paste

½ cup (120 ml) dry red wine

Two 28-ounce (794-gram) cans Italian
plum tomatoes, preferably San
Marzano, with the juice, pureed in a
food processor or food mill

1 teaspoon kosher salt, or more to taste

½ teaspoon crushed red pepper flakes,
or more to taste (optional)

2 tablespoons kosher salt

1½ pounds (680 grams) spaghetti
or linguine

very gentle simmer; if the sauce boils, the fat will separate from the meat and they will dry out. When you think they are done, remove one from the pot and cut into it with a paring knife. If it is still pink in the middle, continue to cook until done, another 10 to 15 minutes.

Just prior to serving, fill a 10-quart stockpot with 7 quarts (6.5 liters) of water and bring to a boil. Add the 2 tablespoons of salt and spaghetti and cook until al dente. Drain, add to the pan with the meatballs and sauce, and carefully toss to coat. Serve immediately.

tips: To see if you've added enough salt and pepper to the meatball mixture, before shaping the meatballs, bring a small pot of water to a boil. Pinch off a grape-sized piece of meatball mixture, roll it into a ball, and drop it in the pot. When it is cooked through, in about 2 minutes, taste it and adjust the seasoning before rolling all of your meatballs.

To roll nice round meatballs without having the meat stick to your hands, moisten your hands with cold water before you start, and then again as necessary.

wine: This calls for a solid but not murderously expensive Chianti. No need to buy a Riserva; just don't buy anything in a straw-covered bottle. If an American wine is in order, try a good Zinfandel from Ridge Vineyards.

mark's mom's meat loaf revisited

POLPETTONE DELLA MAMMA

mark · My meat loaf is straightforward, just like my mom's, but I've learned a few tricks since I watched her make it at home. Instead of chopping the onions by hand, I puree them in the food processor. That way, they disappear into the meat loaf, and their juice flavors the meat and keeps it moist. To balance the sweetness of the onions and meat, I add some mustard and horseradish to the mix. Double-smoked bacon is an artisan product available at better butcher shops, specialty food stores, and online (see Resources, page 306). It imparts its intense flavor to the meat loaf without any of the aftertaste of most supermarket bacons, which have been treated with liquid smoke and artificial flavorings. · SERVES 6 AS A MAIN COURSE

2 pounds (908 grams) ground round

2 large onions, pureed in a food
   processor

2 garlic cloves, minced

4 large eggs

2 tablespoons kosher salt

1 tablespoon freshly ground
   black pepper

1 cup (4 ounces/114 grams) freshly
   grated Parmigiano-Reggiano cheese

1 cup (60 grams) bread crumbs
   (page 303) or store-bought
   unseasoned bread crumbs

1/2 cup (20 grams) chopped fresh
   Italian parsley

1/2 cup Dijon mustard

1/2 cup grated horseradish

1/2 cup (120 ml) ketchup

10 slices (about 8 ounces/228 grams)
   double-smoked bacon

PREHEAT THE OVEN to 350 degrees (175°C). Line a rimmed baking sheet with aluminum foil.

Combine the ground round, onions, garlic, eggs, salt, pepper, cheese, bread crumbs, parsley, mustard, and horseradish in a large mixing bowl and mix with your hands until well blended.

Shape the mixture into a 9-by-5-inch (23-by-13-cm) loaf and place on the prepared baking sheet. Use a pastry brush to cover the loaf with the ketchup. Arrange the bacon slices crosswise over the loaf, overlapping them slightly, to completely cover the surface of the loaf. Use a spatula to tuck the ends of the bacon underneath the loaf.

Bake until the bacon is crisp and the internal temperature of the loaf registers 160 degrees (70°C), about 1 hour.

Let stand for 10 minutes, then slice and serve.

wine: A Chianti from Col d'Orsca is a great drinking wine for this meat loaf.

Pino makes his meatballs (page 52)

fresh pasta with meatballs and mushrooms

PASTA ALLA CHITARRA CON POLPETTINE AI FUNGHI

pino • Here is my answer to American spaghetti and meatballs, a delicate dish of fresh pasta with small rounds of veal flavored with mushrooms, sweet peas, and mint—and no tomato sauce in sight. Pasta alla chitarra is my first choice here, because the short strands are easiest to eat with the meatballs. But fresh tagliolini will also be delicious. • SERVES 6 AS A MAIN COURSE

FOR THE MEATBALLS

8 ounces (228 grams) ground veal

¼ cup (1 ounce/28 grams) freshly grated Parmigiano-Reggiano cheese

1 large egg yolk

½ cup (30 grams) bread crumbs (page 303) or store-bought unseasoned bread crumbs

1 small garlic clove, minced

2 teaspoons chopped fresh Italian parsley

Kosher salt and freshly ground black pepper

1 cup plus 2 tablespoons (270 ml) olive oil, plus more for drizzling (optional)

1 medium onion, chopped

12 ounces (342 grams) white button mushrooms, wiped clean, stems removed, and sliced ½ inch (1.3 cm) thick

Kosher salt and freshly ground black pepper

1½ cups (200 grams) fresh sweet peas or thawed tiny frozen peas

½ cup (120 ml) vegetable stock or vegetable broth made with Knorr powdered bouillon

6 fresh mint leaves

1½ pounds (680 grams) pasta alla chitarra or tagliolini made from Fresh Egg Pasta Dough (page 94)

4 tablespoons (112 grams) unsalted butter

¼ cup (1 ounce/28 grams) freshly grated Parmigiano-Reggiano cheese

TO MAKE THE MEATBALLS

Place the meat in a large bowl, add the Parmigiano, egg yolk, bread crumbs, garlic, and parsley, and season well with salt and pepper. Mix thoroughly but delicately so as not to compress the meat, which would toughen it.

Take a piece of the meat mixture about the size of a small grape and roll the mixture between the palms of your hands into a small ball. Place on a plate, and repeat with the remaining meat mixture.

Line a large shallow plate with paper towels. Set aside.

Heat 1 cup of the olive oil in a 10- to 12-inch skillet over medium heat. Place only as many meatballs in the pan as you can without crowding them and panfry until browned and crisp on one side, about 3 minutes. Flip and cook until the other side is browned and crisp, about 2 minutes more. Remove the meatballs from the pan with a spatula and place on the prepared plate to drain. Repeat with any remaining meatballs.

Heat the remaining 2 tablespoons olive oil in another large skillet over medium-high heat. Add the onion and sauté until translucent, about 4 minutes. Add the mushrooms, season with salt and pepper, and sauté 5 minutes. Add the peas, toss, and cook until the mushrooms release their liquid, about 2 to 3 minutes. Add the stock and mint and cook for another 5 minutes. Taste and, if necessary, adjust the seasoning. Add the meatballs, toss well, and set aside, covered, to keep warm.

Fill a 10-quart stockpot with 7 quarts (6.6 liters) of water. Add 2 tablespoons kosher salt and bring to a boil. Add the pasta and cook until al dente.

Reserve ½ cup of the cooking liquid, then drain the pasta and stir it into the sauce. Add the butter, the Parmigiano, and a few tablespoons of the reserved cooking water, and heat over very low heat. Taste and adjust the seasoning, then toss thoroughly, drizzling with more olive oil if desired.

wine: A young sparkling Prosecco from the Veneto may seem an unusual selection for meatballs, but because these are made with veal, it's the perfect choice here.

turkey meatballs in spicy tomato sauce

POLPETTINE DI TACCHINO IN SALSA PICCANTE

mark • Turkey is very low fat, and my Upper East Side customers like that. But that's not really why I use it in this recipe. I'm a big fan of spicy tomato sauces, and turkey, which is very mild, pairs well with the assertive, acidic sauce. It's a nice change from traditional meatballs, familiar but a little bit different.

Meatballs made with turkey are less firm than those made with beef or pork. Refrigerating the balls before cooking will help them hold together. I also like to crisp them up on the outside by coating in a mixture of cheese and bread crumbs and panfrying them before they get simmered in the sauce. Panfrying gives them a crunchy crust so they don't fall apart, while the simmering keeps them moist inside. To temper the hot pepper, follow this with a Bibb or Boston lettuce salad dressed with lemon juice and a little extra-virgin olive oil.

Grana Padana is a delicious grating cheese similar in flavor and texture to Parmigiano-Reggiano but made outside the strictly defined zone in and around Italy's Parma region. Less expensive than Parmigiano, it's a smart choice when you're using a large quantity, as in this recipe. • MAKES 30 MEATBALLS, SERVING 6 AS A MAIN COURSE

FOR THE MEATBALLS

2½ cups (150 grams) bread crumbs (page 303) or store-bought unseasoned bread crumbs

1 cup (240 ml) plus 2 tablespoons (30 ml) olive oil

4 ounces (114 grams) turkey bacon, minced

2 leeks, white part only, thoroughly washed and minced

3 shallots, minced

1½ pounds (680 grams) ground turkey

1 pound (454 grams) turkey sausage (about 4), removed from casings and crumbled

2½ cups (10 ounces/280 grams) freshly grated Grana Padano cheese

3 large eggs

1 large egg yolk

½ teaspoon kosher salt

½ teaspoon crushed red pepper flakes, or more to taste

[INGREDIENTS CONTINUE]

TO MAKE THE MEATBALLS

Preheat the oven to 350 degrees (175°C).

Spread 1 cup of the bread crumbs on a rimmed baking sheet and toast, stirring once or twice, until golden, about 10 minutes. Set aside to cool completely, then transfer to a large bowl.

Heat a 10- to 12-inch skillet over medium heat, and when it is hot, add 2 tablespoons of the olive oil. Add the bacon, leeks, and shallots and sauté until the vegetables are soft and golden, 5 to 7 minutes. Set aside to cool.

Add the turkey, turkey sausage, cooled leek mixture, 2 cups of the cheese, the eggs, egg yolk, salt, and red pepper flakes to the toasted bread crumbs and mix with your hands until thoroughly combined. Form the mixture into Ping-Pong-ball-sized meatballs, place them on a large plate, and cover with plastic wrap. Refrigerate until firm, 1 hour.

Line a baking sheet with paper towels and set aside.

Place the remaining 1½ cups of bread crumbs and remaining ½ cup cheese in a large shallow bowl or pie pan and mix to combine. Roll the meatballs in the bread mixture to coat, and place back on the plate.

Heat a 10- to 12-inch skillet over medium heat, and when it is hot, add the remaining 1 cup oil. Add the meatballs, in batches if necessary, and fry until just browned, about 2 minutes per side. Remove the meatballs to the paper-towel-lined baking sheet.

[CONTINUED]

2 tablespoons (30 ml) extra-virgin
olive oil

4 garlic cloves, thinly sliced

1 cup (120 grams) minced white onion

1 cup (240 ml) dry white wine

Two 28-ounce (794-gram) cans Italian
plum tomatoes, preferably
San Marzano, with their juices

1 to 2 teaspoons crushed
red pepper flakes

1 cup (30 grams) loosely packed sliced
fresh basil leaves (about 1 bunch)

½ cup (20 grams) chopped fresh Italian
parsley

TO MAKE THE SAUCE

Place a 7- to 8-quart Dutch oven over medium-low heat, and when it is hot, add the olive oil. Add the garlic and cook until fragrant, about 30 seconds. Add the onion and cook until softened, about 3 minutes. Add the wine, tomatoes, and red pepper flakes.

Once the sauce starts to simmer, add the meatballs and cook until the sauce thickens and the meat is cooked through, 45 minutes to 1 hour. Add the basil and parsley and cook 2 minutes more. Taste the sauce for salt and pepper, and serve immediately.

tips: You can vary this by using some ground chicken in place of the turkey, which will give the flavor another dimension. If you want meatballs with more body, add a little ground veal.

Cut off the rind from your Grana Padano and cook it in the sauce for extra flavor. If you do this, you might not need additional salt, since the rind will release its salt into the sauce.

wine: With this dish, you want a white wine with a little more body than a typical Pinot Grigio or Soave—try an off-dry Riesling (such as the Alsatian Trimbach) or a Tocai.

meatballs with amaretti

POLPETTINE SFIZIOSE

pino · Amaretti, the almond cookies manufactured in Piedmont, are often used in savory dishes in that region. They impart their aromatic flavor to several interesting meat dishes, including ravioli with a meat filling and these delicious meatballs. Serve them as an appetizer or snack, warm or at room temperature. · MAKES ABOUT 18 MEATBALLS, SERVING 6 AS AN APPETIZER

1¼ cups (about 2 ounces/56 grams) white bread cubes (crust removed)

½ cup (120 ml) whole milk

½ cup (30 grams) bread crumbs (page 303) or store-bought unseasoned bread crumbs

1½ pounds (680 grams) ground chuck

6 amaretti cookies (from 3 packages), crushed

Grated zest of 1 well-washed lemon

¼ cup (1 ounce/28 grams) freshly grated Parmigiano-Reggiano cheese

1½ tablespoons finely chopped fresh Italian parsley

2 large eggs

1 teaspoon freshly grated nutmeg

1 teaspoon kosher salt

¼ teaspoon freshly ground black pepper

2 cups (480 ml) olive oil

PLACE THE BREAD and milk in a medium bowl and let soak for 5 minutes.

Place the bread crumbs in a large shallow bowl or pie plate. Set aside.

Squeeze the milk out of the bread, discarding the milk and breaking the bread into very small pieces, about the size of small peas, and transfer to a large bowl. Add the beef and crushed amaretti and mix well, using your hands.

Using your fist, create a crater in the middle of the mixture. Add the lemon zest, cheese, parsley, eggs, nutmeg, salt, and pepper and mix with your hands until well blended. Once you think the mixture is well combined, continue mixing for another minute or two.

To make the meatballs: Take a piece of the meat mixture about the size of a large grape, roll the mixture into a ball between the palms of your hands, and then flatten it slightly into a patty about 1½ inches (37 cm) in diameter. Repeat with the remaining meat. Roll each meatball in the bread crumbs to coat, and place on a baking sheet or large plate.

Line a large shallow plate with paper towels. Set aside.

Heat the oil in a 10- to 12-inch skillet over medium heat. Place only as many meatballs in the pan as you can without crowding them and panfry until browned and crisp on one side, about 3 minutes. Flip and cook until the other side is browned and crisp, about 2 minutes more. Remove the meatballs from the pan with a spatula and place on the prepared plate to drain. Repeat with the remaining meatballs, and serve immediately.

wine: Prosecco is a suitably festive match when you are serving these meatballs as a party snack.

antonio's neapolitan lasagne

LASAGNE NAPOLETANE ALL'ANTONIO

pino · My father passed away a few months before we began writing this book. After his funeral, my brother and I exchanged our happy memories of him, and most of mine were set in the kitchen. During the summers we spent at the beach, I helped him make his specialty, a Neapolitan-style lasagne. It was a real labor of love, an extravagant layering of eggplant, tomato sauce, hard-cooked egg, mozzarella, and meatballs. My mother never cooked this type of dish. Her style was more spare and reserved. But my father was from Naples, and after being separated from his sisters, growing up in an orphanage, and joining the army, he returned to their house and learned to cook from them. He loved to spend a day of his summer vacation making this dish for his kids and showing us where he came from.

On vacation, my mother was happy to sit back and watch the family enjoy a different type of food, more rustic and well suited to the outdoors. We'd reserve a pergola on the beach and she would set the table with cloth napkins, real plates, and silverware. At noon, my father would bring down the lasagne. I can call up very vividly the feeling of dining in the shade of the pergola, wind blowing on our tan skin, and the sea just a few yards away. Those were wonderful days.

Maybe because I ate this dish as a child, it is the one way I truly love eating meatballs and pasta together. When the meat is baked between layers of pasta, with the melting cheese holding everything together, the result is a cohesive dish where the sum is definitely greater than the parts.

I make this in an extra-large baking pan, as my father did. If you'd like, you can assemble it in two smaller pans, and even freeze one for later. · SERVES 10 TO 12 AS A MAIN COURSE

FOR THE MEATBALLS

1 pound (454 grams) ground beef

2 large eggs

2 tablespoons (14 grams) freshly grated Parmigiano-Reggiano cheese

2 tablespoons minced fresh Italian parsley

1 teaspoon kosher salt

1/2 teaspoon freshly grated nutmeg

1/2 cup (120 ml) extra-virgin olive oil

FOR THE EGGPLANT

3/4 cup (9.5 grams) all-purpose flour

1 teaspoon kosher salt

2 large eggs

1/2 cup (120 ml) extra-virgin olive oil

1 pound (454 grams) eggplant, sliced lengthwise into 1/4-inch-thick slices

TO MAKE THE MEATBALLS

Place the beef, eggs, cheese, parsley, salt, and nutmeg in a large mixing bowl and, using your hands, knead the ingredients together for 4 minutes. Cover and refrigerate for 10 minutes.

Line a baking sheet with paper towels and set aside.

Roll the meat mixture between moistened palms to form balls no larger than 1 inch (2.5 cm) in diameter, and place on a plate. You should have about 24 meatballs.

Heat the olive oil in a 10- to 12-inch skillet over medium heat. When it is hot, add the meatballs and cook, turning occasionally, until browned on all sides, 5 to 7 minutes. Transfer to the towel-lined baking sheet.

TO MAKE THE EGGPLANT

Line another baking sheet with paper towels and set aside. Place the flour and 1 teaspoon of salt in a large shallow bowl and mix well. Place the eggs in a large shallow bowl and beat well.

Heat a 10- to 12-inch skillet over medium heat, and when it is hot, add 6 tablespoons of the olive oil. When the oil is hot, dredge 1 slice of eggplant in the flour and then in the egg, place in the oil, and cook until browned,

2 tablespoons kosher salt

2 pounds (908 grams) dried lasagne
   sheets (18 to 20)

3 cups (720 ml) canned plum Italian
   tomatoes, preferably San Marzano,
   drained and pureed

1 pound (454 grams) mozzarella,
   thinly sliced

2 cups (8 ounces/228 grams) freshly
   grated Parmigiano-Reggiano cheese

6 hard-cooked large eggs, sliced

 30 fresh basil leaves

1 to 2 minutes per side. (You can cook more than 1 slice of eggplant at a time, but be careful not to crowd the pan.) Transfer to the towel-lined baking sheet. Repeat until all the eggplant is cooked.

TO COOK THE LASAGNE NOODLES

Fill a 10-quart stockpot with 7 quarts (6.5 liters) of water and bring to a boil over high heat. Fill a large bowl with ice water. Add 2 tablespoons of salt to the boiling water. Add the lasagne noodles 2 or 3 at a time and cook until al dente, about 5 minutes. Remove with a slotted spoon to the ice water.

TO ASSEMBLE THE LASAGNE

Preheat the oven to 350 degrees (175°C). Use your hands and the remaining 2 tablespoons of olive oil to coat the bottom and sides of a baking pan measuring 24 to 28 inches by 12 to 14 inches with 4-inch-high sides. Or use two 9-by-13-inch pans.

Arrange a layer of noodles on the bottom of the pan, close together but not overlapping. Top the noodles with a layer of eggplant, using half of the eggplant, then spread one-third of the tomatoes on top of the eggplant. Arrange one-third of the mozzarella slices over the tomatoes and sprinkle with one-third of the Parmigiano-Reggiano. Follow that with another layer of pasta, another one-third of the tomato sauce, and another one-third of the mozzarella. Arrange all of the meatballs over the mozzarella, and top with all of the hard-boiled egg slices. Sprinkle with another one-third of the Parmigiano-Reggiano, then 10 of the basil leaves. Cover with the remaining noodles, then the remaining eggplant, tomatoes, mozzarella, Parmigiano, and basil leaves. Cover the pan tightly with aluminum foil.

Transfer the pan to the middle rack of the oven and bake until the sauce is bubbling and the cheese is melted, 45 minutes to 1 hour.

Remove the pan from the oven and pierce the lasagne with a fork in a few spots. Return the uncovered pan to the oven and cook for an additional 20 minutes. Let the lasagne rest for about 1 hour before serving.

wine: My father drank only red wine, most often Chianti, with his lasagne. Today I like a full-bodied Chardonnay with lots of fruit and vanilla.

3

dried pasta

and the unification of the two meatballs

Saranno i maccheroni, ve lo giuro, a unire l'Italia.
—GIUSEPPE GARIBALDI

When Giuseppe Garibaldi invaded Naples from Sicily in 1860 with the hopes of making it a part of a new and united Italian state, he declared, "I swear to you, macaroni will unite Italy." Since Garibaldi's declaration, dried pasta, invented in the south, has certainly won over every corner of the country. It has made significant inroads in the United States as well—which perhaps can be traced back to Garibaldi's stay on Staten Island in 1848, where he lived briefly and became a U.S. citizen.

If only dried pasta could have the same unifying effect on the two of us. What is the place of dried pasta at the table? How should you match pasta shapes and sauces? Which brands are best? We'll never agree completely.

pino In America, dried pasta is a cheap and quick way to fill your belly. In Italy, it is a way of life.

mark That's ridiculous. No one has done more to put dried pasta on a pedestal in the last twenty-five years than Americans.

pino Really? Go to Italy, and you'll never see pasta dishes called "appetizers." They have their own section on the menu. It's called the pasta course.

mark Well, here in America, we don't usually make pasta a first course, or a pasta course, or whatever you Italians want to call it, and then serve a piece of meat or fish after it. We put it front and center, making it the main dish.

pino Yes, so you can eat more of it. There you go, filling your belly with carbohydrates instead of considering variety in a meal.

mark And there you go, making dinner more complicated than most of us want it to be. For most Americans, pasta is the perfect one-dish meal. Just grab a box off the supermarket shelf on your way home from work, and make a quick sauce with a can of tomatoes and maybe even some leftovers. . . .

pino Stop! Even *you* have to admit that the choice of pasta is important. The shape, first of all. You want to make sure you have a pasta shape that captures the sauce, so the sauce and pasta don't stay separate. That's why I can't stand the gigantic meatballs on top of the spaghetti. But it's true of every kind of pasta dish. Sauces with chunks of vegetables, like cauliflower and broccoli, need a short shape like cavatelli so the sauce can grab on to the pasta instead of just sliding off. Loose tomato sauces (hold the meatballs, please) are better with long, thin pastas like spaghetti, which gets coated and soaks up the liquid.

mark Then explain spaghetti alle vongole. That's a perfect match of chunky clams and long, thin spaghetti. There goes your rule, right in the garbage with the clam shells.

pino Have you forgotten the liquid from the clams? That's your sauce, and it's so loose it's practically the consistency of water! Shellfish is always paired with spaghetti in Italy.

mark I'm just saying I don't like strict rules. Yes, I agree with you that loose tomato sauces are great with spaghetti. But if my customers asked me to serve my tomato sauce with penne because it's neater to eat and results in fewer tomato stains on their silk ties, I wouldn't refuse. And I wouldn't say it compromises the integrity of the dish!

pino Next you'll be saying just buy whatever spaghetti's on sale at the supermarket.

mark As a matter of fact, I don't think there's anything wrong with the less expensive domestic dried pastas. But I will admit that I've tried expensive artisanal pasta from Italy, and I love it.

pino At last, a reasonable opinion. If I could get people to change their thinking about dried pasta as a cheap commodity and start spending a few extra dollars a pound for artisanal pasta, then they would see how much the pasta itself, its flavor and texture, can contribute to a finished dish. Artisan brands—I like Martelli and Latini—are made from the highest quality of wheat, and when you cook them, you can see from the clear water left when you strain them that they release less starch. Totally different from the cloudy water you get when you boil cheap pasta. You can taste the nuttiness of the wheat and feel the firmness of the semolina in your mouth.

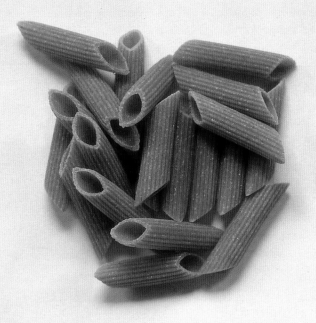

penne rigate (whole wheat)

farro penne

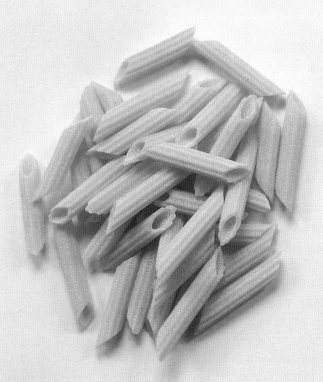

pennette

cavatelli

mezzi-rigatoni #20

farro

bucatini

rigatoni with butcher's sauce

RIGATONI DEL MACELLAIO

mark · This sauce is called "butcher's sauce" because it's made with odds and ends, like the sauce a butcher would make after he closed up shop for the day and brought home some leftovers to feed the family. I always liked the idea because it's practical. We don't like to waste anything at the restaurant, so I came up with this version—using a small amount of bacon, a little leftover pot roast, a glass of red wine—tailoring the idea to take advantage of what we have sitting around in the kitchen. Another thing I like about it—it is quick to prepare. But I don't save the recipe for when I have leftovers. I like it so much that when I'm planning a weeknight dinner, I'll go out and buy a little bit of sausage and a little bit of steak, just so I can have this meaty pasta dish at home. It's a more moderate way to eat meat than sitting down to a big steak, but just as satisfying. Rigatoni or any other large tubular pasta shape is good for catching bits of the chunky sauce. · MAKES ABOUT 5 CUPS (1.2 LITERS) SAUCE, SERVES 4 TO 6

1 to 2 tablespoons (15 to 30 ml) extra-virgin olive oil

1 hot Italian sausage (about 4 ounces/ 114 grams), removed from casing and crumbled

1 medium garlic clove, sliced

1/2 cup (30 grams) minced bacon or pancetta

1/2 medium red onion, thickly sliced

1/2 cup (120 ml) dry red wine

3 cups (720 ml) canned tomato puree

12 Gaeta or Niçoise olives, pitted and coarsely chopped

1 cup (115 grams) shredded leftover Tuscan Pot Roast (page 187) or cooked skirt or flank steak

1/2 cup (30 grams) minced salami (any kind)

Pinch of crushed red pepper flakes

1/2 teaspoon freshly ground black pepper

2 tablespoons kosher salt, plus more to taste

1 pound (454 grams) rigatoni, ziti, or other large tubular pasta

2 tablespoons chopped fresh Italian parsley

1/4 cup (1 ounce/28 grams) freshly grated Pecorino Romano cheese

PLACE A 10-INCH SKILLET over medium-high heat, and when it is hot, add 1 tablespoon of the olive oil. Add the sausage and sauté until the meat is cooked and has given up its liquid, about 7 minutes. Using a slotted spoon, remove the sausage to a paper-towel-lined plate and set aside.

Drain off all but 1 tablespoon of fat from the pan. Or, if the sausage hasn't given off a tablespoon of fat, add an additional tablespoon of oil to the skillet and heat over medium heat. Add the garlic, bacon, and onion and sauté until the onion is soft and golden, 5 to 7 minutes. If the mixture starts to brown, turn down the heat. Add the wine, tomato puree, olives, sausage, pot roast or steak, salami, red pepper flakes, and pepper and gently simmer until the sauce starts to thicken, about 20 minutes. Add salt to taste.

While the sauce is cooking, fill a 10-quart stockpot with 7 quarts (6.5 liters) of water and bring to a boil over high heat. Add the 2 tablespoons kosher salt. Add the pasta, stir, and cook until al dente.

Reserve 1/2 cup of the pasta cooking water, and drain the pasta. Add the pasta to the pan with the sauce, then add the parsley and toss over low heat until the pasta is well coated, about 2 minutes. If the pasta looks dry, add the reserved cooking water about 1 tablespoon at a time, tossing to combine between additions. Serve immediately, with the Pecorino Romano on the side.

wine: With this dish, I'd drink a Barbera from one of my favorite producers, Vietti. It's not a grand red wine and it won't overwhelm the flavors of the sauce. (I refuse to call it "humble"—I go crazy when I hear Pino call any wine humble, because to me, wine, even if it's meant for everyday drinking, elevates food.)

rigatoni with game sauce

RIGATONI ALLA CACCIATORA

mark • The most difficult thing about this recipe is shopping for it. Making the sauce is easy. It might seem extravagant to use venison, rabbit, *and* wild boar in one recipe, but my feeling is if you are going to take the trouble to buy one of these meats, it's just as easy to buy a variety. So go to a good butcher and ask for a little bit of each. As my mother used to say to me, "If you don't ask, you don't get." If your butcher can give you only one or two, or offers you guinea hen or pheasant as a substitute, use any combination that works for you. If he can't get you any game at all, you can order it online at www.dartagnan.com. • MAKES ABOUT 5 CUPS (1.2 LITERS) SAUCE; SERVES 4 TO 6

3 tablespoons (45 ml) extra-virgin olive oil, plus more for drizzling

4 ounces (114 grams) boneless venison stew meat, cut into 1/4-inch (0.6-cm) cubes

4 ounces (114 grams) boneless rabbit meat, cut into 1/4-inch (0.6-cm) cubes, plus 6 rabbit legs, boned and cut into 1/4-inch (0.6-cm) cubes

4 ounces (114 grams) boneless wild boar from the shoulder, cut into 1/4-inch (0.6-cm) cubes

1/2 red onion, minced

1 garlic clove, sliced

6 cups (1.4 liters) dry red wine

2 fresh rosemary sprigs, leaves chopped

2 whole cloves

1/4 teaspoon freshly grated nutmeg

Pinch of ground mace

1 cup (240 ml) canned crushed Italian plum tomatoes, preferably San Marzano

2 tablespoons kosher salt, plus more to taste

Freshly ground black pepper

1 pound (454 grams) rigatoni

PLACE A 10-TO 12-INCH SKILLET over medium heat, and when it is hot, add the olive oil. Add the meats and cook, stirring occasionally, until they are no longer pink on the outside, 2 to 3 minutes. Add the onion and garlic and cook, stirring occasionally, until the onion is softened, about 5 minutes. Add the wine, rosemary, and spices and bring to a boil. Reduce the heat to medium-low and simmer for 5 minutes. Add the tomatoes and cook until the meat is tender and starting to fall apart, 15 to 20 minutes. Add salt and pepper to taste.

While the sauce is cooking, fill a 10-quart stockpot with 7 quarts (6.5 liters) of water and bring to a boil over high heat. Add the 2 tablespoons kosher salt. Add the pasta, stir, and cook until al dente.

Reserve 1/2 cup of the pasta cooking water, and drain the pasta. Add the pasta to the pan with the sauce. If the pasta looks dry, add the reserved cooking water 1 tablespoon at a time, tossing to combine between additions. Serve immediately, drizzling each portion with olive oil.

wine: Game is hearty and strong, so I like a full-bodied red for this dish, preferably a California Cabernet. The reasonably priced Cabernet from Rabbit Ridge is a good bet.

bucatini with pancetta and onion ragu

BUCATINI ALL'AMATRICIANA

pino · This classic recipe traces its origins to the town of Amatrice, southeast of Rome, where cured pork products like pancetta and *guanciale* (pig jowls) are a specialty. I remember eating it at the beach as a child on August 15, at Ferragosto (Feast of the Assumption), the most important summer holiday in Italy. It's unusual, because most pasta sauces with pork aren't considered summertime food, but this one is. I thought long and hard about including it in this book. After all, it has been a standard for many years in cookbooks and on restaurant menus. Is there any need for another recipe for it? Well, the answer is yes, because I'm an opinionated person, and I feel there are a few aspects of this dish in its authentic form that have never been translated for American home cooks. The original is most often made with guanciale, but that can be hard to find in the United States. Pancetta (see Tips) is a good substitute, but it's important to have it sliced ¼ inch thick, not paper-thin. Chunky pieces of pancetta give the sauce its texture. Likewise, I strongly believe in cutting the onion into large dice, not mincing it. You don't want it to melt into the sauce when it's cooked, but to keep its shape. Spaghetti is too fine for a sauce with this much texture. Bucatini (or *perciatelli,* which is dialect for the same long tubular shape) is just right here. · MAKES ABOUT 4 CUPS (960 ML) SAUCE; SERVES 4 TO 6

1 tablespoon (15 ml) extra-virgin olive oil

4 ounces (114 grams) thick-cut pancetta, cut into ¼-inch dice

1 large red onion, cut into ½-inch dice

½ teaspoon crushed red pepper flakes, or more to taste

2 tablespoons plus 1 teaspoon kosher salt, or more to taste

1 cup (240 ml) dry red wine

2½ cups (480 ml) canned Italian tomato puree, preferably San Marzano

1 small hot chili pepper, such as a jalapeño, stemmed, seeded, and quartered

1 pound (454 grams) bucatini or perciatelli

¼ cup (1 ounce/24 grams) freshly grated Pecorino Romano cheese

PLACE A 10- TO 12-INCH SKILLET over medium heat and when it is hot, add the olive oil and pancetta. Cook until the pancetta softens and releases some fat, about 2 minutes. Add the onion and cook, stirring frequently, until it softens and becomes translucent and the mixture becomes powerfully fragrant, about 4 minutes. Add the crushed red pepper flakes and 1 teaspoon of the salt and stir well. Add the wine and cook until about half of it has evaporated, about 7 minutes.

Add the tomato puree and cook, stirring constantly, until the mixture comes to a boil. Reduce the heat to low and simmer until the sauce is thick and fragrant, about 30 minutes. Remove the sauce from the heat, and season with additional salt if necessary.

While the sauce is cooking, fill a 10-quart stockpot with 7 quarts (6.5 liters) of water and bring to a boil over high heat. Add the remaining 2 tablespoons salt and the chili pepper. Add the pasta, stir, and cook until al dente.

Reserve ½ cup of the cooking water, and drain the pasta. Remove and discard the chili pepper. Add the pasta to the pan with the sauce and raise the heat to medium. Toss until the sauce and pasta are well combined. If the pasta looks dry, add the reserved cooking water about 1 tablespoon at a time, tossing to combine between additions. Transfer to a serving platter, sprinkle with the Pecorino Romano, and serve immediately.

baked penne with radicchio and sausage

PENNE PASTICCIATE

pino · I first had this dish in Bolzano, in northern Italy. I was with my kids on a ski vacation and the cook at the pensione where we were staying heated up what was probably some leftover casserole for us to eat when we arrived. Leftover or not, it was delicious and just right for the cold weather. Here the radicchio, often combined with game or roasted meat in northern Italy, brings a wonderful smoky flavor to the dish. The sausage and milk give it richness, and the cheese sprinkled on top becomes deliciously crunchy when baked. · SERVES 4 TO 6

8 ounces (228 grams) sweet Italian sausage (about 2), removed from casings and crumbled

8 ounces (228 grams) hot Italian sausage (about 2), removed from casings and crumbled

1 small head radicchio, thinly sliced

2 tablespoons kosher salt, plus more to taste

1 pound (454 grams) penne

1 1/2 cups (360 ml) whole milk

2 large eggs, lightly beaten

3/4 cup (3 ounces/85 grams) freshly grated Parmigiano-Reggiano cheese

PREHEAT THE OVEN to 375 degrees (190°C). Lightly butter an 8-by-12-inch baking dish.

Heat a 10- to 12-inch skillet over medium heat. When it is hot, add the sausage. Cook, breaking up the sausage into small pieces with a wooden spoon, until the fat is rendered and the sausage has lost its pink color. Pour off all but 1 tablespoon of the fat. Add the radicchio, stir well, and cook, stirring until it is soft and well blended with the sausage, about 4 minutes. Season with salt to taste, and transfer to a large mixing bowl.

Meanwhile, fill a 10-quart stockpot with 7 quarts (6.5 liters) of water and bring to a boil over high heat. Add the 2 tablespoons salt. Add the pasta, stir, and cook until al dente. Drain the pasta and add to the bowl with the sausage. Add the milk and eggs and mix well. Pour into the prepared dish and sprinkle the top with the Parmigiano-Reggiano.

Transfer to the oven and bake until the top looks a bit crunchy and golden, 20 to 25 minutes. Let rest for 15 minutes before serving.

wine: A rich dish with bitterness from the radicchio, this requires a full and intense red like Brunello di Montalcino. Two of my favorite estates are Argiano and Colombini Barbi. If you choose a different estate, make sure that the wine is at least 5 or 6 years old.

linguine with zucchini, garlic, black olives, and toasted bread crumbs

LINGUINE CON ZUCCHINE E PANGRATTATO

mark · One of the great joys of being in the restaurant business is talking food with customers and listening to their memories of meals past. I must admit that not only do I love hearing people's anecdotes, but I often find they inspire menu ideas. That was the case with this recipe, which was my attempt to re-create a dish described to me by one of my loyal customers. It was his grandmother's specialty, and grandmothers are indeed the essence of Italian cooking. The honest flavors of the olives, garlic, onions, and herbs appealed to me instantly. And I like how the zucchini cooks down very softly—Grandma didn't know from al dente vegetables.

In Italy, bread crumbs are often used on pasta in place of cheese to save money. Buy un-seasoned bread crumbs from a local bakery—they'll taste much better than the ones you buy in the supermarket. Or make your own (see page 303). · MAKES 2 CUPS (480 ML) SAUCE; SERVES 4 TO 6

2 tablespoons kosher salt, plus more to taste

1 pound (454 grams) linguine

¼ cup (60 ml) extra-virgin olive oil

3 garlic cloves, peeled

1 large red onion, thinly sliced

4 medium zucchini, sliced lengthwise in half and then into paper-thin half-moons

20 Gaeta or Niçoise olives, pitted

1½ teaspoons dried oregano, preferably Sicilian

½ teaspoon crushed red pepper flakes, or more to taste

½ cup (30 grams) bread crumbs (page 303) or store-bought unseasoned bread crumbs

FILL A 10-QUART STOCKPOT with 7 quarts (6.5 liters) of water and bring to a boil over high heat. Add the 2 tablespoons kosher salt. Add the pasta, stir, and cook until al dente.

Meanwhile, heat a 10- to 12-inch skillet over medium-low heat. When it is hot, add the olive oil and garlic and cook, stirring frequently, until the garlic is lightly browned, 3 to 5 minutes. Add the onion and zucchini and cook, stirring frequently, until they are soft and just starting to color, about 5 minutes. Adjust the heat as necessary to keep the dish from browning. Add the olives, oregano, and crushed red pepper flakes, and season to taste with kosher salt.

Reserve ½ cup of the cooking water, and drain the pasta. Add it to the pan with the sauce and toss to combine. If the pasta looks dry, add the reserved cooking water 1 tablespoon at a time, tossing to combine between additions. Transfer the pasta to a large serving platter. Sprinkle on the bread crumbs, and serve immediately.

wine: Greco di Tufo, a southern Italian white made from grapes introduced to Italy by the Greeks more than two thousand years ago, would be terrific here. It's a fruity wine, not aged in oak. Try the one from Mastroberardino.

4

fresh pasta like mamma used to make

essential techniques and well~matched sauces

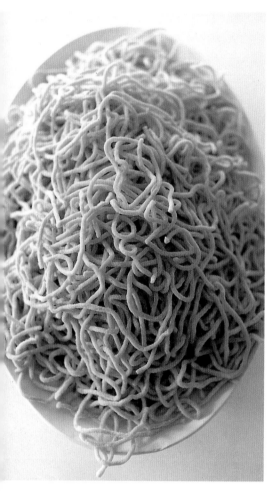

Dried and fresh pastas are fundamentally different
in the way they combine with sauces. Dried pasta, while a vehicle for
sauce, stands apart from it with its firm texture and assertively wheaty
flavor. Fresh pasta, in contrast, has a more yielding texture and mellow
richness from egg, absorbing sauce and almost becoming one with
it, so when you take a bite you can't separate the flavors of the two.

The recipes in the previous chapter demonstrate how dried pasta
catches sauce and carries it to the mouth: The rigatoni served with
butcher's sauce, for example, traps little chunks of sausage, salami,
and chopped olive in their large holes. Strands of whole wheat linguine
intertwine beautifully with small, soft bits of roasted vegetables. With
fresh pasta, we choose sauces that are more creamy, lighter, and more
saucy—for instance a simple mixture of emulsified butter, olive oil, and
melted Parmesan to flavor fettuccine, or a sauce of softened, citrus-
scented carrots for ravioli—designed to meld with the pasta as a proper
sauce should.

As we agreed in the previous chapter, it is well worth it to seek
out top-quality artisanal dried pasta for its superior texture and flavor.
Unfortunately, we have no such simple recommendation when it comes
to fresh pasta. It is true that in Italy good-quality fresh pasta is made

with the same simple ingredients as homemade—eggs and flour—by small shop owners who knead and roll and cut it as if they were in their own kitchens. Busy Italians can buy pasta as good as what they could make at home and skip right to preparing the sauce. But that shortcut is not an option for Americans. Even in the most expensive specialty food markets here, the so-called fresh pasta is a commercial product, unpleasantly thick, with such a doughy, gooey texture that it's not worth eating.

So in this chapter, before we present our favorite sauces for fresh pasta, we want to show you how to make excellent pasta at home. Not only have we studied pasta-making technique with many Italian *mamma* (more on this later), but we have worked hard over many years to adapt traditional methods, using a hand-cranked pasta machine, to make them as easy and quick as possible. With the benefit of our experience, you will be able to produce the thinnest, most tender and yielding, best-tasting fresh pasta possible. (If you want to try any of the sauce recipes here, but are not interested in making your own pasta, we suggest you substitute dried egg pasta from the supermarket. Our favorites are Barilla and Buitoni dried egg fettuccine, arranged in little nests inside their packages. Our second choice would be to replace the fresh pasta with dried semolina pasta. Just be aware that the dishes will be very different made with dried pasta.)

Beyond egg pasta, Italians have many wonderful recipes for *gnocchi* (dumplings made with potatoes or semolina), *ravioli nudi* (spinach and walnut dumplings), and *scialatielli* (rustic egg and milk pasta from southern Italy). The chapter concludes with our best recipes for these simple but satisfying homemade pasta dishes, appropriately sauced.

Making fresh pasta will never be as quick and convenient as opening up a box of dried pasta. So what can we say to convince you to do it? Only that it is absolutely a magical experience to transform a rough ball of dough into ethereal strands of tagliolini or into sheets of lasagne so thin that you can see through them when you hold them up to the light. Nothing else in the repertoire of Italian cooks can match this handmade food for its delicacy and delicious flavor.

pino I first learned to make pasta from my mother, who had all kinds of tricks for getting the most out of her dough. She used to say that when she thought the dough had been kneaded enough, she'd take a deep breath and knead it for another few minutes. That extra kneading is what gave it the elasticity to stretch so thin.

mark It's like making bread dough. When you knead, you develop the protein, called gluten, in the dough. That's what makes dough stretchy. Without gluten, pasta dough and bread dough would both break apart, not stretch.

pino Another thing I remember is how she would let it sit for a half hour after kneading before trying to roll it out. I would wake up late on the weekend, and the ball of dough would be resting on the counter. Then I could start to look forward to lunch. The resting time was as important as the kneading time, my mother would say.

mark The resting allows the gluten strands to relax. Unrested dough is like a short, thick rubber band, which will resist and pull back when you try to stretch it. Rested dough is like a long, thin rubber band with a lot of give.

pino My mother had a special technique for rolling it into a thin sheet. She would only roll in one direction, wrapping two-thirds of the dough around the rolling pin and then rolling it away from herself, rotating the dough a little, and repeating this wrapping and rolling until she had made her way completely around the dough.

mark Rolling that way, moving outward all the time, happens to be the most productive method for stretching the dough. If you tried to roll first away from yourself and then toward yourself, the way many people roll out pie dough, you'd create very tense strands of gluten fighting against each other and bouncing back toward the center.

All these tricks she taught you—kneading a long time, letting the dough rest, rolling it in a single direction—have a basis in flour science. She wasn't a food scientist, but she knew intuitively how to develop the gluten in the flour and work with it so that it would stretch as far as possible. Her expertise came from years of experience, and that's something that no amount of studying can give you. The more experience you have, the better equipped you are to judge by look and feel whether you have kneaded the dough enough, whether one way of rolling is better than another.

When I was working in Germany—where they make fantastic fresh egg pasta, by the way—the most important thing I learned was how to judge my dough. Was it too dry? Was it well kneaded? Was it thin enough when rolled? I learned by making literally thousands of pounds of egg noodles by hand. You're not going to be able to judge anything the first time you do it. The more batches you have under your belt, the more nuances about pasta making you will understand.

pino Yes, absolutely. It's my mother's experience, day after day, week after week, that inspired me to open my restaurant Le Madri ("the mothers" in Italian). The idea was to serve food like the homemade pasta my mother used to make, and to actually staff the kitchen with Italian women with similar experience: one Italian mother, a grandmother, and two younger women who had learned pasta making from their mothers and grandmothers.

mark Maria Fillabozzi, who later worked at Le Madri, taught me how to make Italian-style pasta one summer in East Hampton, at Sapore di Mare. She came from Rome to visit her son, who is a doctor in the city, and he asked you to give her a job to get her out of the house.

pino She didn't speak much English, did she?

mark We communicated very well after I figured out that she only wanted to hear three things: "Yes, Maria," "No problem, Maria," and "Thank you, Maria."

pino You figured her out, all right. Not only did she teach you to make beautiful pasta, at the end of two months she was doing your laundry!

mark I'll never forget how she would put a sheet of pasta on top of the newspaper. If you could still read the paper through the pasta, it was thin enough. She didn't use a rolling pin, though. I distinctly remember a mixer with a dough hook and a hand-cranked pasta machine.

pino Well, even four Italian women with four rolling pins wouldn't be able to make enough pasta to serve an entire restaurant. What I wound up doing was asking one of them, Marta Pollini, to figure out a way to duplicate handmade pasta using a mixer to knead the dough and a hand-cranked machine to roll and cut it. She knew what the dough was supposed to look and feel like every step of the way, and she made sure that the recipe using the machines produced pasta as close to handmade as possible. The other women, Maria, Margarita Aloi, and Allessandra Buitoni, kept the recipe honest.

mark Well, I love that machine, and it's absolutely not cheating to use one.

pino I'll agree, with this caution: Use only a hand-cranked machine. Electric machines that you attach to a mixer extrude the dough rather than rolling it, and the elasticity and resilience are not the same. What Marta and the others discovered was the importance of gradually reducing the thickness of the pasta sheets. If you rush and try to go from ¼ inch to ⅛ inch with one crank, you'll tear the dough.

mark You can also save time by kneading the dough in an electric mixer, with the dough hook attachment. Artisan bread bakers use these machines. There's no reason why artisan pasta can't be kneaded this way.

pino Sure, sure. That will work. Marta's technique included sufficient kneading time in the mixer, just as if you were kneading by hand.

mark I've tried kneading dough in the food processor, but the result is nowhere near that of hand kneading. The food processor blade just cuts through the dough, rather than really kneading it to develop that gluten. So food processor pasta doesn't have the elasticity, and will never stretch as thin as dough kneaded by hand or in a mixer.

pino But to be a purist, knead the dough by hand and stretch it with a rolling pin. I'd like everyone to try it just once, for the experience. Then you'll have something to compare to your machine-made dough. The two pastas will be related but will have a different texture in your mouth. Fettuccine made by hand is never slippery the way machine-cranked pastas are. It's pleasantly grainy. Try it to experience the authentic old style.

mark Just be prepared for a good upper-body workout.

pino It's hard work, yes. But it's a key to understanding a certain time in northern Italy. When you make pasta, you'll have a taste of life as it was when I was growing up. It is a taste of the Italian weekend, when we slowed down a little, went to mass, or a soccer game, and then sat down to a family meal. If you walked through a town square in Tuscany early on a Sunday afternoon, the streets would be empty, and you would be able to hear plates and glasses clinking through the open windows as everyone enjoyed some pasta. You have to experience it to appreciate it. Asked how he was able to capture the ineffable Italian spirit on film, Fellini said, "Life is a combination of magic and pasta."

mark Pino, you are sentimental beyond belief. Now can we get to the nuts and bolts of making pasta?

getting ready

BECAUSE WE WANT TO MAKE SURE THIS ITALIAN LEGACY is accurately reflected in the recipes, we're giving you a complete and detailed description of what you need to make fresh pasta dough.

equipment

There are two options for each of the two steps involved in making egg pasta. First, you can choose to knead the pasta dough by hand or to knead it using a stand mixer fitted with the dough hook. Second, you can choose to roll it out and cut it by hand, using a rolling pin and a knife, or to roll it out and cut it using a hand-cranked pasta machine.

TO KNEAD PASTA DOUGH BY HAND

• **Wooden cutting board.** You will need a large work surface, preferably wooden. (Stainless steel or marble will work, but since they are colder, they may make the dough a little tougher to knead.) In Italy, most homes have a special pasta board— a wooden board with a wooden lip two inches wide nailed to the side. The lip fits against the edge of a table or counter and holds the board in place, which is useful both for kneading the dough and for rolling it out. If you become truly dedicated to making pasta, you might want to make one of these, but we find that a wooden cutting board at least 12 by 24 inches (30 by 60 cm) works just fine. (If you plan both to knead and to roll out the pasta dough by hand, you will need a 24-by-30-inch surface to roll out the dough—use that for kneading it as well.) If you have a corner area on your countertop, that's a good place to set the cutting board, as the corner will hold the board in place.
• **Bench scraper.** You will need a bench scraper for cleaning the work surface. A bench scraper is a tool that consists of a stiff rectangular stainless steel blade attached to a wooden or plastic handle.

TO KNEAD PASTA DOUGH USING A STAND MIXER

• **Stand mixer with a dough hook.** Far and away the sturdiest and most reliable brand of home stand mixers is KitchenAid. Do not even attempt this with a hand-held mixer. All you'll get is a big wad of unmixed dough and a burned-out motor.
• **Wooden cutting board.** You will need a wooden cutting board at least 12 by 24 inches (30 by 60 cm) or an equivalent work surface. You will want to knead the dough briefly by hand after the machine has done most of the hard work.

TO ROLL AND CUT PASTA DOUGH BY HAND

• **Large work surface.** You will need a large work surface, at least 24 by 30 inches (60 by 75 cm), preferably wood. You can use the same work surface to knead and roll out the dough by hand. Be sure to scrape it clean with the bench scraper, wash it, and let it dry in between, while the dough is resting. Any bits of dough left on the surface will stick to the pasta dough as you are rolling it out and mar the surface of the dough.
• **Rolling pin.** The best type of rolling pin for this is the wooden dowel type, also known as a French rolling pin, 1 to 2 inches (2.5 to 5 cm) in diameter and at least 24 inches (60 cm) long.
• **Chef's knife.** You should always keep your knives sharp, but in this case it's particularly important. A dull blade will tear the edges of the noodles when you cut them and leave them ragged.
• **Baking sheets.** You will find it useful to line two baking sheets with parchment and transfer the pasta to them as you reach the desired thickness, especially if you are working in a small kitchen without much counter space.

TO ROLL AND CUT PASTA DOUGH USING A HAND-CRANKED MACHINE

- **Pasta machine.** A hand-cranked or electric crank pasta machine is an ingenious little gadget. On one end it has a set of rollers that are used to thin the dough into almost transparent "tongues" of pasta. The rollers are adjusted to numbered widths using a knob, usually from 8 (the widest) to 1 (the narrowest). By turning the knob from the widest to the narrowest setting (always in one-step increments) and then feeding through the dough, you thin the pasta. The other end of the machine has at least two and often more cutting blades. By feeding the tongues of pasta through the blades, you cut the sheet into noodles of varying widths. Determining the cut for your noodles is as simple as placing the crank in the correct hole. An electric crank machine operates on the same principle, but a motor turns the rollers so you don't need to crank by hand.
- **Baking sheets.** You will find it useful to line two baking sheets with parchment and transfer the pasta to them as you reach the desired thickness, especially if you are working in a small kitchen with little counter space.

ingredients

Homemade egg pasta contains eggs and flour, and that's all. Since pasta has only two components, their quality is paramount. Naturally, fresher eggs will result in better-tasting pasta. Be sure to use large eggs, not jumbo, extra-large, medium, or small. Eggs count as liquid in a recipe, and we tested the recipe with large eggs.

Use imported Italian 00 flour if you can find it. In Italy, flour is classified as 1, 0, or 00, with 00 being the most refined. This type of flour is so finely milled that it disintegrates like talcum powder if you rub it between your fingers. If you cannot buy 00 flour—more and more gourmet stores are stocking it—unbleached all-purpose flour is extremely similar and an excellent choice as well.

We know that some cooks add things to the dough. Even in Italy, you will find pasta colored (and supposedly flavored, but we never really taste a difference) with spinach or squid ink. But to us, this feels like trying to reinvent the wheel. The beauty of pasta lies in its simplicity. Gilding the lily by adding anything other than the eggs and flour only makes your work harder and the resulting pasta heavier.

fresh egg pasta dough

PASTA ALL'UOVO

Over the twenty years we have worked together, we have disagreed on many things, but this was one recipe we easily wrote in tandem.

A dough made with five eggs is the maximum amount that a home cook can comfortably knead, and it's not worth the effort to make less. If you want to make more, work it in two batches. You will notice that this recipe yields a generous 1½ pounds, but most of our recipes call for only 1 pound of pasta. We suggest either rolling and cutting all the dough and storing individually wrapped packets of noodles in the freezer, or simply rolling out the excess dough and cutting it into *maltagliati* (literally, "badly cut"), irregular pieces of pasta, often roughly diamond-shaped and about ½ inch across at their centers, that can be frozen and then later added to soups directly from the freezer.

To start, you will be using one hand to mix the ingredients together—this is your "working hand." You need to keep the other hand clean to pick up tools and sprinkle in flour as needed. We consider this the most efficient, neatest way to handle the process. Of course, once you start kneading, you will be using both hands. • MAKES 1 POUND 10 OUNCES (740 GRAMS)

3½ cups (1 pound/454 grams) Italian 00 flour or unbleached all-purpose flour, plus about 1 cup (125 grams) for dusting the work surface and your hands

5 large eggs

kneading pasta dough

TO KNEAD PASTA DOUGH BY HAND

Wash and dry your hands (remove any jewelry) and the work surface before beginning. Your work surface—a counter or table—should be at a comfortable height for kneading.

Shape the flour into a mound on the work surface. Have the flour for dusting in a small mound to the side of the work surface. Using your fist, create a well, or crater, in the center of the large mound of flour large enough to hold the eggs comfortably, 8 to 10 inches (20 to 25 cm) in diameter. Place the eggs in the center of the well [see page 96].

For this part of the process, you will use one hand as your working hand (use your favored hand, i.e., your right hand if you're right-handed) and keep the other clean to pick up ingredients and tools as needed. Using your working hand, break the yolks by "pinching" them together with the whites. Then, while continuing to pinch the eggs, use the fingertips of your hand to begin pulling flour into the eggs from the inside perimeter of the well. Pull in small amounts of flour at a time—your goal is to keep the wall of the well intact until the mixture is no longer runny. Continue incorporating small amounts of flour and pinching it into the mixture until the mass turns into a thick paste. Then, with the palm of your working hand, slowly begin to scrape the remaining flour from the well into the mixture, squeezing it gently until it is incorporated, 3 to 4 minutes. The dough will come together to form a sticky, pale yellow mass, with some flour and small pieces of dough remaining on the work surface; your working work hand will be well coated.

Using your clean hand, scrape and clean the working surface with a bench scraper, bringing all the remaining flour and dough particles toward the dough mass. Still using your clean hand, grab some of the unused flour from the work surface and sprinkle it over your working hand, then rub your hands together aggressively over the work surface. The flour should work as an abrasive to remove dough particles. Both hands should now be "working clean."

Using both hands, gather the remaining flour into the dough mass and then begin to knead it, using moderate pressure while pressing and stretching the dough forward and away from your body using the heels of your hands. Knead it several times this way to form an oval shape.

Turn the oval so that a narrow end is toward you. Hold down one end with the palm of your "non-working" hand and use the heel of your other hand to press and stretch the dough forward, then roll it back on itself against the palm of your hand. Do this 10 times, then turn the oval so that a long side is parallel to you, and roll it to smooth the seams. Turn the oval so that a narrow end is once again facing you and repeat the kneading process until you have an amalgamated dough that is only slightly sticky, 5 minutes. Incorporate the remaining flour and particles, and continue kneading until the dough is smooth and firm, 10 to 15 minutes total. When the dough is ready, it will be firm, very smooth, and pale yellow. When pressed, it should bounce back to its original shape. You may be tempted to stop kneading, because it's hard work, but keep going. When you think you're done, give it an additional 3 minutes.

Shape the dough into a rough ball and wrap it tightly in plastic wrap. Let the dough rest at room temperature for 30 minutes to 1 hour before rolling it out. Sufficient resting time is critical: after the resting period, the dough will be more elastic and easier to roll out.

TO KNEAD PASTA DOUGH USING A STAND MIXER

Place the eggs and flour in the bowl of the mixer. Use a fork to whisk them together roughly.

Attach the dough hook to the mixer and fix the bowl in place. Turn the mixer to speed 2 (low) and knead until the ingredients are amalgamated and the dough is firm and is just starting to form a ball and pull away from the sides of the bowl, about 2 minutes.

Lightly flour a wooden cutting board or other work surface, turn out the dough, and knead by hand until it is soft and supple and the surface is smooth, about 2 minutes.

Shape the dough into a rough ball and wrap it tightly in plastic wrap. Let it rest at room temperature for 30 minutes to 1 hour before rolling it out. Sufficient resting time is critical: after the resting period, the dough will be more elastic and easier to roll out.

rolling and cutting pasta

TO ROLL AND CUT PASTA DOUGH BY HAND

Line two baking sheets with parchment paper and set aside. Dust your work surface very lightly with flour.

Place the dough in the center of the work surface. With your hands, flatten the dough slightly. Place the rolling pin on the center of the dough and roll it away from you. Turn the dough a quarter turn and repeat.

Continue rolling the dough away from you, turning a quarter turn each time, until you have a large circle that is ⅛ inch (0.3 cm) thick. The dough should be roughly circular and the thickness should be fairly even.

To begin thinning, place the rolling pin on the edge of the dough opposite you (at 12 o'clock). Roll up the dough toward you, wrapping two-thirds of it up on the rolling pin, then quickly unroll the sheet, pressing down with the pin and smoothing the pasta with your hands as you unroll it. Turn the sheet of pasta slightly and repeat. It should take 12 turns to make your way completely around the circle of dough. If the dough sticks to the rolling pin or itself, sprinkle very lightly with flour. An expert pasta maker can thin the dough enough with just 1 trip around, but it may take you 2 or 3 to reach the right state of transparency. When the dough begins to tear in spots, that indicates that you have stretched it as far as it can go. Set the sheet aside and allow it to dry slightly before cutting it.

To cut the dough into noodles, roll up the dough into a flat cylinder 3 inches (7.5 cm) wide. Hold the dough with one hand while you cut it with the other, using a sharp knife. Then fluff the noodles to separate them, and transfer to the baking sheets until you are ready to cook them. For lasagne noodles, don't roll up the dough. Simply cut it to the size you want. Do the same for farfalle, and then pinch each rectangle firmly in the center to shape the noodles. The method for ravioli appears on page 110.

TO ROLL AND CUT PASTA DOUGH USING A HAND-CRANKED MACHINE (OR ELECTRIC CRANK)

Line two baking sheets with parchment and set aside. Set the rollers on the machine to the widest setting, probably 8, and insert the crank.

Cut off a golf-ball-sized piece of dough. Rewrap the remaining dough in the plastic wrap. Lightly flour the piece of dough. Insert it into the opening between the rollers and turn the crank smoothly. A flattened piece of dough will emerge from the other side.

Remove the flattened dough, fold it in half, lightly flour it again, and then feed it through the rollers on the same setting. Repeat this process until the pasta dough is perfectly smooth and does not shred or have "fringe" on the sides. Then turn the dial on the pasta machine to the next thinnest setting, lightly flour the dough, and pass it through the rollers once.

Continue to put the dough through the rollers, reducing the machine's thickness setting each time. Do not fold the dough again, but continue to flour it lightly. When you have passed it through the thinnest setting (with the exception of spaghetti alla chitarra, which should be thinned to the next-to-last level; see page 93), set the sheet aside and repeat with the remaining dough (do not stack the sheets).

Hand-stretched and -cut tagliatelle

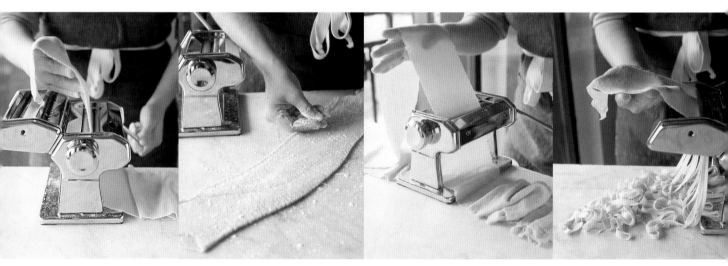

Machine-stretched and -cut tagliatelle

When all the dough has been rolled, to cut the noodles insert the crank into the hole for appropriate cutting blade and run each piece of dough through the machine. Fluff the noodles and transfer to the parchment-lined baking sheets, arranging them in a single layer so they don't stick together. For lasagne and farfalle see page 102; for ravioli, see the individual recipes.

APPROXIMATE PASTA SIZES

Pappardelle	1 inch (2.5 cm) wide
Tagliatelle	½ inch (1.3 cm) wide
Fettuccine	¼ inch (0.6 cm) wide
Tagliolini	⅛ inch (0.3 cm) wide
Farfalle	1-by-2-inch (2.5-by-5-cm) rectangles, pinched in the middle
Lasagne	6-by-12-inch (15-by-30-cm) rectangles
Spaghetti alla chitarra	⅛ inch (0.3 cm) wide

storing fresh pasta

Sometimes you will want to cook the pasta right away, or within an hour after cutting it. In that case, simply leave it at room temperature on the parchment-lined pans. In fact, if you let the surface of the pasta dry a little bit, it's easier to handle.

If you are not going to cook it within 1 hour but will use it within 24 hours, cover the pans loosely with plastic wrap and store in the refrigerator.

For long-term storage, freeze pasta immediately after cutting it. The best way we've found is to wrap individual portions in two layers of plastic wrap. Pasta will keep frozen like this for several weeks. Do not thaw frozen pasta before cooking—drop it, still frozen, directly into boiling, salted water.

cooking fresh pasta

Abundant water is particularly important when cooking fresh pasta, because the dough is delicate. If pieces bump against each other, they may tear.

To cook 1 pound (454 grams) of pasta, to feed 4 to 6 people (which most of these recipes call for), you need 7 quarts (6.5 liters) of water. Since adding pasta to the water will increase the volume, you want your pot a little more than three-quarters full with water, which is why we recommend a 10-quart pot. You should be able to see the pasta moving around freely in the water.

We recommend salting this amount of cooking water with 2 table-spoons salt. That may look like a lot of salt to you, but much of it is washed away when you drain the pasta, and you want your cooking water to be flavorful, so that if you use it to loosen the sauce it doesn't flatten the taste. This is not such an exact amount that you need to measure it out (unless you want to). In Italian homes, as well as in professional kitchens, salt is stored in a large jar or container, and the cook just grabs

tagliolini

fettuccine

tagliatelle

pappardelle

spaghetti alla chitarra

lasagne

farfalle

it by the handful. If you try this method a few times, you will soon recognize the correct amount by feel. We recommend kosher salt for cooking pasta. Kosher salt does not contain any additives, so it lends a cleaner flavor. Sea salt is another acceptable choice.

Fresh pasta needs to be watched very closely, because it cooks in 2 to 3 minutes. Generally, when fresh pasta floats to the surface, it's ready to come out. Ravioli are an exception because they are thicker and they expand as the filling heats, so they need to sit on the surface a little longer. Fresh pasta that isn't homemade—the kind you buy in the grocery store—needs to cook about 50 percent longer, because it is thicker and doughier.

You need to taste pasta to know whether it's cooked. Fresh pasta is one of the all-time great comfort foods because of its tender texture, but you don't want it to be *too* soft, or mushy. Take it off the heat when there is still a touch of resistance—that's the true meaning of *al dente*.

When pouring the pasta into a colander in the sink, work slowly and gently so it doesn't tear. The new pasta pots with built-in strainers are particularly useful for delicate fresh pastas.

We value pasta cooking water, and so should you. Right before you drain the pasta, use a ladle to remove a little of the cooking water—$\frac{1}{2}$ cup— that you can then use to loosen the sauce if necessary. The starch in the cooking water helps unite the sauce with the pasta, and the cooking water is already seasoned with salt and flavored from the pasta, so it won't dilute the flavor of your sauce the way plain water would.

fettuccine carbonara

FETTUCCINE ALLA CARBONARA

pino • In my youth, I was an actor and I traveled around Italy with a theater troupe. We were all good cooks—food was our second passion, after acting. The perfect fettuccine alla carbonara became our Holy Grail. When we were on the road, we'd finish a performance and then find a local restaurant where we'd ask the owner to make the dish, or, if it was late enough and the place was empty, we'd just ask to go into the kitchen and cook for ourselves. We competed fiercely to see who could come up with the best version, and we built on each other's refinements. More than two decades later, I am still using the recipe I developed with my fellow actors, and it remains a stand-out carbonara.

Making a great carbonara is like making a great stir-fry: It's all about the timing and assembly. If you have all of your ingredients ready, you can quickly put everything together. Tossing the cooked pasta with the onions and olive oil before adding the eggs lets the pasta cool slightly, reducing the chance that the eggs will scramble when you stir them in. Whipping the eggs with a whisk loosens them up so that they completely coat the pasta instead of separating into strands. Using a stainless steel or glass mixing bowl also helps. Ceramic bowls hold too much heat, and if you use them, you risk curdling the eggs. Speaking of eggs, since their flavor is prominent here, you want to use farm-fresh organic eggs if you can find them.

I haven't stopped experimenting with the details. Just recently, I substituted some apple-smoked bacon for the pancetta and liked its smoky flavor so much that I recommend it as an alternative here. • SERVES 4 AS A MAIN COURSE OR 6 AS AN APPETIZER

2 tablespoons kosher salt

8 ounces (225 grams) ¼-inch (0.6-cm) slices pancetta or apple-smoked bacon, cut into ¼-inch (0.6-cm) dice

1 medium red onion, thinly sliced

1 large egg

3 large egg yolks

1 pound (454 grams) fettuccine made from Fresh Egg Pasta Dough (page 94) or store-bought dried egg fettuccine or semolina bucatini

2 tablespoons extra-virgin olive oil

¼ cup (2 ounces/56 grams) freshly grated Pecorino Romano cheese

¼ cup (2 ounces/56 grams) freshly grated Parmigiano-Reggiano cheese

1 tablespoon freshly ground black pepper

FILL A 10-QUART STOCKPOT with 7 quarts (6.5 liters) water and bring to a boil over high heat. Add the salt, stir, reduce the heat to low, and cover the pot.

Place a 10-inch skillet over low heat. Add the pancetta or bacon and cook, stirring frequently to prevent sticking, until it has given up its fat and is beginning to color and crisp, 5 to 7 minutes. Add the onion, reduce the heat, and cook, stirring occasionally, until the onion is soft and beginning to color and the pancetta or bacon is crisp, about 7 minutes.

While the pancetta and onion are cooking, place a large stainless steel or glass bowl next to the stove. Pour the egg and egg yolks into a medium bowl and whisk until pale and increased in volume, 3 to 5 minutes. Set the bowl with the eggs next to the larger bowl.

When the pancetta and onions are cooked, remove them from the heat. Raise the heat under the pot of water and bring it back to a boil.

Add the pasta and cover the pot until the water begins to bubble. Lift the lid and immediately taste the pasta. When the pasta is al dente, about 2 minutes (longer if using dried pasta), scoop out about ½ cup of the cooking water, then drain the pasta and add to the large bowl. Add the onion mixture and olive oil and mix gently but thoroughly with tongs or a wooden spoon.

Add the eggs to the pasta and mix very quickly and thoroughly. (If you aren't fast here, the eggs will scramble.) If the pasta looks dry at this point, add some of the reserved cooking water 1 tablespoon at a time, mixing between additions. Stir in the cheeses and pepper and mix again. Transfer the pasta to a serving dish and serve immediately.

tip: I couldn't afford truffles in my younger days, but occasionally I will shave about 4 paper-thin slices of either fresh black truffles or (much cheaper and more convenient) jarred black truffles in olive oil onto each serving of the finished dish. The woodsy flavor of the truffles goes beautifully with the richness of the egg yolks.

wine: A southern Italian white wine such as a Fiano d'Avellino is sharp enough to clean the palate after the egg yolks.

Pino makes Fettuccine Carbonara (page 104)

fettuccine with butter and cheese

FETTUCCINE AL BURRO E PARMIGIANO

pino • At first glance, fresh pasta tossed with butter and cheese might not seem like much of a recipe. But it is the technique for combining the three ingredients that transforms them into a coherent dish. Grate the cheese on the large holes of a box grater or a rasp grater, so the larger flakes will cling to and melt on the surface of the pasta. Don't pass additional cheese at the table. There is just enough in the recipe to season the pasta; any more would make the dish too dry. And resist oversalting the dish before serving. The sweetness of the butter, fruitiness of the olive oil, and tang of the cheese should be the primary flavors here, not salt added at the end. The ground cinnamon is optional (you can also use ½ teaspoon ground cumin or ¼ teaspoon grated nutmeg), but its spiciness combines wonderfully with the sweetness of the butter.

• SERVES 4 AS A MAIN COURSE OR 6 AS AN APPETIZER

4 tablespoons (56 grams) unsalted butter, cut into small pieces

2 tablespoons (30 ml) extra-virgin olive oil

½ cup (2 ounces/56 grams) freshly grated Parmigiano-Reggiano cheese (grate it in the large holes of a box grater)

½ teaspoon ground cinnamon (optional)

2 tablespoon kosher salt, plus more to taste, if necessary

1½ pounds (680 grams) fettuccine made from Fresh Egg Pasta Dough (page 94) or store-bought dried egg fettuccine or semolina spaghetti

FILL A 10-QUART STOCKPOT with 7 quarts (6.5 liters) water and bring to a boil over high heat. While the water is heating, place a heatproof bowl large enough to hold the pasta on top of the uncovered pot. Put the butter, olive oil, cheese, and cinnamon, if using, in the bowl, and stir occasionally as the butter melts.

When the water is boiling, use oven mitts to transfer the bowl to a heatproof surface. Scoop out about ½ cup of the boiling water, and pour 6 tablespoons of it into the bowl.

Add the 2 tablespoons salt and then the pasta to the pot, and cover the pot. When the lid starts to dance, remove it. Stir the pasta and cook until al dente, about 3 minutes (longer if using dried pasta).

While the pasta is cooking, whisk the sauce vigorously to emulsify.

When the pasta is cooked, reserve ½ cup of the cooking water. Drain the pasta, add it to the bowl, and toss very well with tongs or two large forks to coat. If the pasta looks dry, add some of the reserved cooking water 1 tablespoon at a time, tossing between additions. Season with salt if necessary and serve immediately.

wine: The butter and cheese here call out for a buttery Chardonnay from California.

pappardelle with lamb ragu

PAPPARDELLE AL SUGO DI AGNELLO

pino • Wide noodles like pappardelle are the best choice for rich, meaty ragus. At 1 inch wide, they wrap themselves nicely around pieces of lamb, and their surfaces are good for absorbing sauce. Here a slow simmer tenderizes what can sometimes be a tough cut, and the addition of cloves enhances the lamb's rich flavor. This makes a generous amount of sauce; leftovers can be frozen for another meal. • SERVES 6 AS A MAIN COURSE OR 8 AS AN APPETIZER

2 tablespoons (30 ml) extra-virgin olive oil

1 medium carrot, finely minced

2 medium celery stalks, finely minced

½ small red onion, finely minced

2 pounds (908 grams) boneless lamb (from the shoulder or leg), cut into ½-inch cubes

4 bay leaves

4 whole cloves, wrapped in cheesecloth and tied

½ teaspoon freshly ground black pepper, or more to taste

1 cup (240 ml) dry red wine, such as Chianti

1 cup (240 ml) Chicken Stock (page 29) or canned low-sodium organic chicken broth

2 cups (480 ml) canned Italian plum tomatoes, preferably San Marzano, with their juice, pureed in a food processor or food mill

1 teaspoon dried thyme

2 tablespoons kosher salt, plus more to taste

1½ pounds (680 grams) pappardelle made from Fresh Egg Pasta Dough (page 94) or dried semolina bucatini

½ cup (2 ounces/56 grams) freshly grated Pecorino Romano or Parmigiano-Reggiano cheese

PLACE A 10- TO 12-INCH SKILLET over medium heat, and when it is hot, add the oil. Add the carrot, celery, and onion and cook until soft, 5 to 7 minutes.

Add the lamb, raise the heat to high, and cook, stirring frequently, until the meat has lost its raw appearance, about 5 minutes. Stir in the bay leaves, cloves, and pepper, then continue cooking, stirring constantly, until the meat has browned, about 5 minutes. Add the wine and continue stirring until it has almost completely evaporated, 5 minutes.

Add the stock and tomatoes, stir well, and bring to a boil. Add the thyme and reduce the heat to low. Cover the skillet with a tight-fitting lid and simmer gently until sauce has begun to thicken, about 30 minutes.

Remove the cover and cook until the sauce is thickened and no longer soupy but not dry, about 15 minutes.

Taste the sauce and season with salt if necessary. Remove the clove sachet and bay leaves and discard. Set the sauce aside while you cook the pasta.

Fill a 10-quart pot with 7 quarts (6.5 liters) water and bring to a boil over high heat. Add the 2 tablespoons kosher salt, and then drop in the pasta. Cook the pasta until tender but still al dente, about 3 minutes (longer if using dried pasta).

Drain the pasta and transfer to a large bowl. Add the sauce to the pasta 1 cup at a time, tossing gently to combine between additions, until the sauce coats the pasta. Sprinkle with the grated cheese and serve immediately.

tip: In Tuscany, a sauce like this is often made with wild boar, which is a very sweet meat, not at all gamy. If you'd like to try it, use boar meat from the leg or shoulder, cut into ½-inch (1.3-cm) cubes. If you have trouble locating boar, you can mail-order it in 1-pound packages from D'Artagnan (see Resources, page 306).

wine: The obvious choice here is a good vintage Brunello di Montalcino. Look for a 2001 or a 2002, which can go toe-to-toe with something as meaty as lamb.

fresh carrot and ricotta ravioli with carrot and orange sauce

RAVIOLI DI CAROTE AL SUGO D'ARANCIA

mark · In the cooking of Emilia-Romagna, tortellini are often stuffed with winter squash. Inspired by the bright orange color of the filling, I substituted carrots and ricotta cheese in this springtime version. A sauce of fresh orange juice and thinly sliced multicolored baby carrots makes this dish a visual stunner. (The Carrot-Orange Soup on page 23 has similar flavors and the same brilliant color.)

Egg pasta dough rolled out into sheer sheets serves as a wrapper for all kinds of stuffed pasta, including ravioli. When you have the dough in sheets, you put the filling on one sheet in regular rows, place another sheet on top, and seal the sheets together with your fingers. Be sure to press hard—you may want to go over them twice—or the filling may leak into the cooking water. Then you simply cut the ravioli. You can cut ravioli with a regular knife, but using a pastry wheel seals them a little more firmly. I like to use a ravioli cutter, a metal ring or square with handles that makes fast work of a sheet of ravioli. Pino says his mother used the rim of a small drinking glass for the same result. Uncooked ravioli freeze beautifully (place them on baking sheets in the freezer until frozen hard, then transfer to zipper-lock bags; they can be kept frozen for up to 2 weeks). · SERVES 4 AS A MAIN COURSE OR 6 AS AN APPETIZER

FOR THE FILLING

6 large carrots (1½ pounds/
680 grams), cut into chunks

1 tablespoon (14 grams)
unsalted butter

2 tablespoons sugar

1 teaspoon kosher salt, plus more
to taste

1 pound (2 cups/454 grams)
fresh ricotta

½ teaspoon freshly grated nutmeg

1¼ cups (5 ounces/140 grams) freshly
grated Parmigiano-Reggiano cheese

¼ teaspoon freshly ground
black pepper

1½ pounds (680 grams) 12-by-4-inch
(30-by-10-cm) pasta sheets made
from Fresh Egg Pasta Dough
(page 94)

2 large eggs, lightly beaten,
for egg wash

TO MAKE THE FILLING

Place the carrots, butter, sugar, and 1 teaspoon of the salt in a small saucepan, cover with water, and bring to a boil over high heat. Reduce the heat and simmer until the carrots are very soft, about 20 minutes.

Drain the carrots and transfer to a food processor. While the machine is running, add the ricotta ¼ cup at a time. Add the nutmeg, the Parmigiano-Reggiano cheese, pepper, and salt, to taste. Set aside to cool.

TO ASSEMBLE THE RAVIOLI

Lightly dust a baking sheet with flour and set aside. Place 1 pasta sheet on a floured work surface. Scoop the carrot filling into a pastry bag without a tip. (Alternately, use a plastic bag with one corner snipped off.) Starting 1½ inches (40 cm) from one end, pipe teaspoons of filling every 3 inches (7.5 cm) down the center of the pasta sheet. Brush egg wash onto another sheet of pasta and place the second sheet on top of the first, egg-washed side down. Use your fingers to seal the top sheet to the bottom sheet, pressing out any air pockets. Cut the ravioli into 3-inch (7.5-cm) squares with a decorative pastry wheel, a ravioli cutter, or a knife, and transfer to the prepared baking sheet. Repeat until the pasta and filling are used up. (The ravioli can be refrigerated for up to 3 hours before cooking.)

When you are ready to cook the ravioli, fill a 10-quart pot with 7 quarts (6.5 liters) of water and bring to a boil over high heat.

1 tablespoon (14 grams) unsalted
  butter

½ teaspoon grated orange zest

Juice of 1 medium orange

8 baby carrots, preferably multicolored,
  thinly sliced

Kosher salt and freshly ground
  black pepper

2 tablespoons kosher salt

8 fresh sage leaves

½ cup (2 ounces/56 grams) freshly
  grated Parmigiano-Reggiano cheese

Place an 8-inch skillet over medium heat and add the butter, orange zest, and juice. When the butter has melted, add the baby carrots. Cook until the carrots are tender, about 1 minute. Season with salt and pepper to taste. Remove from the heat and cover to keep warm.

Meanwhile add the 2 tablespoons salt to the boiling water. Use a slotted spoon to gently place the ravioli into the water. When the ravioli are just tender, 4 minutes, using the slotted spoon, transfer them to a large serving bowl.

Pour the sauce over the ravioli, garnish with the sage, and sprinkle on the Parmigiano-Reggiano cheese and serve immediately.

wine: A Greco di Tufo is fruity enough to balance the carrots here.

fred's spaghetti

SPAGHETTI ALLA FRED

mark · Popular demand keeps this dish on the menu at Fred's, the restaurant at Barneys, the chic Manhattan department store where I serve as chef. The fashionable clientele loves pasta but prefers sauces made with vegetables. This one is a lightened version of a traditional Genovese pasta dish with pesto, potatoes, and green beans. In my version, I get rid of the potatoes (too many carbs) and add some sun-dried tomatoes for color and bright, acidic flavor.

Spaghetti alla chitarra is slightly thicker than other noodles. Originally in Italy it was made with a wire-stringed instrument that resembled a guitar, hence the name (in this country, you can buy one at Sur la Table; see Resources, page 306). It is sometimes still made this way, but it is also made with a pasta machine: When rolling the dough, leave it slightly thicker, working down to the next-to-last setting, and then feed it through the narrowest pasta cutter on the machine. The width and height of spaghetti alla chitarra should be more or less equal; in other words, if you look at the end of one piece, it should be square. You can also purchase dried spaghetti alla chitarra or use semolina spaghetti for this dish. · SERVES 4 AS A MAIN COURSE OR 6 AS AN APPETIZER

---

2 tablespoons plus 1 teaspoon kosher salt, or more to taste

8 ounces (228 grams) green beans, trimmed

¼ cup (60 ml) extra-virgin olive oil

2 garlic cloves, sliced

24 shiitake mushrooms (12 ounces/ 340 grams), stems removed and discarded, caps cut into julienne,

1 pound (454 grams) spaghetti alla chitarra made from Fresh Egg Pasta Dough (page 94) or store-bought dried spaghetti alla chitarra (preferably Setaro brand) or dried semolina spaghetti

½ cup (120 ml) Pesto (page 33)

½ cup (2 ounces/56 grams) freshly grated Pecorino Romano cheese

12 fresh basil leaves

FILL A 3-QUART SAUCEPAN with water and bring to a boil. Add 1 teaspoon of the salt and the green beans and cook for 3 minutes. Drain and set aside. When the green beans are cool, use a sharp paring knife to halve them lengthwise.

Place a 12-inch skillet over medium heat, and when it is hot, add the olive oil. Add the garlic and cook until golden, about 1 minute. Add the mushrooms and sauté until soft and deep brown, about 5 minutes. Add the green beans, reduce the heat, and cook until heated through, 2 minutes. Remove from the heat. Set aside.

Meanwhile, fill a 10-quart pot with 7 quarts (6.5 liters) water and bring to a boil over high heat. Add the remaining 2 tablespoons kosher salt, stir, and toss in the spaghetti. Cook until al dente, 2 to 3 minutes (longer if using dried pasta).

While the pasta is cooking, add the pesto to the skillet with the vegetables and stir well. Taste and season with more salt if necessary (beware: some sun-dried tomatoes are very salty).

When the pasta is cooked, reserve ½ cup of the cooking water, and drain the pasta. Add the pasta to the skillet and toss to combine. If the pasta looks dry, add the reserved pasta cooking water 1 tablespoon at a time, tossing to combine between additions.

Garnish with the cheese and fresh basil leaves and serve immediately.

wine: This dish is a luncheon favorite at Fred's, where Chardonnay is a popular, and appropriate, accompaniment.

tagliolini with sweet sausage and black truffle

TAGLIOLINI CON SALSICCIA E TARTUFO NERO

pino • This is a luxurious dish, appropriate for New Year's Eve or another celebratory occasion. The sausage keeps the truffles from being too fussy, and the truffles elevate the sausage with their exquisite flavor. If you have never eaten fresh black truffles, you are in for a treat—their flavor is unique.

A truffle slicer is a small metal gadget that looks like a cheese slicer and has a very sharp blade. Truffles are always cut very thin, which releases their flavor and makes the best use of them, given their cost. If fresh black truffles aren't available, or are simply out of your reach financially, you can use black truffles preserved in olive oil or even black truffle puree. • SERVES 4 AS A MAIN COURSE OR 6 AS AN APPETIZER

2 tablespoons (30 ml) extra-virgin olive oil

1 medium red onion, thinly sliced

1 pound (454 grams) sweet Italian sausage (about 4), casings removed

1/2 teaspoon freshly grated nutmeg

1 teaspoon freshly ground black pepper

1 cup (240 ml) heavy cream

2 tablespoons kosher salt

1 pound (454 grams) tagliolini made from Fresh Egg Pasta Dough (page 94) or store-bought dried egg fettuccine or dried semolina penne

1/4 cup (1 ounce/28 grams) freshly grated Parmigiano-Reggiano cheese

1 ounce (28 grams) fresh black truffle, or 3 tablespoons black truffle puree (preferably Urbani brand)

PLACE A 12-INCH SKILLET over medium heat, and when it is hot, add the olive oil. When the oil is hot, add the onion and cook, stirring frequently, until soft, about 5 minutes. Add the sausage, raise the heat to high, and cook, crumbling the meat with a fork and then stirring occasionally until the sausage is no longer raw, about 6 minutes. Add the nutmeg and pepper, stir well, and cook, stirring occasionally, until the meat is cooked through, about 3 minutes. Add the cream and stir, then lower the heat to low and cook for 2 minutes. (The sauce will still be very liquid.) Remove the skillet from the heat and set aside.

Fill a 10-quart pot with 7 quarts (6.5 liters) of water and bring to a boil over high heat. Add the salt, then add the pasta, stir and cook until al dente, about 3 minutes (longer if using dried pasta).

Reserve 1/2 cup of the pasta cooking water, and drain the pasta. Add the pasta to the skillet with the sauce, return the skillet to medium heat, and toss well to coat the pasta. If the pasta seems dry, add some of the reserved cooking water 1 tablespoon at a time, tossing to combine between additions. Stir in the cheese 1 tablespoon at a time.

Transfer the pasta to a large serving platter. Using a truffle slicer, slice the fresh black truffle over the pasta, or add the truffle puree and toss to combine. Serve immediately.

wine: I suggest an Aglianico, a great red wine from the south that is deep in flavor and rich in taste. Importers have recently discovered Aglianico in a big way, and it is now widely available here.

tagliolini with chicken livers and onion

TAGLIOLINI ALLA CIBREO

pino • I am addicted to *cibreo,* one of the great Florentine dishes. It consists of chicken livers sautéed with red onion and white wine. It is usually served as a spread on crostini but, at one of those times when necessity is the mother of invention, I discovered that it also works well as a luscious pasta sauce. To vary the basic recipe, try adding a tablespoon of chopped capers—but if you do, omit the Parmigiano-Reggiano at the end. • SERVES 4 AS A MAIN DISH OR 6 AS AN APPETIZER

3 tablespoons (45 ml) extra-virgin olive oil, plus 1 to 2 tablespoons for drizzling

1 large red onion, thinly sliced

2 pounds (908 grams) chicken livers, trimmed and coarsely chopped

1 cup (240 ml) dry white wine, such as Sauvignon Blanc

1 teaspoon freshly ground black pepper

1 1/2 cups (480 ml) Chicken Stock (page 29) or chicken broth made from Knorr powdered bouillon

1 tablespoon minced fresh thyme

1 tablespoon minced fresh sage

2 tablespoons plus 1 teaspoon kosher salt

1 pound (454 grams) tagliolini made from Fresh Egg Pasta Dough (page 94) or store-bought dried egg fettuccine or dried semolina rigatoni

1/4 cup (1 ounce/28 grams) shredded Parmigiano-Reggiano cheese (grate it on the largest holes of a box grater)

PLACE A 10- TO 12-INCH SKILLET over medium heat, and when it is hot, add the olive oil. Add the onion and cook until soft and golden, 5 to 7 minutes.

Raise the heat to high and add the chicken livers. Cook, stirring constantly with a fork and pressing down on the chicken livers, until they break apart into small pieces, about 2 minutes. Reduce the heat to low and continue cooking, all the while pressing down on the livers, for 3 minutes longer. Add the wine and pepper and cook until the wine is reduced by half, about 5 minutes. Add the chicken stock, thyme, sage, and 1 teaspoon of the salt. Reduce the heat to medium-low and simmer for 5 minutes. Taste for seasoning. Set the sauce aside.

While the sauce is cooking, fill a 10-quart stockpot with 7 quarts (6.5 liters) water and bring to a boil over high heat. Add the remaining 2 tablespoons kosher salt. Add the pasta, stir, and cook until al dente, about 3 minutes (longer if using dried pasta).

Reserve 1/2 cup of the pasta cooking water, and drain the pasta. Add it to the pan with the sauce and toss over low heat until well coated, 2 minutes. If the pasta looks dry, add the reserved cooking water 1 tablespoon at a time, tossing to combine between additions. Serve immediately, with the Parmigiano-Reggiano cheese on the side and drizzle with olive oil.

wine: A young Dolcetto or Nebbiolo from the Piedmont region will balance this rich pasta dish.

ribollita-filled ravioli

RAVIOLI CON RIBOLLITA AL POMODORO E PARMIGIANO

pino • *Ribollita,* a thick vegetable soup, was the food of my childhood. Although I tend to make mostly Tuscan classics, this dish is something new I created for my restaurant Tuscan Square. I was looking to please my customers, who more and more request vegetarian pasta dishes. Rather than fill my ravioli with the usual spinach or broccoli, I thought about what would be more tasty. When I looked at a bowl of ribollita, so flavorful from the kale, so thick that a spoon could stand up in it, I suspected that it would be a wonderful ravioli filling—and I was right. The pasta has the same smoky, rich taste that Italians find so satisfying. If you have some leftover ribollita, give this a try. If you don't, here's your excuse to make a pot of the delicious soup, which you can eat throughout the week after you have your pasta. • SERVES 4 AS A MAIN COURSE OR 6 AS AN APPETIZER

1½ pounds (680 grams) 12-by-4-inch (30-by-10-cm) pasta sheets made from Fresh Egg Pasta Dough (page 94)

1 cup leftover Ribollita (page 31), cold

FOR THE SAUCE

3 tablespoons (45 ml) extra-virgin olive oil

1 medium red onion, thinly sliced

1½ cups (360 ml) canned Italian plum tomatoes, preferably San Marzano, with their juice, pureed in a food processor or food mill

½ cup (240 ml) vegetable stock or vegetable broth made with Knorr powdered bouillon

2 tablespoons plus 1½ teaspoons kosher salt

¼ cup (1 ounce/28 grams) freshly grated Parmigiano-Reggiano cheese

LIGHTLY DUST A BAKING sheet with flour and set aside.

TO MAKE THE RAVIOLI

Place 1 pasta sheet on the work surface. Starting 1½ inches (40 cm) from the end, spoon tablespoons of ribollita every 3 inches (7.5 cm) down the center of the pasta sheet. Using a finger, dampen the pasta sheet around the filling. Place a second sheet of pasta on top of the first one and seal the two sheets together by pressing firmly around the filling with your fingertips, pressing out any air pockets. Cut the ravioli into 3-inch (7.5-cm) squares with a decorative pastry wheel, a ravioli cutter, or a knife, and transfer to the prepared baking sheet. Repeat until the pasta and filling are used up. (The ravioli can be refrigerated for up to 3 hours before cooking.)

TO MAKE THE SAUCE

Place a 12-inch skillet over medium heat, and when it is hot, add the olive oil. Add the onion and cook, stirring occasionally, until soft, about 3 minutes. Add the tomatoes, vegetable stock, and 1½ teaspoons salt and cook over low heat until thickened, about 12 minutes. Remove the skillet from the heat.

When you are ready to cook the ravioli, fill a wide deep pot three-quarters full with water. Bring the water to a boil and add the 2 tablespoons salt. Using a slotted spoon, gently place the ravioli in the water, no more than 3 at a time, and cook until al dente, about 3 minutes after they bob to the top. As they are done, remove them with the slotted spoon and place them in the skillet with the sauce.

When all the ravioli are cooked and in the sauce, turn the heat to medium and very gently toss the ravioli in the sauce until coated, about 2 minutes. Sprinkle with the Parmigiano-Reggiano cheese and serve immediately.

wine: This very wintry dish screams for a good vintage super Tuscan.

cannelloni with asparagus and mortadella

CANNELLONI CON ASPARAGI E MORTADELLA

mark • When I began traveling to Italy, I was a little surprised—and disappointed—to discover that what I had thought of as "Italian food" when I was growing up in Queens was rarely on the menu. I missed the stuffed shells and cannelloni I loved as a child. Then, on a trip to Bologna, I discovered these delicate pasta packages filled with asparagus and the local mortadella, a sausage with a distinctive pink color, studded with cubes of creamy fat and pistachio nuts. Like much of the food of Emilia-Romagna, this dish is rich almost to the point of decadence. But there is no better way to spoil your friends and family than by serving it as a first course or side dish for a festive spring meal. For a long time, Italian mortadella wasn't exported to the United States, but it is now available in gourmet and specialty food stores, and it is far superior to domestic mortadella in taste and texture. • SERVES 6 AS AN APPETIZER OR SIDE DISH

2 tablespoons plus 1 teaspoon kosher salt

2 pounds (908 grams) asparagus, trimmed and cut into 1/2-inch pieces

Twelve 2-by-3-inch (5-by-7.5-cm) pasta rectangles made from Fresh Egg Pasta Dough (page 94) or 12 dried cannelloni shells

One 8-ounce (227-grams) log plain goat cheese

2 cups (10 ounces/255 grams) minced mortadella

1 1/2 cups (6 ounces/170 grams) freshly grated Parmigiano-Reggiano cheese

1 1/2 cups (360 ml) heavy cream

4 large eggs

Freshly ground black pepper

1 tablespoon (14 grams) unsalted butter

PREHEAT THE OVEN to 350 degrees (175°C).

Bring a large pot of water to a boil. Add 1 tablespoon of the salt, add the asparagus, and blanch for 1 minute. Drain and set aside to cool.

Place a large bowl of ice water on the counter. Fill a 6-quart pot with 4 quarts (4 liters) of water and bring to a boil over high heat. Add 1 tablespoon of the salt, then add the pasta and cook until just tender. With a slotted spoon, remove the sheets or cannelloni shells to the ice water to cool completely.

TO MAKE THE FILLING

Combine the asparagus, goat cheese, mortadella, 1 cup of the Parmigiano-Reggiano, 1/2 cup of the heavy cream, 2 of the eggs, 1/2 teaspoon of the salt and black pepper to taste in a large mixing bowl. Stir well.

Butter a 15-by-12-inch lasagne pan. If using pasta sheets, place 1 sheet on a work surface with a long side toward you. Place about 2 tablespoons of the filling across the center of the sheet. Roll up the sheet and place it seam side down in the lasagne pan. Repeat with the remaining pasta sheets and filling, placing the cannelloni side by side in the pan. If using dried cannelloni shells, simply fill the tubes with the asparagus mixture and arrange side by side in the pan.

Whisk together the remaining 1/2 cup cheese, 1 cup cream, 2 eggs, and 1/2 teaspoon salt in a bowl. Pour over the cannelloni.

Bake until browned on top, about 30 minutes. Let rest for 5 minutes, and then serve.

wine: A bright rosé from Bandol, in France, will cut the richness of the cannelloni and refresh the palate between bites.

maria's lasagne

LASAGNE ALLA MARIA

mark • I named this lasagne after Maria Fillabozzi, who taught me how to roll sheets of pasta so thin I could read a newspaper through them. I'm sure the fineness of the noodles is one of the reasons I get more requests for this recipe than any other. It's also the alchemy of the dish— how, during baking, the layers of meat sauce, cheese, and pasta come together harmoniously instead of fighting each other for attention. The top layer of pasta adds an element of crunch to the creaminess below the surface.

This recipe looks complicated because the ingredients list is long, but each of the components—the meat sauce, the béchamel, and the pasta—can be prepared in advance. To save a little time, I simply mix the béchamel and meat sauce together before layering, rather than layering them separately. I also like the way they taste when they're mixed together. You can assemble the entire lasagne up to 2 days before you plan to serve it, cover, and refrigerate. Bring to room temperature before baking. • SERVES 6 AS A MAIN COURSE OR 8 AS AN APPETIZER

FOR THE MEAT SAUCE

¼ cup (56 ml) extra-virgin olive oil

8 ounces (228 grams) lean ground beef

8 ounces (228 grams) ground veal

8 ounces (228 grams) ground pork

2 garlic cloves, minced

½ large red onion, minced

½ medium carrot, minced

1 large celery stalk, minced

1½ teaspoons chopped fresh rosemary

1 teaspoon dried thyme

1 bay leaf

½ to 1 cup (120 to 240 ml) dry red wine, such as Chianti

Two 28-ounce (794-gram) cans Italian plum tomatoes, preferably San Marzano, with their juices, pureed in a food processor or food mill

TO MAKE THE MEAT SAUCE

Place a 10- to 12-inch skillet over medium-high heat, and when it is hot, add 2 tablespoons of the olive oil. Add the meat and cook, stirring to break up any lumps, until just browned, about 5 minutes. With a slotted spoon, remove the meat to a colander set over a plate to drain.

Wipe out the skillet with paper towels (be careful not to burn yourself). Reheat the skillet over medium-high heat, and when it is hot, add the remaining 2 tablespoons oil. Add the garlic, onion, carrot, celery, rosemary, thyme, and bay leaf and cook, stirring, until the vegetables are soft and golden, 5 to 7 minutes. Add the meat, wine, and tomatoes, mix well, and bring to a gentle boil. Reduce the heat to a bare simmer and cook, uncovered, until thickened, about 1 hour. Remove from the heat and discard the bay leaf.

TO MAKE THE BÉCHAMEL

Place the milk, onion, bay leaf, nutmeg, salt, and pepper in a 4- to 6-quart saucepan and heat over low heat until hot, about 5 minutes. Do not allow the milk to boil; if it begins to bubble, turn down the heat.

While the milk is heating, melt the butter in an 8-inch skillet over medium heat, being careful not to let it brown. Add the flour 1 tablespoon at a time, whisking all the while. Gradually whisk in the hot milk mixture and whisk together. Simmer very gently until thickened to the consistency of sour cream, 5 to 7 minutes. Do not let the sauce boil or color; reduce the heat if necessary. Remove from the heat and discard the onion and bay leaf.

4 cups (1 quart/960 ml) whole or
2%-fat milk

1 small onion, peeled and studded with
3 whole cloves

1 bay leaf

½ teaspoon freshly grated nutmeg

½ teaspoon kosher salt

½ teaspoon freshly ground
white pepper

14 tablespoons (1¾ sticks/56 grams)
unsalted butter

¼ cup (30 grams) unbleached
all-purpose flour

1 pound (454 grams) 6-by-12-inch
(15-by-30-cm) lasagne noodles
made from Fresh Egg Pasta Dough
(page 94) or noodles cut from
store-bought pasta sheets or dried
lasagne noodles

2 tablespoons kosher salt

2 tablespoons (30 ml) extra-virgin olive
oil for brushing the pasta sheets

1 cup (4 ounces/114 grams) freshly
grated Parmigiano-Reggiano cheese

1 cup (240 ml) heavy cream

1 cup (240 ml) canned crushed Italian
plum tomatoes, preferably San
Marzano, or Pomi brand strained
tomatoes

2 tablespoons chopped fresh
Italian parsley

Fill a 10-quart pot with 7 quarts (6.5 liters) of water and bring it to a boil over high heat. Meanwhile, prepare a large bowl of ice water. Add the salt to the boiling water. Cook the pasta in batches of noodles at a time until just tender, about 3 minutes. Remove the noodles with a slotted spoon and place them in the bowl of ice water. When all the noodles are cooked, lay a sheet of waxed paper on a counter or work surface and brush with oil. Remove 1 noodle from the ice water and blot dry with a paper towel. Brush the noodle with olive oil and place it on the waxed paper. Repeat with the remaining noodles, arranging them on the waxed paper and then stacking them on top of each other; do not pile more than 4 layers of noodles together, as the weight could cause them to stick. Set aside.

Preheat the oven to 350 degrees (175°C). Lightly oil a 9-by-12-inch baking dish.

Place the meat sauce and béchamel in a large bowl and mix to combine. Line the bottom and sides of the baking dish with lasagne noodles. Spread a thin layer of sauce over the noodles, and sprinkle cheese over the sauce. Cover with a layer of pasta, a layer of sauce, and a sprinkling of cheese, and repeat until you have used all the ingredients, ending with cheese on top.

Cover the dish with aluminum foil and bake until heated through, about 30 minutes. Remove the foil and bake until the top is brown, about 10 additional minutes. Let the lasagne rest for at least 15 minutes before serving.

Shortly before serving, place the cream and tomatoes in a 9- or 10-inch skillet and bring to a boil over medium heat. Reduce the heat and simmer until reduced by half, about 12 minutes.

Cut the lasagne into serving portions and transfer to individual plates. Pour the pink sauce over the lasagne, sprinkle on the parsley, and serve immediately.

wine: A super Tuscan, such as a Tignanello or Sassicaia, will be much appreciated with this dish, and you deserve a glass for putting it all together, too.

farfalle with heirloom tomato sauce

FARFALLE AL TELEFONO

mark • I remember how excited I was when heirloom tomatoes first came to the farmers' markets in New York City. In general, they're not as watery as beefsteak tomatoes and they have so much more flavor than fresh plum tomatoes sold in supermarkets. I especially like their texture in sauces—some can be a little bit mealy, which helps to thicken the sauce. Use as many colors as possible—red, yellow, purple—for the most beautiful dish. And include some green ones, which give the sauce a bright acidity.

My kids love this pasta, which combines the tomatoes with smoked mozzarella cheese. They like to stretch the cheese with their forks, making telephone wires, just like kids in Italy—this is traditionally a children's favorite in the south, where the dish is called *pasta al telefono*. I use farfalle because it's one of the easiest shapes to make, and kids love it. Just cut the pasta into squares and pinch each square together in the middle. The smoked mozzarella is unconventional—in Italy, Parmigiano is the choice—but I like its smoky flavor, which contrasts well with the acidic tomatoes. If you are not a fan of smoked cheese, you can substitute buffalo mozzarella or fresh goat cheese. The latter won't stretch as well, but it is delicious. • SERVES 4 AS A MAIN COURSE OR 6 AS AN APPETIZER

¼ cup (60 ml) extra-virgin olive oil

3 garlic cloves, thickly sliced

3 pounds (1.4 kilos) heirloom tomatoes (yellow, red, purple, and green), chopped into small dice, with their juices

2 tablespoon plus 1 teaspoon kosher salt

1 pound (454 grams) farfalle made with Fresh Egg Pasta Dough (page 94) or dried farfalle

8 ounces (228 grams) smoked mozzarella, cut into ¼-inch cubes

1 large bunch chopped fresh basil leaves

HEAT A 12-INCH SKILLET or large Dutch oven over medium heat. When it is hot, add the olive oil and garlic and cook until the garlic is golden brown, 3 to 5 minutes. Add the tomatoes, with their juices, and 1 teaspoon of the salt, then reduce the heat to low and simmer for 10 minutes.

While the sauce is cooking, fill a 10-quart stockpot with 7 quarts (6.5 liters) of water and bring to a boil over high heat. Add the remaining 2 tablespoons salt. Add the pasta, stir, and cook until al dente, 2 to 4 minutes (longer if using dried pasta).

Reserve ½ cup of the pasta cooking water, and drain the pasta. Add it to the pan with the sauce, tossing to combine. If the pasta looks dry, add the reserved cooking water 1 tablespoon at a time, tossing to combine between additions. Gradually stir in the cheese and then the basil until the cheese is incorporated throughout. Transfer to a large serving platter and serve immediately.

tip: Fresh pasta, especially this bowtie shape, is so fragile that it's best to serve on a platter rather than in a deep bowl. In a bowl, the weight of the sauce will undo the pinches of the farfalle.

wine: A straightforward Sicilian red like Duca di Salaparutta, from Corvo, would pair well with this boldly flavored pasta dish.

gnocchi with two mushroom sauces

GNOCCHI DI PATATE AL SUGO DI FUNGHI

pino • The word *gnocco* simply means a single dumpling (or the bump you get after a knock on the head). *Nudi,* or "naked" ravioli (page 126), are a kind of gnocchi, as are semolina-based gnocchi alla romana (page 124). In northern Italy, potato gnocchi are served every Thursday, although no one quite knows what gave rise to this tradition.

Potato gnocchi are so easy to make. Since they don't involve rolling out a dough to super-thin transparency, they take less time than egg pasta. They are also meant to be somewhat irregular in shape and size, so the work of shaping and cutting them goes quickly. When properly made, gnocchi are soft to the bite, but not mushy or gluey. Italians never chew gnocchi; they simply press them between their tongues and palates and let them dissolve.

When you are boiling the potatoes for the gnocchi, pierce them only once or twice to check for doneness. If you poke too many holes in them, they will absorb too much water. Don't overdo mashing the potatoes either, or your gnocchi will become gummy. To make the dough, you will need a large, preferably wooden work surface (although not as large as the one required to make egg pasta), an offset spatula, and a sharp knife. You will also need a strainer for scooping them out of the cooking water. You will know you've added the right amount of flour to the dough when it doesn't stick to your hands anymore. This recipe serves 8 generously, because I believe that if you are going to go to the trouble of making gnocchi, you should make a lot, but you can freeze any extra gnocchi if necessary (see below).

Gnocchi marry well with a variety of sauces, including any simple tomato sauce. Below are two possibilities, both with mushrooms, whose earthy flavors match well with the potatoes. I serve the tomato-based sauce in the summer and the cream sauce in the winter. • MAKES ABOUT 120 PIECES, SERVING 8 GENEROUSLY

---

2 pounds (908 grams) Yukon Gold or russet potatoes (6 medium), scrubbed

1½ cups (187 grams) unbleached all-purpose flour, plus additional for dusting

3 tablespoons (21 grams) freshly grated Parmigiano-Reggiano cheese

2 tablespoons plus ½ teaspoon kosher salt

Pinch of freshly grated nutmeg

Pinch of freshly ground black pepper

1 large egg, lightly beaten

Wild Mushroom Sauce or Mushroom Cream Sauce (recipes follow), warm

3 tablespoons (21 grams) freshly grated Parmigiano-Reggiano cheese, if using the Mushroom Cream Sauce

PLACE THE POTATOES in a 6-quart stockpot and cover with 3 inches of cold water. Cover the pot and bring to a boil, then reduce to a gentle simmer. Cook until the potatoes are tender and easily pierced with the tip of a paring knife, about 25 minutes. (Do not test too often, or you will waterlog the potatoes.) Drain the potatoes.

Line two baking sheets with parchment paper. Wash and dry your hands (remove any jewelry) and the work surface. A wooden surface is recommended for best results, but stainless steel or marble may also be used.

Lightly flour the work surface. As soon as the potatoes are cool enough to handle—they should still be very warm—peel them. Place the potatoes on the work surface, and slightly mash them. Sprinkle with the flour, Parmigiano-Reggiano cheese, ½ teaspoon of the salt, the nutmeg, and pepper. Place the egg in the center of the mixture. Working quickly, gently knead and squeeze the ingredients together until incorporated, about 1 minute. Avoid overworking the dough.

(CONTINUED)

Dust your hands with 2 tablespoons of flour and rub them together aggressively over the work surface. Dough particles should fall to the surface, and both hands should now be "working clean." Roll the dough mass gently around the work surface to incorporate any remaining flour and dough particles, then shape it into a large log. The dough should still be warm to the touch. Sprinkle with flour. Unlike fresh egg pasta dough, gnocchi dough should not rest, but should be shaped immediately.

Dust the work surface very lightly with flour. Cut the dough into 8 equal parts. Working with one at a time, roll the pieces into logs ½ inch (1.3 cm) in diameter and 10 to 12 inches (25 to 30 cm) long. As you finish each log, move it away from you and dust it generously with flour.

Lightly flour the work surface and roll 4 of the logs toward you, moving them through the flour to coat them. Line up the 4 logs parallel to one another; then, holding your hand perpendicular to the work surface, separate the logs from each other with the tips of your fingers. Cut the logs on the bias into ½-inch (1.3-cm) pieces. Gently scrape the work surface with an offset spatula, lifting the gnocchi up and tossing them in the flour on the work surface, and then use the spatula to transfer the gnocchi to one of the prepared baking sheets. Arrange them in a single layer.

Repeat with the remaining 4 logs of dough. You should have about 10 dozen gnocchi in all. The gnocchi can be stored in a cool, dry place for up to 2 hours; do not refrigerate. (The gnocchi may also be frozen for up to several weeks. Freeze them on the baking sheets in a single layer. When they are frozen, place them in a strainer in small batches and sift off excess flour, then portion into freezer bags or containers. Do not thaw before cooking, but when cooking frozen gnocchi, boil them in small batches, or they will drop the temperature of the cooking water too rapidly.)

Fill a 10-quart pot with 7 quarts (6.5 liters) of water and bring to a boil over high heat. Add the remaining 2 tablespoons kosher salt. Place the warm sauce in a large shallow ceramic bowl that's been warmed.

Lift one-third of the gnocchi off the pans, shaking them to sift off any excess flour as you do so, and add to the boiling water. At first the gnocchi will sink to the bottom of the pot. Do not stir them. As the water returns to a boil, after 1 to 2 minutes, the gnocchi will float to the surface. Gnocchi are the rare pasta that is not cooked al dente: the ideal cooked texture is soft and pillowlike, with just enough solidity to hold together without becoming chewy. This is normally achieved after 1 to 2 minutes of cooking time, or as soon as they rise to the surface of the cooking water. Scoop the gnocchi from the boiling water using a strainer, draining them well, and transfer to the bowl containing the sauce.

Before adding the next batch of gnocchi to the pot, gently stir the boiling water with the strainer: any gnocchi remaining in the water should rise to the surface—scoop them out. Wait for the water to return to a boil, and then cook another one-third of the gnocchi. (Since gnocchi cook quickly, even when cooked in 3 batches, they will still be hot when they are served.)

Season with salt and pepper, as desired. Swirl the bowl to combine. Avoid using a utensil to toss the gnocchi, as cooked gnocchi are very delicate and damage easily. Sprinkle the cheese over the top, if using, and serve immediately.

wine: I'd open an unoaked Chilean Chardonnay if serving the gnocchi with the tomato-mushroom sauce. If serving them with the cream sauce, I'd choose a red that won't overwhelm the sauce, probably a nice, young Chianti—the most recent vintage.

wild mushroom sauce · MAKES 4 CUPS (960 ML)

SUGO AL FUNGHETTO DI BOSCO

2 tablespoons (30 ml) extra-virgin olive oil

2 garlic cloves, chopped

2 pounds (908 grams) mushrooms (oyster, shiitake, hen-of-the woods, chanterelle, or porcini, or a combination of two or more), stems removed, caps wiped clean and thinly sliced (about 4 cups)

1½ teaspoons kosher salt

1 teaspoon freshly ground black pepper

1 tablespoon fresh thyme leaves

¼ cup (60 ml) dry young red wine, such as Chianti

2 cups (480 ml) canned Italian plum tomatoes, preferably San Marzano, with their juices, pureed in a food processor or food mill

PLACE A 12-INCH SKILLET over medium heat, and when it is hot, add the olive oil. Add the garlic and cook until it releases its fragrance, about 1 minute. Add the mushrooms, salt, pepper, and thyme, mix gently, and cook until the mushrooms have released all their liquid and are very soft, about 10 minutes.

Add the wine and bring to a simmer, 2 minutes. Add the tomatoes, reduce the heat to low, and cook, stirring occasionally, until most but not all of the liquid has evaporated, about 10 minutes.

mushroom cream sauce · MAKES 4 CUPS (960 ML)

SUGO DI CREMA E FUNGHI

2 tablespoons (30 ml) extra-virgin olive oil

2 garlic cloves, finely chopped

2 pounds (908 grams) cremini mushrooms, stems removed, caps wiped clean and finely chopped (the food processor works well; about 4 cups chopped)

½ cup (120 ml) dry white wine

1 teaspoon kosher salt, or more to taste

2 teaspoons freshly ground black pepper, or more to taste

½ cup (120 ml) heavy cream

PLACE A 12-INCH SKILLET over medium heat, and when it is hot, add the olive oil. Add the garlic and cook until lightly colored, 2 to 3 minutes.

Add the mushrooms and cook, stirring constantly, until they have released all their liquid and cooked down, about 10 minutes. Add the wine, salt, and pepper and cook until the alcohol from the wine has evaporated, about 2 minutes. Add the cream and cook, stirring frequently, until it has reduced and blended with the mushrooms, 5 minutes. Taste for salt and pepper.

roman-style baked semolina gnocchi

GNOCCHI ALLA ROMANA

mark • This dish originated in Rome, but it has become popular all over Italy. I first tasted it at a restaurant called Osteria Vecchio Castello in the hills outside Montalcino. Part of the reason I enjoyed the dish so much is that I was relieved to finally find the restaurant—it's in the middle of nowhere. I drove 2½ hours from Montalcino, but I swear I traveled only about 30 kilometers (about 19 miles). The whole route is up and down.

Semolina is durum wheat flour, the same kind of flour used to make dried pasta. Gnocchi made from semolina have a texture similar to polenta (or Cream of Wheat). Baked with a rich and creamy mushroom sauce, they are a sublime first course. A drizzle of truffle oil is a relatively inexpensive way to enjoy some truffle flavor and aroma. Look for the oil in gourmet stores and Italian markets or order it online (see Resources, page 306). • SERVES 6 AS AN APPETIZER

FOR THE GNOCCHI

4 cups (1 quart/0.9 liters) whole, skim, or low-fat milk

Pinch of kosher salt

2 cups (240 grams) Italian semolina

¼ cup (1 ounce/28 grams) freshly grated Parmigiano-Reggiano cheese

2 large egg yolks

Pinch of freshly grated nutmeg

FOR THE SAUCE

1 tablespoon (14 grams) unsalted butter, plus more for buttering the casserole

3 tablespoons (45 ml) extra-virgin olive oil

2 tablespoons minced onion

½ garlic clove, minced

12 ounces (342 grams) assorted mushrooms (a combination of cremini, shiitake, oyster, pleurotte, chanterelle, and/or hedgehog), stems removed and any large caps roughly chopped (2 firmly packed cups)

1 teaspoon kosher salt

½ cup plus 2 tablespoons (150 ml) heavy cream

Freshly ground black pepper

2 tablespoons white truffle oil (preferably Urbani brand), for drizzling

LIGHTLY OIL A 10-inch baking pan.

TO MAKE THE GNOCCHI

Place the milk in a 6- to 8-quart stockpot and add the salt. Slowly bring the milk to a boil over medium heat, then gradually stir in the semolina, letting it fall in a thin stream from one hand as you stir with the other. Cook, stirring constantly, until the semolina thickens and pulls away from the sides of the pot, 8 to 10 minutes.

Stir in the cheese, and remove from the heat. Whisk in the egg yolks and nutmeg with a heavy-duty whisk (a flimsy wire whisk will break in the stiff mixture). Immediately spread the warm semolina 2 inches thick on the prepared pan. Set aside to cool to room temperature.

Cover the cooled semolina loosely with plastic wrap. Refrigerate for at least 2 hours, or up to 2 days.

When you are ready to cook the gnocchi, preheat the oven to 350 degrees (175°F). Lightly butter an 18-by-13-inch casserole dish and set aside.

Using a sharp knife, working right on the cookie sheet, cut the semolina into 2-inch squares, dipping your knife into hot water if necessary to prevent sticking. Arrange the gnocchi in a single layer in the casserole dish, transfer to the oven, and bake until warmed through, 10 minutes.

WHILE THE GNOCCHI ARE BAKING, MAKE THE SAUCE

Place a 10-inch skillet over medium heat, and when it is hot, add the olive oil. Add the onion and garlic and sauté until soft and golden, about 3 minutes. Add the mushrooms and salt and sauté until the mushrooms begin to give off their liquid, about 5 minutes. Add the cream and butter, bring to a simmer and ,stirring constantly, simmer, until thick, about 5 minutes. Taste for salt and season with pepper.

Remove the gnocchi from the oven and spoon the mushrooms and sauce over them. Return to the oven and bake until the sauce coats the gnocchi, about 2 minutes.

Drizzle with the truffle oil and serve immediately.

wine: Pair a Pinot Noir from Oregon with this dish. There is logic to this, even if the geography doesn't add up: Oregon is home to an enormous mushroom industry (mushrooms grow in the same forests that have made the state so key to the American timber industry). It's fun to seek out wines made in the same area that produces a main ingredient in a dish—their flavors will work well together.

"naked" ravioli with walnuts, sage, and butter

RAVIOLI NUDI CON NOCI E SALVIA AL BURRO

pino • Light yet complex, *nudi*, ("naked" dumplings) are a quintessential Florentine dish, as emblematic of my native city as Ghiberti's bronze doors on the Duomo. They're called *nudi* because they're essentially a ravioli filling without the pasta casing. They're simpler to make than ravioli for the obvious reason that you don't have to make, roll out, and cut the pasta dough. I have veered slightly from the classic preparation by including walnuts, because I love the way their crunchiness contrasts with the soft texture of the dumplings. Sage loves nuts, so it is a natural addition.

Ricotta cheese can be very watery, especially if you buy it at an Italian market where they make it themselves (I recommend this—it's much better than commercial ricotta cheese sold at the supermarket). You can get rid of the excess water by letting it drain in a paper-towel-lined strainer set over a bowl for 30 minutes. • SERVES 4 AS A MAIN COURSE OR 6 AS AN APPETIZER

FOR THE DUMPLINGS

1 cup (125 grams) all-purpose flour

1 pound (454 grams) spinach
  (2 bunches), trimmed of tough
  stems, rinsed, steamed until
  tender, squeezed dry, and chopped

1 cup (245 grams) whole-milk ricotta,
  preferably fresh, strained
  (see headnote)

4 teaspoons kosher salt

1 teaspoon freshly grated nutmeg

1 teaspoon freshly ground black pepper

FOR THE SAUCE

4 tablespoons (112 grams) unsalted
  butter

10 fresh sage leaves, chopped

1 cup (4.4 ounces/125 grams) walnuts,
  toasted and finely chopped

¼ cup (1 ounce/28 grams) freshly
  grated Parmigiano-Reggiano cheese

TO MAKE THE DUMPLINGS

Spread ½ cup of the flour evenly over a work surface (preferably metal or marble) in a rough 8-by-11-inch rectangle. Distribute the chopped spinach over the surface of the flour, then spread the ricotta over the spinach. Sprinkle with 2 teaspoons salt and the nutmeg and pepper. Begin to knead the ingredients together the way you would a pastry dough—folding the dough over and then giving it a quarter turn, incorporating the flour as you go. Continue kneading until the mixture is well amalgamated and firm, 3 to 4 minutes.

Dust a baking sheet with flour. Dust your hands with flour as well. Place 2 tablespoons of the mixture in the palm of one hand and gently roll your palms against each other until you create a 2-inch (5-cm) oval dumpling. Place it on the prepared sheet. Repeat with the remaining mixture. You should have 12 dumplings. Slide the sheet into the refrigerator and let the dumplings rest for 1 hour.

Preheat the oven to 375 degrees (190°C).

Fill a wide pot three-quarters full with water. Bring the water to a boil and add the remaining 2 teaspoons kosher salt. Use a slotted spoon to place the dumplings gently into the water, and cook for 2 minutes.

WHILE THE DUMPLINGS ARE COOKING, MAKE THE SAUCE

Place a 12-inch skillet over medium heat and add the butter. Once the butter has melted, stir in the sage and walnuts.

Remove the dumplings from the water with the slotted spoon (reserve the pan of cooking water) and gently arrange them in a single layer in the skillet with the butter. Cook for 1 minute, using a spoon to baste the dumplings with the butter. If the dish looks dry, drizzle on a little of the cooking water 1 tablespoon at a time.

Transfer the dumplings to individual serving plates, sprinkle on the Parmigiano-Reggiano cheese, and serve immediately.

wine: For this very Florentine dish, nothing beats a local wine: Go with a good Chianti or any good red Tuscan table wine.

scialatielli with roasted peppers and cherry tomatoes

SCIALATIELLI CON PEPERONI E POMODORINI

pino • *Scialatielli* is a rustic variety of fresh pasta typical of the Campania region of Italy, which includes Naples. Although native to the south, scialatielli may incorporate milk, eggs, and even grated cheese and fresh herbs, more characteristic of the north. What differentiates this and other homemade pastas of the south from their northern egg pasta cousins is the texture—while northern pasta is smooth and silky, southern pasta, even if made with eggs, is always dense and chewy. The shape of scialatielli can also vary, although they tend to be rather short.

The characteristic cut and texture make scialatielli ideal for finishing in a sauté pan with a sauce that they can absorb. They're terrific with vegetable preparations and simple tomato sauces. This sauce, a simple combination of roasted bits of sweet red pepper and halved cherry tomatoes, is one of my favorites. It has some of the dominant flavors of southern Italian cooking. The roasted vegetables, which are transferred to a sauté pan after roasting and cooked further to soften them up, cling very nicely to the pasta, which absorbs their flavors like a sponge. • SERVES 4 AS A MAIN COURSE OR 6 AS AN APPETIZER

FOR THE PASTA

2 1/3 cups (290 grams) all-purpose flour

6 1/2 tablespoons (95 ml) whole milk

1 large egg

2 tablespoons (30 ml) extra-virgin olive oil

1 tablespoon freshly grated Pecorino Romano cheese

2 fresh basil leaves, minced

1/2 teaspoon kosher salt

Pinch of freshly ground black pepper

(INGREDIENTS CONTINUE)

TO MAKE THE PASTA

Before beginning, wash and dry your hands and the work surface: I recommend wood for best results, but you can also use stainless steel or marble. (Remove any jewelry.) Have a bench scraper ready.

Arrange the flour in a mound on the work surface. Using your fist, make a well large enough to hold the liquid ingredients, about 6 to 8 inches in diameter. Place the milk, egg, oil, cheese, basil, salt, and pepper in the center of the well. You will use one hand as your working hand and keep the other clean to pick up ingredients and tools as needed. Using your working hand, begin combining the ingredients in the center of the well by "pinching" them together. When the mixture begins to thicken, use the fingertips of your working hand to pull the flour into the eggs from the inside perimeter of the well, keeping the wall intact. Continue incorporating small amounts of flour and pinching it into the mixture until a sticky dough forms. Then, with the palm of your working hand, slowly begin scraping the remaining flour from the well into the mixture, squeezing it gently to incorporate it. This should take about 1 minute. The dough will come together and will be slightly sticky, with some flour and small pieces of dough remaining on the work surface.

Using your clean hand, scrape and clean the work surface with the bench scraper, bringing all the remaining flour and dough particles toward the dough mass. Grab the unincorporated flour from the work surface and sprinkle it over your working hand, then rub your hands together aggressively over the work surface, using the flour as an abrasive to remove dough particles. Both hands should now be "working clean."

(CONTINUED)

Using both hands, gather the dough particles and flour into the dough mass and then begin to knead it, exerting moderate pressure while pressing and stretching the dough forward and away from your body using the heels of your hands. Knead it several times to form an oblong shape.

Turn the dough so that a narrow end is toward you. Hold down one end with the palm of your "non-working" hand and use the heel of your other hand to press and stretch the dough forward, then roll it back on itself against the palm of your hand. Do this about 4 times, then turn the dough so that a long side is toward you, and roll it to smooth the seams. Turn the oblong so that a narrow end is once again facing you and repeat the kneading process, just until the dough is smooth, firm, and pliable, 2 to 3 minutes. Do not overwork the dough: this dough is rolled out much thicker than the Fresh Egg Pasta Dough (page 94) and so requires less kneading. It is also a slightly moister, softer dough.

Shape the dough into a ball and lightly dust with flour. Wrap tightly in plastic wrap and let rest at room temperature for 30 to 45 minutes. Sufficient resting time is critical: after the resting period, dough can be stretched and will retain its stretched shape with less retraction.

Line two baking sheets with parchment paper and sprinkle with flour.

Remove the plastic wrap, and dust the dough and the work surface lightly with flour. Flatten the ball slightly and, using a wooden rolling pin, begin rolling it out into a rectangle: Roll 4 to 6 strokes and then rotate the dough a quarter turn, lifting it gently to prevent sticking. Repeat the process until the dough measures 12 by 13 inches (30 by 33 cm) and is about ⅛ inch (0.3 cm) thick.

Cut the dough lengthwise into 3 strips. Turn one of the dough strips horizontally in front of you and cut it into noodles about ½ inch (1.3 cm) wide. Sprinkle the cut noodles with a little flour, lifting them gently to separate, and place on one of the prepared pans. Repeat with remaining 2 strips of dough. (The pasta can be frozen. Freeze in a single layer on the baking sheets immediately after cutting, then portion into freezer bags or containers and freeze for up to several weeks. Do not thaw before cooking—drop while still frozen directly into boiling salted water.)

3 yellow bell peppers, cored, seeded, and cut into very small dice

3 red bell peppers, cored, seeded, and cut into very small dice

5 tablespoons (75 ml) extra-virgin olive oil

1 pound (454 grams) cherry tomatoes, halved

2 teaspoons finely chopped fresh thyme

1 medium red onion, finely chopped

½ cup (120 ml) vegetable stock or vegetable broth made with Knorr powdered bouillon

2 tablespoons kosher salt

½ cup (2 ounces/56 grams) freshly grated Pecorino Romano cheese

Kosher salt and freshly ground black pepper

TO MAKE THE SAUCE

Preheat the oven to 325 degrees (165°C).

Place the red and yellow peppers on a rimmed baking sheet, drizzle with 2 tablespoons of the olive oil, and toss to coat. Roast until softened, about 10 minutes. Remove the baking sheet from the oven and set aside.

Place the cherry tomatoes on a rimmed baking sheet, sprinkle with the thyme, drizzle with 2 tablespoons of the olive oil, and toss to coat. Roast until very soft, about 15 minutes. Remove the baking sheet from the oven and set aside to cool.

Heat a large skillet over medium-high heat. When it is hot, add the remaining tablespoon of olive oil and the onion. Turn the heat down to medium and sauté until the onion is very soft and brown, about 10 minutes. Add the vegetable stock and bring to a simmer, scraping up any brown bits on the bottom of the pan with a wooden spoon. Add the roasted peppers and simmer until they fall apart.

While the sauce is cooking, fill a 10-quart stockpot with 7 quarts (6.5 liters) of water and bring to a boil over high heat. Add the 2 tablespoons salt. Add the pasta, stir, and cook until al dente.

Reserve ½ cup of the pasta cooking water, and drain the pasta. Add it to the pan with the sauce. Add the roasted cherry tomatoes, reduce the heat to low, and toss continuously until the pasta has absorbed the sauce and is well combined, about 3 minutes. If the pasta looks dry, add the reserved cooking water 1 tablespoon at a time, tossing to combine between additions. Stir in the cheese. Season to taste with salt and pepper (you may not need any salt at all, because the cheese can be quite salty). Transfer to a serving platter and serve immediately.

wine: Go with a dry, lighter white, such as a Sauvignon Blanc, which is good with light vegetable sauces.

5

risotto and farrotto

While serving as ambassador to the Court of Savoy

(now in northern Italy), Thomas Jefferson fell in love with the rice of the Po Valley. The Savoiardi carefully guarded their prize, making sure it wasn't exported so it could be cultivated somewhere else. But when Jefferson returned to the United States, he smuggled out four pounds of it and planted it in his backyard. We completely understand Jefferson's obsession. If Arborio and other varieties of Italian rice weren't now widely available, we would consider planting it ourselves so that we could make risotto, the creamy rice dish unique to Italy, for our families and customers.

Sadly for Americans, Thomas Jefferson didn't bring back any *farro*, an ancient grain related to wheat, along with the rice. Cheaper than rice, farro was grown in Tuscany, Umbria, and Abruzzo and used in place of rice in these areas to make *farrotto*, sometimes called poor man's risotto. It is unknown to most Americans, but so was risotto twenty-five years ago. We'd like to change this, because we think Americans, who more and more choose whole-grain brown rice over white, will like its resilient texture and nutty flavor. Farrotto is no longer a cheap alternative to risotto, but it is an alternative to it when you want something similar in style yet completely different in texture and flavor.

mark Risotto isn't a dish you generally see on menus in restaurants south of Rome.

pino Of course not. This is another example of how Italian cooking has to be discussed by region. Rice doesn't grow in the south; it grows near the Po River, which flows west to east from Piedmont to the area close to Venice. So that's where the tradition of risotto is the strongest.

mark It may be a regional dish in Italy, but it's certainly spread to every Italian restaurant in this country. When I first started cooking Italian food in the 1980s, Arborio rice was kind of hard to find. Now it's in every supermarket. You don't have to be like Thomas Jefferson and pack it in your suitcase when you leave Italy. And that's great, because risotto is such a perfect dish for enjoying at home.

pino Arborio rice certainly is everywhere. I'd like to see other less well-known Italian rices getting some attention. In Italy, everyone has a favorite—Italians will argue about which kind of rice is the best the same way they argue about the best soccer teams. Personally, I like Vialone Nano, which has the shortest grain of any Italian rice. When I'm doing risotto with quail or mushrooms, I want to use a rice that's exceptionally strong, resilient, and holds up well in cooking. Vialone Nano's grains stay firm during cooking without having to add too much liquid, whereas Arborio is so soft and starchy that it falls apart. You have to look harder for these types of rice, or you can order them online (see Resources, page 306), but when you cook with them, you'll notice and really enjoy the differences.

mark I'd say be careful, though, about buying the less well-known varieties off the shelf, unless you know that the store has a high turnover. Even if you love Vialone Nano, if it's fresher, Arborio will make a better risotto. Rice is an agricultural product and has a limited shelf life, though people tend to think it will last forever. It won't. If you're buying from bins or have had rice in your pantry for a long time, hold some in your hand and see how much of it is broken and cracked. That will tell you if it's old. When rice is fresh, it is very white and slightly translucent, but it begins to change color after three months. It won't hurt you to eat older rice, but I have noticed that it doesn't result in as creamy or silky a risotto, so I always try to use the freshest rice available—which is often Arborio.

pino But we must be clear—it's not the rice on its own that is creamy. It's the cooking method that transforms it. Risotto is not another word for rice, it's a particular way of preparing rice. If you simply boil Arborio or Vialone Nano or Carnaroli rice, you're not going to get that result.

mark Let's talk about technique. A misconception about making risotto is that you have to stir it all the time. I've found that if you stir it just often enough so the starch that's extracted from the rice during cooking can move around and doesn't stick to the bottom of the pan—once every minute or so, not constantly—you'll wind up with just as thick and rich a mixture as if you had stood there all night stirring. Italian rice is much starchier than other kinds of rice. If you look carefully, you can see a little white dot of starch just inside each rice kernel. As it cooks, a starchy, creamy layer forms on top of the rice. Stir this layer back into the rice, add a little liquid, let the rice cook some more and release more starch, and soon you will have risotto.

pino There's a little more to it than that! First, I disagree with you about stirring. I believe that stirring constantly will release the maximum amount of starch. If you're lazy, you

just won't get the most out of the rice. You have to put in some effort and, just as important, some time. It's like falling in love. You go slowly so as not to overwhelm the process.

mark I can't imagine my risotto any creamier than it already is. And no chef I know has the time to stand there and stir all night. But I'll agree with you that you can't rush it. Don't dump in too much liquid at a time, and never let the mixture come to a full boil. A slow simmer is better for extracting the starch.

pino But back to the beginning— to flavor the rice, you put enough olive oil in the bottom of the pan, add a *soffritto* of finely chopped onions, carrots, and celery, and then . . .

mark You mean butter, don't you?

pino I would never start with butter.

mark That's the Tuscan talking. But let your American colleague point out that a classic risotto milanese starts with butter. Northern Italy, where the rice is from, is dairy country. There are cows, and so there's butter. Cooking the grains of rice in butter before you add any liquid allows them to soak up that great dairy flavor that you're not going to get from olive oil. To me, oil is too fruity for this job.

pino Well, if you're going to make a risotto milanese, yes. For most other risottos, I start with olive oil. Tuscany is the land of rocks, hills, and olive trees and, of course, olive oil. I like the vegetal taste that the oil gives the rice grains, connecting them back to the earth. I'll stir in a little butter at the end, to bring the dish together, but butter at the beginning? That style is too rich for me.

mark Well, if it's a question of style, I choose Milanese opulence. But beyond butter and rice, there are other ingredients you need to transform rice into risotto. A little sautéed onion or shallot is essential, to give the dish an underlying sweetness. And wine—that's where risotto gets its slightly acidic bite and pleasant musty flavor.

pino And there's the cooking liquid. In addition to wine, you need something else. This is a case where I'll use homemade chicken stock. I don't like it in soup, but I think it adds body to what could be bland with just water.

mark Thank you! You'll be using my recipe for stock?

pino Of course. But if I don't have any in the freezer, I fall back on Knorr chicken bouillon. To me it has a purer taste than canned chicken broth, which always carries unwanted flavors from whatever seasonings they are cooking the chicken with at the factory.

mark Low-end brands taste terrible, I agree. But the new organic broth made with free-range birds is just fine for making risotto, although I wouldn't use it in my chicken soup.

pino And let's not forget a handful of grated Parmigiano-Reggiano cheese to bring everything together.

mark Yes, just the way it can bring two meatballs together in the end.

Making risotto or farrotto is a little like making bread. The first time you do it, you'll certainly enjoy the results, but without any experience, you won't know if you've gotten it quite right. After several more attempts, you'll have a basis for comparison. You will become sensitive to the rice or farro and how it absorbs the liquid, learning over time the rate at which you'll need to add liquid to make the creamiest risotto or most fluffy farrotto, and how long you should let it cook at the end so that it's not too soupy but not too dry. So try the range of recipes in this chapter—risotto with mushrooms, or with quail, or seafood; farrotto with Pecorino or cherry tomatoes and goat cheese. Every time you make a new recipe, you will also be working on your technique.

In Italy, risotto and farrotto are served as first courses, but there is no reason that they can't become the centerpiece of a meal. We like the way they hold the heat in ceramic bowls. You can enjoy them while you linger over a glass of wine with friends.

risotto with quail

RISOTTO CON QUAGLIE

pino • I first ate this dish in the trattorias of Montalcino and Montalto di Castro, two Tuscan villages where the local quail are grilled, roasted, and braised in risotto in the fall. The tender, lean, slightly gamy quail over a risotto of onions and Pecorino cheese is just as mouthwatering. If your quail aren't deboned when you purchase them, ask your butcher to do it. • SERVES 4 AS A MAIN COURSE

Four 4.5 ounce (128-gram) semi-boneless quail, rinsed and patted dry

1 teaspoon kosher salt

1/2 teaspoon freshly ground black pepper

4 fresh sage leaves

4 slices pancetta

1 cup (240 ml) dry white wine

6 cups (1.4 liters) Chicken Stock (page 29) or chicken broth made with Knorr powdered bouillon

2 tablespoons (30 ml) olive oil

1 medium red onion, thinly sliced

2 cups (454 grams) Vialone Nano, Carnaroli, or Arborio rice

1 tablespoon fresh thyme leaves

1/2 cup (56 grams) freshly grated Parmigiano-Reggiano cheese

PREHEAT THE OVEN to 200 degrees (95°C).

Sprinkle the quail with 1/2 teaspoon of the salt and 1/4 teaspoon of the pepper. Place a sage leaf on the breast of each quail and tightly wrap in a slice of pancetta. Place a 10- to 12-inch skillet over medium-high heat, and when it is hot, add the quail and sear until well browned, 4 to 5 minutes on each side. Turn the quail breast side up. Pour the wine over the quail and simmer, covered, until the wine evaporates, 4 to 5 minutes. Transfer the quail to a plate and cover loosely with foil to keep warm while you make the risotto. Wipe the pan clean with a paper towel.

Meanwhile, pour the stock into a 2½- to 3-quart saucepan and bring to simmer. Keep warm over low heat.

Return the skillet to medium heat, and when it is hot, add the olive oil. When the oil is hot, add the onion and sauté, stirring with a wooden spoon, for 2 minutes. Add the rice, the thyme, and the remaining 1/2 teaspoon salt and 1/4 teaspoon pepper and cook, stirring, until all the grains of rice are coated with oil, 2 to 3 minutes. Using a ladle, gradually add 2 cups of the hot stock to the rice and stir gently until it is absorbed by the rice, 8 to 10 minutes. Continue adding stock, 1 cup at a time, stirring until it is absorbed by the rice each time, another 8 to 10 minutes. The risotto should be very moist but not soupy, and the rice grains should show a tiny little white dot, or "the soul," in the center. Remove from the heat and stir in the Parmigiano-Reggiano cheese. Spoon the risotto onto a large shallow serving platter and arrange the quail on top. Serve immediately.

wine: A young Dolcetto from Cerreto, in Piedmont, has a sweetness that's not overpowering, just right for this mildly flavored creamy but light dish.

risotto cakes

SUPPLI DI RISO

To make risotto cakes with leftover risotto, take about 1/4 cup (56 grams) of risotto for each cake and tap it back and forth between your palms until it is like a flat compact patty. Lightly dust it with flour. Place 1/2 cup (240 ml) olive oil in a skillet, and when it is hot, gently add the risotto cakes and fry until browned, 2 to 3 minutes on each side. Drain on paper towels.

For cheesier cakes, add some grated Pecorino cheese to the mixture before you form it into cakes.

risotto pizza-maker-style

RISOTTO DEL PIZZAIOLO

mark · I always thought that cooking for my constantly dieting customers on the Upper East Side of New York was challenging—until I had kids. Getting kids to eat something new or unusual is an ever bigger challenge. I remember driving in Italy and seeing a billboard of a little girl trying to negotiate a long strand of mozzarella from a bowl of penne. And I thought, that's a good way to get kids to eat—give them something they can play with. So I developed this risotto, along with Farfalle al Telefono (page 120), especially for my kids, who like to lift forkfuls of food to their mouths just to see if they can stretch the cheese without snapping it. This risotto is a little more sophisticated than the pasta. Its pretty pale pink color and creaminess remind me of good tomato soup. I put it on the menu at Coco Pazzo, and I was surprised at how many diners abandoned their diets to enjoy it. Even if you are counting calories, don't omit the cream at the end: it brings the whole dish together. Two tablespoons of cream now and then never changed anyone's dress size. • SERVES 6 AS A MAIN COURSE

5 to 6 cups (1.2 to 1.4 liters) Chicken Stock (page 29) or low-sodium canned organic chicken broth

2 tablespoons (28 grams) unsalted butter

1 medium red onion, minced

2 cups (454 grams) Arborio rice

1 cup (240 ml) dry white wine, such as Trebbiano or Sauvignon Blanc

2 cups (454 grams) canned tomato puree

1 cup loosely packed fresh basil leaves (about 2 bunches), chopped

2 tablespoons (30 ml) heavy cream

1/2 cup (2 ounces/56 grams) finely grated Parmigiano-Reggiano cheese

4 ounces (114 grams) smoked mozzarella cheese, cut into small cubes

Kosher salt and freshly ground black pepper

POUR THE CHICKEN STOCK into a 2 1/2- to 3-quart saucepan and bring to a simmer. Keep warm over low heat.

Place a heavy-bottomed 5- to 6-quart pot over medium heat, and when it is hot, add 1 tablespoon of the butter. Add the onion, stir well with a wooden spoon, and sauté until soft and golden, 5 to 7 minutes. Add the rice and stir until all the grains are coated, about 2 minutes. Gradually add the wine, stirring constantly. When the rice has absorbed the wine, add the tomato puree and mix well. Add 1/2 cup of the chicken stock and simmer, stirring, until it has been absorbed. Continue adding stock 1/2 cup at a time and stirring until all the stock has been absorbed and the rice is al dente, 15 to 18 minutes. Add the remaining tablespoon of butter, the basil, cream, and cheeses and stir until the cheeses are well incorporated. Add salt and pepper to taste and serve immediately.

wine: A nice Sicilian red would make sense with the southern Italian flavors of this risotto. Look for a Pitola from Sicily, a simple red with a lot of fruit.

farro cooked risotto-style

FARROTTO AL PEPOLINO

pino • *Al pepolino* means with Pecorino, tomatoes, and fresh oregano, all ingredients available to the ancient Etruscans, who prepared farro centuries ago. They would presoak the grain in cold water to soften it up, and so do I. • SERVES 4 AS A MAIN COURSE OR 6 AS AN APPETIZER

3 cups (600 grams) farro

2 tablespoons (30 ml) olive oil

1 small red onion, thinly sliced

¼ teaspoon freshly ground black pepper, or more to taste

2 cups (480 ml) canned tomato puree

2 cups (480 ml) Chicken Stock (page 29) or chicken broth made with Knorr powdered bouillon

1 tablespoon finely chopped fresh chives

1 tablespoon chopped fresh Italian parsley

1 tablespoon chopped fresh oregano (or 1 teaspoon dried)

¼ cup (1 ounce/28 grams) finely grated Pecorino Toscano cheese, preferably 3 months old—sweet but a bit sharp

1 tablespoon unsalted butter

Kosher salt

PLACE THE FARRO in a medium bowl, cover with 6 cups (1.5 liters) cold water (it should be covered by 1 inch) and refrigerate for at least 1 hour, or up to 24 hours. The farro will have absorbed most, if not all, of the water. Place it in a strainer and gently shake from side to side to remove any excess water.

Place a 10- to 12-inch skillet over medium heat, and when it is hot, add the olive oil. Add the onion and pepper and sauté until the onion is soft and golden, 5 to 7 minutes. Add the farro and stir until the grains are coated with oil, about 2 minutes. Add 1 cup of the tomato puree and 1 cup of the stock, bring to a simmer, and simmer, stirring occasionally, until all the liquid has been absorbed by the farro, 6 to 8 minutes. Stir in the chives, parsley, and oregano and mix well. Add the 1 remaining cup each tomato puree and stock and let simmer, stirring occasionally, until the mixture starts to thicken. Then continue simmering, stirring constantly but slowly, until all the liquid has been absorbed and the farro is al dente, about 25 minutes. The mixture will look smooth and silky.

Remove from the heat, fold in the cheese and butter, and season with salt and pepper to taste. Serve immediately.

wine: This is a dish for all seasons, so my wine selection is the one that will be good for all seasons: Chianti Classico from Tuscany from Fontodi or Monsanto. Gaja, one of Italy's most renowned wineries, is now making a blend of Cabernet and Sangiovese grapes, called Promise, that is absolutely incredible and well worth seeking out for this dish.

risotto with green and white asparagus

RISOTTO CON ASPARAGI

mark • Asparagus is great in risotto. It's very watery, and as it cooks in the rice, its liquid is released and flavors the rice. Take advantage of the bounty of spring and use two kinds of asparagus. The green has a more assertive, earthy flavor, and the white brings its own delicacy to the dish. Black truffle puree is one of my favorite packaged foods. A little of it goes a long way. If you have some around, use it here to add luxury to this vegetarian dish. If you don't, I encourage you to buy some so you can see what it does for food. • SERVES 4 AS A MAIN COURSE OR 6 AS AN APPETIZER

4 to 5 cups (960 ml to 1.2 liters) Chicken Stock (page 29) or low-sodium canned organic chicken broth

2 tablespoons (28 grams) unsalted butter

1 medium white onion, minced

1 pound (454 grams) green asparagus, woody ends removed and cut into ½-inch (1.3-cm) pieces

1 pound (454 grams) white asparagus, woody ends removed and cut into ½-inch (1.3-cm) pieces

2 cups (454 grams) Arborio rice

1 cup (240 ml) dry white wine

1 tablespoon black truffle puree (optional)

¼ cup (1 ounce/28 grams) freshly grated Parmigiano-Reggiano cheese

Kosher salt and freshly ground black pepper

1 tablespoon chopped fresh Italian parsley

POUR THE CHICKEN STOCK into a 2½- to 3-quart saucepan and bring to a simmer. Keep warm over low heat.

Place a heavy-bottomed 5- to 6-quart pot over medium heat, and when it is hot, add 1 tablespoon of the butter. When the butter foams, add the onion and asparagus, mix well with a wooden spoon, and sauté until softened, 5 to 7 minutes. Add the rice and stir until all the grains are coated with butter, about 2 minutes. Gradually add the wine, stirring constantly. When the rice has absorbed most of the wine, add ½ cup of the broth and simmer, stirring, until it has been absorbed. Continue adding stock ½ cup at a time and stirring until all the stock has been absorbed and the rice is al dente, about 18 minutes.

Stir in the remaining 1 tablespoon butter, the truffle puree, if using, and the Parmigiano-Reggiano cheese. Add salt and pepper to taste, stir in the parsley, and serve immediately.

wine: You don't want a grassy white wine like a Sauvignon Blanc, which would compete with the grassy flavor of the asparagus. I'd choose a buttery or oaky white, such as a California Chardonnay or a white Burgundy from France.

mushroom risotto

RISOTTO AI FUNGHI

pino • Porcini mushrooms, available fresh in the fall, are one of nature's great gifts, and this risotto showcases their flavor beautifully. To intensify their earthiness, I add a little bit of dried mushrooms to the risotto. The perfume of this dish is incredible. Don't be tempted to mix other mushrooms with the porcini. I love chanterelles and morels, and I'll make risotto with them, but I like to use them singly, so their unique flavors don't get mixed and muddied. If you'd like to substitute chanterelles here, just leave out the dried porcini and stir in a pinch of saffron, which complements their subtle woodsiness. Morels are so delicate that I keep the preparation simple, stirring them into the risotto without the dried porcini or any herbs that might obscure their flavor. • SERVES 4 AS A MAIN COURSE

4 to 5 cups (960 ml to 1.2 liters) Chicken Stock (page 29) or chicken broth made from Knorr powdered bouillon

1 ounce (28 grams) dried porcini mushrooms

1 cup (240 ml) very hot tap water

2 tablespoons (30 ml) olive oil

1 medium red onion, finely minced

1 pound (454 grams) fresh porcini mushrooms, thinly sliced

2 cups (454 grams) Vialone Nano, Carnaroli, or Arborio rice

1 tablespoon fresh thyme leaves

4 teaspoons freshly grated Parmigiano-Reggiano cheese

2 tablespoons (28 grams) unsalted butter

Kosher salt to taste

1/2 teaspoon freshly ground black pepper

POUR THE CHICKEN STOCK into a 2½- to 3-quart saucepan and bring to a simmer. Keep warm over low heat.

Place the dried porcini mushrooms and hot water in a cup or small bowl and set aside to soak for 15 minutes. Remove the mushrooms and set aside. Strain the soaking liquid through a cheesecloth-lined sieve or a coffee filter and reserve.

Place a heavy-bottomed 5- to 6-quart pot over medium heat, and when it is hot, add the olive oil. Add the onion and fresh mushrooms, mix well with a wooden spoon, and sauté until softened, 5 to 7 minutes. Add the rice and cook until all the grains are coated with the oil, about 2 minutes. Add the dried porcini, then gradually add 2 cups of the stock, stirring constantly. When the rice has absorbed the liquid, add the remaining stock and then the porcini water, ½ cup at the time, stirring constantly and slowly, and simmer until the rice has absorbed all the liquid, about 15 minutes. The risotto should be very moist but not soupy, and the rice grains should show a tiny little white dot, "the soul," in the center. Remove from the heat, and add the thyme, cheese, butter, salt, and pepper. Stir, and serve immediately.

tip: If you can't get fresh porcini, chanterelles, or morels, or if they are too expensive for your budget, use cremini or white mushrooms, adding the dried porcini (which are always available and relatively inexpensive) for a rich, deep flavor.

wine: A great estate, Santi in the Veneto, makes an Amarone that has the intensity and bouquet to stand up to the porcini. If you are using chanterelles or morels, switch to a Santi Valpolicella, which is a more gentle, delicate red.

farro with button mushrooms, cherry tomatoes, and goat cheese

FARROTTO CON FUNGHI, POMODORINI, E FORMAGGIO

mark • Chefs often overlook plain old button mushrooms, but when you want real mushroom flavor (as opposed to the meatiness of shiitakes or the nuttiness of porcini), you can't do better. Their earthy flavor goes well with farro, which also has an earthy, wholesome flavor. Goat cheese has an earthiness of its own, which is why I chose it for this recipe. The cherry tomatoes bring a little bit of acidity and sweetness. • SERVES 4 AS A MAIN COURSE OR 6 AS AN APPETIZER

3 cups (600 grams) farro

3 cups (720 ml) Chicken Stock (page 29) or low-sodium canned organic chicken broth

2 tablespoons (28 grams) unsalted butter

1 tablespoon (15 ml) extra-virgin olive oil

1 medium red onion, minced

1 garlic clove, minced

2 cups (115 grams) thinly sliced button mushrooms

1 pint (285 grams) red cherry tomatoes

1 cup (130 grams) yellow cherry tomatoes

2 fresh marjoram or rosemary sprigs, leaves chopped

1 teaspoon kosher salt, or more to taste

1/2 teaspoon freshly ground black pepper, or more to taste

1 cup (240 ml) dry white wine

4 ounces (114 grams) fresh goat cheese, cut into small pieces

1 tablespoon finely chopped fresh Italian parsley

PLACE THE FARRO in a 3-quart bowl, cover with about 6 cups (1.5 liters) cold water (it should be covered by 1 inch), and refrigerate for at least 1 hour, or up to 24 hours. The farro will have absorbed most, if not all, of the water. Place it in a strainer and gently shake from side to side to remove any excess water.

Pour the chicken stock into a 2½- to 3-quart saucepan and bring to a simmer. Keep warm over low heat.

Place a 10- to 12-inch skillet over medium heat, and when it is hot, add 1 tablespoon of the butter, the oil, onion, and garlic. Sauté until the onion is soft and golden, 5 to 7 minutes. Add the farro and stir until the grains are coated with oil and butter, about 2 minutes. Add the mushrooms, tomatoes, marjoram or rosemary, salt, and pepper and stir for 1 minute. Add the wine and let simmer, stirring occasionally, until the rice absorbs the liquid and the mixture starts to thicken. Gradually add ½ cup of the stock, stirring constantly. When the farro absorbs the liquid, continue adding stock ½ cup at a time, and simmer, stirring constantly and slowly, until all the stock has been absorbed and the farro is al dente; about 20 minutes. The mixture will look smooth and silky.

Remove from the heat and stir in the remaining 1 tablespoon butter, the goat cheese, and parsley. Season with salt and pepper if necessary and serve immediately.

wine: Sancerre, from the Loire Valley in France, pairs well with goat cheese, as do other Sauvignon Blancs.

6

two meatballs go fishing

In Italy, fish restaurants are traditionally closed on Mondays because no fishing boats go out on Sunday. *"Domenica è Domenica"* (Sunday is Sunday), Italians say. Even fishermen get the day off. So on just one day of the week, people have to eat something else if they're eating out. Italians wouldn't dream of eating fish that wasn't fresh.

In coastal areas, Italians have always eaten fish several times a week, sometimes daily. For people living inland, fresh fish used to be a treat reserved for seaside holidays, because otherwise it simply wasn't available straight off the boat. In recent years, because of improvements in transportation, fresh fish can be found in Italian towns far from the sea, and fish has become a regular part of the national diet even in the mountains and farmlands. And Italians all over the country have not had trouble learning to prepare fish, because the traditional regional preparations are so simple and very easy to incorporate into regular shopping and cooking routines. It doesn't matter if it's a bass (*branzino*), sardines (*sarde*), or squid (*calamari*), seafood in Italy is prepared in a simple, straightforward way, without difficult sauces and fancy accompaniments.

Although fresh fish is increasingly available across the country, home cooks here don't have the same commitment to it. It's a rare household where fresh fish is prepared several times a week. Only on a summer vacation by the sea do Americans have the nerve to cook fish and shellfish on a daily basis. In this chapter, we have chosen recipes that call for fish and shellfish readily available in American markets: striped bass, salmon, swordfish, halibut, sardines, cod, shrimp, mussels, and clams. It is our hope that these recipes will bring together the Italian love of fish and the American desire to cook Italian so that more Americans can enjoy the pleasures and health benefits of eating fish regularly.

pino I once wrote a book called *Fish Talking*, all with recipes using the little guys of the sea—sardines, anchovies, squid. These are some of my favorite fish, but the book didn't do well. I'm guessing it's because Americans, who have mostly been fed on regal tuna, think small fish don't count.

mark If you want to talk small fish, let's talk porgies, whitings, and tilefish. They're easier to get here. You can buy a red snapper that's as small as a pound and a half or as big as eight pounds.

pino In my family, we rarely ate anything more than ten inches long.

mark I agree, smaller is sweeter. We sauté them, we add them to stews (*cacciucco*), and we roast them whole. I don't like great big red snapper, big black sea bass, or grouper. I'm talking eight to ten

pounds and up, when they become very tough. But on the other hand I love halibut. Turbot is another bigger fish I love.

pino Generally I avoid anything that wouldn't fit in my home oven. Americans' worship of these gigantic fish, like tuna, is a mystery to me. Unless it is good canned tuna from Sicily preserved in oil, I don't use too much of it. To me, fresh tuna doesn't taste like the sea. I want to get that taste of the ocean, so I use the little fish.

mark I totally disagree, I really do. I love tuna, I love sushi made with tuna, and I love it raw or cooked. It's an oily fish that needs a strong sauce with it. And anyway, did you know that Italy is the biggest importer of the bonito tuna fished off the coasts of Montauk, Long Island, and New Bedford, Massachusetts?

pino Maybe, but in terms of quality, you can't beat the local Italian tuna. Sicilians have been fishing and canning tuna for hundreds of years; they have achieved perfection. They used to can the tuna right on the boats. They probably still do. All I can tell you is that you open a can of their tuna and you really fall in love with that fish. You have to buy the big cans, because they're the ones that contain a whole piece of the belly, the *ventresca,* which is the most flavorful part. It's the only way I'll eat it.

mark In my opinion, buying local is more important when you are talking about fresh. Sole, flounder, grouper, cod, tilefish—all of them are fished off the northeastern coast, and that's what I use when I can.

sicilian couscous

CUS CUS ALLA SICILIANA

mark · The Greeks, the Romans, and the Normans conquered Sicily at different times, and when they left, they left behind recipes. The Normans left this one, and I discovered it when I stumbled into one of Italy's more exotic food and wine regions on a vacation in the northwestern part of Sicily near Marsala. I was staying in a little hotel in the tiny town of Erice. The place had a dining room with a bit of a reputation and fog, two reasons to stay in for the night. We dined on fish "cus cus" and hung around the hotel drinking Marsala, appreciating the truly indigenous meal, food and drink that could have been eaten in that location hundreds of years ago.

I loved the spicy, lemony flavor of the couscous, which is also flavored with the liquid from the seafood. I knew instantly that this highly flavored, low-fat seafood dish would appeal to my health-conscious customers. · SERVES 4

8 ounces (228 grams) cleaned octopus, cut into 1½-inch pieces

1 tablespoon (15 ml) red wine vinegar

12 littleneck clams, scrubbed

2 tablespoons (30 ml) extra-virgin olive oil

2 garlic cloves, thickly sliced

1 pound (454 grams) cleaned squid, bodies cut into ½-inch-wide (1.3-cm) rings

1 red onion, finely diced

2 celery stalks, finely diced

1 carrot, cut into small dice

Pinch of crushed red pepper flakes

8 mussels, preferably Prince Edward Island, scrubbed and debearded

1 cup (240 ml) dry white wine

¾ cup (360 ml) Fish Stock (recipe follows), water, or additional wine

Juice of 2 lemons (about ½ cup/120 ml)

2 fresh oregano sprigs, leaves only

4 ounces (114 grams) monkfish fillet, cut into 1½-inch (3.7-cm) pieces

6 ounces (160 grams) cod or blackfish fillet, cut into 1½-inch (3.7-cm) pieces

8 large sea scallops (about 8 ounces/ 228 grams)

12 large shrimp, shelled and deveined

Kosher salt and freshly ground black pepper

One 10-ounce (285-gram) box instant couscous

2 tablespoons chopped fresh Italian parsley

PLACE THE OCTOPUS in a 3- to 4-quart saucepan and cover it with water by 1 inch. Add the red wine vinegar, cover the pan, and bring to a boil over medium-high heat. Uncover the pot and cook at a rolling boil until the octopus is curled and chewy-tender, about 35 minutes. Drain and set aside.

Meanwhile, to clean the clams, place them in a colander and cover with ice cubes. Place the colander in a larger bowl, cover the clams with cold water, and set aside for 20 minutes. Drain.

Place a heavy-bottomed 6- to 7-quart pot over medium-high heat, and when it is hot, add the olive oil. Add the garlic and cook until just golden, about 1 minute. Add the squid, onion, celery, carrot, and red pepper flakes, and sauté until the vegetables are soft, 5 to 7 minutes. Add the octopus, mussels, clams, wine, fish stock, lemon juice, and oregano. Bring the soup to a simmer, then reduce the heat to medium, and cook until the shellfish have opened, 5 to 7 minutes. Add the monkfish and cod or blackfish, pushing them into the simmering liquid to cover. Add the scallops and cook 1 minute, then add the shrimp. When the shrimp are pink and no longer translucent, after about 3 to 4 minutes, remove the soup from the heat. Using a slotted spoon, remove and discard any mussels and clams that did not open. Season with salt and pepper to taste.

(CONTINUED)

Make the couscous following the directions on the box, substituting simmering broth from the soup for the water required. Transfer the couscous to a large serving bowl, and slowly ladle the seafood and broth around it. Sprinkle with the parsley and serve immediately.

wine: Try Bianco Alcamo, a crisp and lively white from Sicily, with this Sicilian-style couscous.

fish stock

At the restaurant, we always use fish stock in seafood dishes to add an extra layer of flavor that would be missing if we used plain water. You can get similar complexity without the trouble if you use wine or bottled clam juice, but for the most intense ocean flavor, fish stock is great. If you have time and a good kitchen exhaust fan (I won't lie, the smell of boiling fish bones can linger), ask the fishmonger for a couple of pounds of bones and give fish stock a try. • MAKES 6 TO 7 CUPS (1.4 TO 1.7 LITERS)

2 pounds (908 grams) white fish bones, such as scorpionfish, porgy, or grouper

1 carrot, coarsely chopped

1 celery stalk, coarsely chopped

1 Spanish onion, coarsely chopped

1 bay leaf

6 peppercorns

1 fresh parsley sprig

8 cups (1.9 liters) water or 4 cups (960 ml) water and 4 cups (960 ml) dry white wine

PLACE ALL THE ingredients in a 5- to 6-quart pot and bring to a gentle boil over high heat. Reduce the heat to low and simmer for 45 minutes.

Strain the stock through a fine strainer. Cover and refrigerate for up to 2 days, or freeze for up to 1 month.

tuscan seafood sauté

FRUTTI DI MARE IN PADELLA

mark · Although we disagree about many things, Pino and I share a love for the food of the Tuscan coast. It's amazing to travel the coastline of this region and taste the different ways they prepare the medley of clams, mussels, octopus, squid, and shrimp that appear in so many soups, pastas, risottos, and main dishes. This very simple, healthy sauté of the seafood, which I first tried in Livorno, is probably my favorite. It fills me up without weighing me down. I've added an American seafood favorite—scallops—but otherwise it's the same as the dish I remember so well. It's beautiful when served family-style on a large platter put in the center of the table. No garnish is necessary, because the seafood itself is so visually appealing. · SERVES 4

4 slices country bread

2 garlic cloves, 1 peeled and left whole, 1 minced

2 tablespoons (30 ml) extra-virgin olive oil

1 cup (240 ml) dry white wine

12 littleneck clams, scrubbed

24 small mussels, preferably Prince Edward Island, scrubbed and debearded

1 cup (240 ml) canned tomato puree

1½ tablespoons (22 ml) red wine vinegar

1 teaspoon dried oregano, preferably Sicilian, or 1 tablespoon chopped fresh oregano

8 large shrimp, peeled and deveined

4 jumbo or 8 medium sea scallops

½ cup (20 grams) finely chopped fresh Italian parsley

Pinch of crushed red pepper flakes (optional)

Kosher salt and freshly ground black pepper

PREHEAT THE OVEN to 350 degrees (175°C).

Rub each slice of bread with the whole garlic clove and place the slices on a baking sheet. Toast until golden. Set aside.

Place a 10- to 12-inch skillet over medium heat, and when it is hot, add the olive oil. Add the minced garlic and sauté until fragrant, about 30 seconds. Add ½ cup of the wine and the clams and mussels. Cover the pot and steam the shellfish until it begins to open, about 4 minutes. Add the tomato puree, the remaining ½ cup wine, the wine vinegar, and oregano. Raise the heat to medium-high and cook, uncovered, stirring, until the sauce thickens slightly, about 3 minutes. Add the shrimp and scallops and cook until the shrimp are curled and pink and the scallops are just firm, about 3 minutes.

Stir in the parsley, crushed red pepper flakes, if using, and salt and pepper to taste. Using a slotted spoon, remove and discard any clams and mussels that have not opened.

Spoon the seafood into four shallow bowls. Place a slice of toasted garlic bread on top of each bowl. Serve immediately.

wine: I like a lighter red, like a Merlot, with this seafood dish. Swanson Merlot from Oakville in Napa is one of my favorites.

oven-roasted grouper with yukon gold potatoes

CERNIA AL FORNO CON PATATE

pino • My mother was a genius at making flavorful meals on a limited budget. She would buy a whole grouper or snapper from her father, a fisherman (he was a socialist, part of a fishing cooperative, and he gave no freebies, not even to his daughter!). She cleaned the fish and placed it in a pan so big it wouldn't fit into our oven, and then surrounded it with potatoes and some-times some mussels. When everything was assembled, my brother, sister, and I would help her carry it to the bakery in the center of town, and for four or five hundred lire (about fifty cents back then), the baker would cook the fish for us. Just putting it in the oven wasn't the whole story—you had to nurture the fish as it cooked. My mother would stay at the bakery, opening the oven, checking the amount of liquid, and watching vigilantly while the fish, potatoes, and mussels cooked.

This is one case where I love a big fish, a whole grouper or red snapper weighing at least 6 pounds, to ensure that it stays moist until everything is cooked through. The mussels release their juices into the pan, giving the potatoes an incredible briny flavor. Now that home ovens are a little bigger, this dish is simple to make. I enjoy serving it on Good Friday and other major family occasions in the spring and early summer. • SERVES 8

2½ to 3 pounds (1.1 to 1.4 kilos) baby Yukon Gold potatoes, well scrubbed

3 tablespoons (45 ml) olive oil

2 large lemons, cut into 5 to 6 slices each

1 whole grouper or red snapper (6 to 8 pounds/2.7 to 3.5 kilos), cleaned, scaled, rinsed with cold water, and patted dry

1 tablespoon kosher salt

1 tablespoon freshly ground black pepper

2 bunches fresh rosemary

2 bunches fresh sage

2 bunches fresh thyme

1 cup (240 ml) dry white wine

16 to 24 mussels, preferably Prince Edward Island, scrubbed and debearded

PREHEAT THE OVEN to 350 degrees (175°C).

Place the potatoes in a 5- to 6-quart pot, cover generously with cold water, and bring to a boil over high heat. Boil for 10 minutes. (The potatoes will not be tender.) Drain and place in a mixing bowl. Add 1 tablespoon of the oil, mix well, and set aside.

Spread 1 tablespoon of the oil evenly over the bottom of a roasting pan larger than the fish, and place 8 of the lemon slices down the center of the pan.

Brush the remaining 1 tablespoon oil on both sides of the fish, making sure the skin is moist. Lay the fish on its side, gently open the cavity, and sprinkle the interior with 1 teaspoon of the salt and ½ teaspoon of the pepper. Stuff the fish with half of the herbs and the remaining lemon slices. Cut 4 diagonal slashes in each side of the fish and tuck in a sprig of each herb. Place the fish in the pan. Season with the remaining 2 teaspoons salt and 2½ teaspoons pepper and scatter the remaining herbs around the fish.

Transfer the fish to the oven and roast until the fish indents slightly when poked with a finger and the flesh in the slashes is almost cooked through, 30 to 40 minutes.

Pour the wine around the fish and then scatter the potatoes and mus-sels around it. Continue roasting until the mussels have opened, the flesh in the slashes is opaque and just cooked through, and the potatoes are tender, about 15 minutes.

Remove the potatoes and mussels to a large platter. Using two sturdy spatulas, carefully lift the fish to the center of the platter. Pour the juices from the baking dish through a strainer into a serving bowl, and serve alongside the fish.

To fillet the fish, with a sharp fillet or other thin flexible knife, cut along the fish's spine, head to tail. Starting at the head, gently peel back the skin toward the tail and remove it. Divide the top fillet by making a lengthwise cut through it, and serve the flesh from both sides, being careful to check for any bones that might have separated from the spine. Then gently grab the tail and, using a knife if needed, separate the spine from the fillet below by lifting and pulling it back toward the head. Inspect the bottom fillet for any bones that may remain, and serve it.

wine: The northeast regions of Italy produce some of the finest white wines. The one I truly love with this dish is the Jerman Estate Chardonnay from the Friuli region, a wine of great bouquet and taste.

steamed halibut fillets with sweet pepper, cucumber, and basil vinaigrette

IPPOGLOSSO AL VAPORE CON PEPERONI, CETRIOLO, E BASILICO

mark · I learned to cook halibut when I worked at the Amstel Hotel in Amsterdam, which is very close to the North Sea, where halibut live. The fish was delivered every morning, so fresh it was still covered in a natural gel that protected it from the cold waters of the North Atlantic (after a day or two out of water, the fish loses this gel and its skin begins to dry out). After hunting in New York for a good fish purveyor, I found a small company called Brown Oyster, where the halibut is as fresh as I had seen it in Amsterdam.

This is a light and healthy dish that can be served either hot or at room temperature, which is how I like it for a summer buffet. The flavors in this recipe really sing—the contrast between the basil and the sweet fish is beautiful. It is also beautiful to look at, vibrant and bright.

To steam the fish, we use a bamboo dumpling steamer placed over a pot of boiling seasoned water. These steamers are inexpensive and widely available at Asian markets and online. Be very careful when checking the fish for doneness. Remove the pot from the heat, and then use tongs to open it, keeping your face far away from the escaping steam so it doesn't scald you. Once you have removed the lid and the initial burst of steam has dissipated, it is safe to take a closer look at the fish. · SERVES 4

FOR THE VINAIGRETTE

1/2 **bunch fresh basil, leaves only (about 1 cup; 30 grams)**

1 **small garlic clove**

1/2 **red bell pepper, cored, seeded, and minced**

1/2 **yellow bell pepper, cored, seeded, and minced**

1/2 **English (seedless) cucumber, peeled, and cut into tiny cubes**

1 **scallion, white part only, thinly sliced**

1 **tablespoon (15 ml) red wine vinegar**

2 **tablespoons (30 ml) extra-virgin olive oil**

1/2 **teaspoon kosher salt**

FOR THE COURT BOUILLON

12 **whole cloves**

1 **small white onion**

6 **cups (1.4 liters) water**

1/2 **cup (120 ml) white wine vinegar**

2 **bay leaves**

3 **juniper berries**

12 **black peppercorns**

3 **fresh rosemary sprigs**

3 **fresh Italian parsley sprigs**

FOR THE FISH

Four 6- to 8-ounce (170- to 225-gram) halibut fillets

1 **teaspoon kosher salt**

4 **lemon slices**

4 **small fresh rosemary sprigs**

Place the basil and garlic in the bowl of a food processor and process until finely chopped, about 1 minute, scraping down the sides of the bowl once or twice as necessary. Transfer to a medium bowl, add the vegetables and scallion and whisk in the vinegar, oil, and salt. Set aside.

TO STEAM THE FISH

Insert the cloves into the onion. Place the onion, water, vinegar, bay leaves, juniper berries, peppercorns, rosemary, and parsley in an 8- to 10-quart stockpot and bring to a boil over high heat. Season the top of each piece of fish wih salt. Place a lemon slice and a rosemary sprig on top of each piece and place in a single layer in a bamboo steamer. Place the steamer over the court bouillon, cover the pot, reduce the heat to medium-high, and cook the fish, maintaining a vigorous steam, until the fish is moist, flaky, and pristine white, 10 to 12 minutes.

Discard the lemon and parsley and transfer the fish to a platter. Spoon the basil vinaigrette on top of and around the fish, and serve immediately.

wine: A Soave from the Pieropan Estate has a bright acidity that complements the vegetables and dressing on this fish.

oven-roasted salmon on savoy cabbage

SALMONE ARROSTO CON LA VERZA

piro • I love the way the cabbage flavors the salmon with some smokiness and the salmon gives the cabbage some richness in this simple dish. Cook the fish and cabbage together in a skillet you can bring to the table. It's wonderful as it is, but I like to add a little black truffle puree, a little savory candy, to the top. • SERVES 4

1 tablespoon (15 ml) olive oil

1 small yellow onion, thinly sliced

2 garlic cloves, thinly sliced

One 2-pound (908-gram) Savoy cabbage, cut into ½-inch (1.3-cm) slices

½ cup (120 ml) dry white wine

¾ cup (180 ml) Chicken Stock (page 29) or chicken broth made with Knorr's powdered bouillon

1 teaspoon kosher salt

½ teaspoon freshly ground black pepper

Four 8-ounce (225-gram) wild or king salmon fillets (1½ inches/3.7 cm thick), skin removed

1 tablespoon plus 1 teaspoon black truffle puree (optional)

PREHEAT THE OVEN to 425 degrees (220°C).

Place a 10- to 12-inch ovenproof skillet over medium-high heat, and when it is hot, add the olive oil. Add the onion and garlic and sauté, stirring occasionally, until soft and golden, 5 to 7 minutes. Add the cabbage in four batches and sauté, stirring constantly, until it is slightly wilted, about 10 minutes.

Add the wine, reduce the heat to medium-low, cover the pan, and cook until the cabbage is very soft, about 15 minutes. Add the chicken stock and cook, stirring, until the cabbage has absorbed most of the liquid, about 15 minutes. Season the cabbage with ½ teaspoon of the salt and the pepper and remove from the heat.

Place the salmon on top of the cabbage and sprinkle the fish with the remaining ½ teaspoon salt. Place 1 teaspoon truffle puree, if desired, over each piece of fish. Cover, transfer to a rack in the middle of the oven, and bake for 12 minutes for rare, or 15 minutes for medium.

Serve immediately, right from the skillet.

wine: A winter dish this rich in flavor needs red, red, red. Brunello di Montalcino is my favorite. For a superior example, look for a Casanova di Neri Estate 2000 or 2001.

baked clams coco pazzo

VONGOLE GRATINATE

mark • When I was a kid, it was our custom to go out for dinner on Sundays. I was never much of a Chinese food fan, so I would try to steer my parents to an Italian restaurant. Along with fried calamari and spaghetti and meatballs, baked clams were a staple on the menu, and I loved them. Years later, when I started working in a restaurant in an affluent neighborhood, I realized that many of my customers had also grown up on this food, and were still dying for it, and that's how I built a following—by being hospitable and cooking what people want to eat, not always trying to force trendy foods on them. My male customers order these clams by the dozens, even as their wives and girlfriends protest that they don't want to eat anything with oil and bread crumbs. But it's a rare dieter who can resist them in the end.

Italians like their baked clams small and sweet, and so do I. The only ones to buy for this dish are littlenecks. • SERVES 4

24 littleneck clams, shucked (you can have the fishmonger do this, if prepared within 2 hours so the clams stay as fresh as possible), 24 shells reserved

¼ cup (112 grams) minced pancetta (optional)

2 tablespoons (28 grams) unsalted butter

2 garlic cloves, minced

2 cups (120 grams) bread crumbs (page 303) or store-bought unflavored bread crumbs

1 tablespoon dried oregano, preferably Sicilian

¼ cup (120 ml) extra-virgin olive oil

¼ cup (1 ounce/28 grams) freshly grated Parmigiano-Reggiano cheese

2 tablespoons chopped fresh Italian parsley

Kosher salt and freshly ground black pepper

1 cup (240 ml) dry white wine

PREHEAT THE OVEN to 450 degrees (230°C). Place the clam shells on a large rimmed baking sheet.

Sauté the pancetta in a small skillet over medium-high heat until crisp. Use a slotted spoon to remove the pancetta and drain on a paper towel–lined plate.

Place a 4- to 5-inch skillet over medium-low heat, and when it is hot, add the butter and garlic and cook until the garlic is softened but not browned, about 1 minute. Remove from the heat.

Place the bread crumbs, oregano, oil, cheese, parsley, and pancetta, if using, in a medium bowl and stir well. Stir in the butter and garlic mixture. Season with salt and pepper.

Place a clam inside each shell and then completely cover with the bread crumb stuffing. Drizzle a little wine on top of each clam, and pour the remaining wine onto the baking sheet.

Bake until the stuffing is crisp and golden and the clams are gently plumped, about 10 minutes. Serve immediately.

tip: This makes great party food. Serve as your guests are first arriving—it's much more fun than cheese and crackers.

wine: A very light Orvieto is just right with these clams.

spicy shrimp scampi

GAMBERI IN UMIDO CON AGLIO E PEPERONCINO

pino • Here is an Italian-American restaurant classic that I've refined for the menu at Centolire. Spiked with crushed red pepper flakes and silky with butter, it's very delicious. Much of the flavor of shrimp is in the shells, so it's important to cook them shell-on. If you can find shrimp with their heads still on, even better. I like the jumbo size, called U8 in the industry because they come eight to the pound. They are tastier and harder to overcook. • SERVES 4

2 tablespoons (30 ml) olive oil

5 garlic cloves, thinly sliced

2 pounds (908 grams) jumbo shrimp in the shell, preferably head on

2 cups (480 ml) dry white wine

1 tablespoon chopped fresh Italian parsley

1 teaspoon kosher salt

1/2 teaspoon crushed red pepper flakes, or more to taste

1 tablespoon (14 grams) unsalted butter

PLACE A 10- TO 12-INCH SKILLET over medium heat, and when it is hot, add the olive oil. Add the garlic and sauté until golden, about 1 minute. Raise the heat to high, add the shrimp, and sauté them quickly until they are bright pink, about 2 minutes. Add the wine, parsley, salt, and red pepper flakes, reduce the heat to medium, and simmer until the wine has reduced by half, 3 minutes.

Add the butter, toss the shrimp well, and serve immediately.

tip: I love to serve this very spicy and garlicky dish with bruschetta, toasted peasant bread. Place the bread on a serving dish and top with the shrimp and then the sauce.

wine: The garlic makes me want to drink a good Gavi from Piedmont, like the Gavi di Gavi from the La Scolca Estate.

cod and yukon gold gratin

GRATIN DI MERLUZZO E PATATE

mark • Cod's reputation has suffered since the 1960s, when it began to be used in frozen fish sticks and fast-food fish sandwiches. But fresh cod, called "day boat cod" because it is caught in the waters off New England and brought to market on the same day, is becoming highly prized by chefs for its clean flavor and beautiful white flesh, and it is one of my personal favorites. This recipe is an homage to *brandade*, the classical French dish of salt cod with cream and potatoes. Salting fish is a way of preserving it, and salt cod has long been a staple of the Italian as well as the French pantry. But now that day boat cod is an option, I choose it over salt cod for a fresher taste. A little anchovy adds a pleasing complexity. The result is real comfort food, but unusual at the same time. • SERVES 6

4 large Yukon Gold potatoes

4 tablespoons (56 grams) unsalted butter

1 medium onion, thinly sliced

2 cups (480 ml) heavy cream

2 garlic cloves, minced

2 anchovy fillets, rinsed and chopped

1/2 teaspoon kosher salt, plus more to taste

1/2 cup (2 ounces/56 grams) grated Fontina Val d'Aosta, Gruyère, or Appenzeller cheese

Four 6- to 8-ounce (170- to 252-gram) codfish fillets

Freshly ground black pepper

PREHEAT THE OVEN to 375 degrees (190°C). Lightly butter a 9-by-13-inch baking dish.

Peel the potatoes and, using a very sharp knife, cut them into 1/2-inch (1.3-cm) slices. Place the slices in a large bowl of ice water (this will keep them from oxidizing) and set aside.

Place a 6- to 8-inch skillet over medium-high heat, and when it is hot, add 1 tablespoon of the butter. Add the onion and sauté, stirring occasionally, until soft and golden, 5 to 7 minutes. Remove from the heat.

Combine the cream, garlic, anchovies, and salt in a small bowl and mix well. Place the potatoes in the prepared baking dish, overlapping them, to make a bed for the fish. Spread the onion on top of the potatoes. Drizzle the potatoes with the cream mixture and sprinkle with the grated cheese.

Transfer to the oven and bake until the potatoes are almost tender, 25 to 35 minutes.

Place the fish on top of the potatoes, pushing the fillets lightly into the bubbling cream. Dot with the remaining 3 tablespoons butter, sprinkle with salt and pepper, and return to the oven. Bake until the fish is just flaky and the cheese is golden and bubbling, 12 to 14 minutes. Let stand for 5 minutes before serving.

tip: Fontina Val d'Aosta is made in the Italian Alps and is similar to Gruyère. Use it in any recipe that calls for Swiss cheese, and you will love the earthy flavor it brings.

wine: Light Italian whites from Friuli, like Tocai or Sauvignon Blanc, would be good choices here. Look for the Schiopetto label, one of my favorite producers of both varietals.

7

meat and poultry

rustic oven cooking

Even though we grew up in two different food cultures, our mothers had similar goals when planning dinner. They didn't want to spend a lot of money. They wanted to make enough food for the night's meal and maybe enough for lunch the next day. And they didn't want to be tied to the stove for hours, since they had housework to do and children to look after. To achieve these goals, they often began with the same technique, oven braising. Slow-cooking was convenient. The oven did much of the work while our moms could get other things done around the house, and if there was leftover pot roast to put into a quick pasta sauce or leftover chicken for sandwiches, that was one less meal to prepare. But slow cooking also brought out the best in inexpensive cuts of meat, tenderizing pot roast and lamb shoulder, brewing a delicious sauce for cut-up poultry while keeping it moist. That's what we remember most fondly about their braises and what we enjoy today when we braise. The aroma of Lamb Shanks Braised with Savoy Cabbage (page 194) or garlicky Chicken Scarpariello (page 199) as they cook slowly in the oven only whets our appetite for a traditional braised dinner. In the last twenty years, American restaurant chefs have discovered what trattoria cooks in Italy have always known, that diners more often than not prefer home-style food to fussy chef creations.

The trattoria is a home away from home for Italians who enjoy eye round pot roast (*stracotto*), osso buco, and oven-braised rabbit (*coniglio alla cacciatora*), sometimes leaving an unfinished bottle of wine at their favorite table to let the proprietor know they'll be back in a night or two. Now Americans can order brisket or braised lamb shanks at many restaurants, including ours, just the way Italians have always gone out to eat food just like the dishes they eat at home. Although we are happy to serve Rabbit Braised in White Wine and Herbs (page 198) or Sausage and Cranberry Beans with Polenta (page 195) to our customers, we truly believe that this food tastes even better when it comes from your own kitchen, where you can enjoy its aroma as it cooks before you sit down to dinner. If there are any leftovers, that's great, because these braised dishes taste even better on the second day.

The recipes in this chapter pay tribute to our mothers, who first schooled us in the traditions of home cooking, including making enough food to last for several days.

pino You grew up in America in the fifties at the same time I was growing up in Italy, during the reconstruction after World War II. Even though our childhoods were drastically different, our parents had that same postwar mentality, that you had to be frugal about everything, including food.

mark My parents were always telling me about food rationing during the war. My grandmother wouldn't throw anything out. If there was a hole in a piece of clothing, she would mend it. We lived in a housing project built right after the war for returning veterans.

pino From our house, you could walk to the end of the sidewalk and directly onto a dirt road, and after that there were fields. In the spring and fall, my mother would walk to them in search of edible greens before she would go to the store to buy them. She'd bring the kids along to look for kale, dandelions, and wild herbs. She'd say, "I may not have much money, but I have plenty of labor. I've got five kids."

mark When my parents started summering in Pennsylvania, we would go berry picking near the house, where there were wild blackberry bushes by the side of

the road. Now you have to pay a premium to go to one of these pick-your-own places, because the area, which was semi-rural, has now been completely developed.

pino Sometimes I feel sad for my three kids, growing up without having to do any of things that necessity taught me. Last time I took them to Italy, we were walking by a field outside a small village, Colonnata, in the Tuscan Alps. I leaned over to pick up some chicory, and my little one, Lorenzo, asked me how I knew what it was and that I could eat it. I told him about our foraging trips with my mother, and how her great

tuscan pot roast

ARROSTO TOSCANO

mark • If I had to choose one dish that represented who I am as a cook, this would be it. I grew up with my grandmother's and my mother's brisket, the gravy rich with caramelized onions and carrots. When I started to cook Italian, I revisited that brisket, cooking it with typically northern Italian plum tomatoes and rosemary. The chicken livers are optional, but they are well loved in Italy. When they are pureed with the sauce, nobody will know they are there, and they give this dish wonderful body and earthiness. • SERVES 6 TO 8

1 brisket (about 5 to 6 pounds/2.3 to 2.7 kilos), trimmed of excess fat

1 teaspoon kosher salt, or more to taste

1/2 teaspoon freshly ground black pepper, or more to taste

2 tablespoons olive oil

2 carrots, diced

2 celery stalks, diced

1 onion, diced

3 garlic cloves, minced

3 chicken livers, membranes removed and cut into 1/2-inch (1.3-cm) pieces (optional)

1 bottle (750 ml) dry red wine

3 cups (720ml) Chicken Stock (page 29) or canned low-sodium organic canned chicken broth

1 cup (240 ml) canned Italian plum tomatoes, preferably San Marzano, lightly crushed

1 bay leaf

3 tablespoons chopped fresh rosemary

2 tablespoons chopped fresh Italian parsley

SET A RACK in the middle of the oven and preheat the oven to 325 degrees (165°C).

Season the brisket with the salt and pepper. Set aside.

In a 7- to 8-quart Dutch oven with a tight-fitting lid, heat the olive oil over medium-high heat. Add the brisket and brown well on both sides, about 10 minutes. Remove to a plate and set aside.

Add the carrots, celery, onion, and garlic to the pot, reduce the heat to medium, and cook, scraping up any browned bits, until all the vegetables are almost soft and the onion is golden, about 5 minutes. Add the chicken livers, if using, and cook, stirring, until they begin to firm, about 2 minutes. Add the wine, stock, tomatoes, bay leaf, and rosemary, then add the brisket and any reserved juices, raise the heat to medium-high, and bring to a simmer.

Cover the pot and place in the middle of the oven. Cook, turning the meat once, until it is fork-tender, 3 to 3½ hours.

Transfer the brisket to a cutting board and lightly cover with aluminum foil. Let stand for 15 minutes.

Meanwhile, spoon off the accumulated fat from the surface of the sauce. Use an immersion blender to puree the sauce right in the pot. Or transfer to a blender or food processor to puree, and return to the pot. Season with salt and pepper, and stir in the parsley.

Slice the meat and serve with the warm sauce on the side. (Alternatively, slice the meat, return it to the pot, and refrigerate overnight. Remove any solidified fat from the surface of the sauce and reheat, covered, in a 300-degree (150°C) oven until piping hot.)

wine: I'd suggest a Rosso di Montalcino, which is like a baby Brunello, an every-day table wine but with a touch of greatness.

pork loin with orange sauce

ARROSTO DI MAIALE ALL'ARANCIA

pino • Pork loin braised in milk is a classic northern Italian dish (see Tip). Here I substitute orange juice for the milk, and, believe it or not, the result is a creamier-tasting sauce for the pork, because of the way the wine and meat juices combine with the orange juice and zest. It's not at all sweet like a duck dish slathered with marmalade. (Like most northern Italian cooks, I don't like the combination of sweet and savory in meat dishes.) Blood orange juice makes a particularly flavorful sauce, but any freshly squeezed orange juice will produce a beautiful dark brown sauce with a slightly smoky orange flavor that is just delicious. • SERVES 6

One 2½- to 3-pound (1.1- to 1.3-kilo) boneless pork loin roast

Two 2-inch-long fresh rosemary sprigs

Kosher salt and freshly ground black pepper

2 tablespoons (30 ml) olive oil

1 medium red onion, thinly sliced

2 garlic cloves, smashed and peeled

2 teaspoons grated orange zest

1½ cups (360 ml) fresh orange juice

½ cup (120 ml) dry white wine

SET A RACK in the middle of the oven and preheat the oven to 325 degrees (165°C).

Trim the thick layer of fat from the meat if the butcher hasn't already done so. Use a sharp paring knife to pierce the meat all over. Tear the rosemary leaves from the sprigs and insert a leaf into each slit. Sprinkle the meat all over with salt and pepper.

Place a 3- to 4-quart Dutch oven over medium-high heat, and when it is hot, add the olive oil. Add the pork loin and sear until deeply browned on all sides, 12 to 15 minutes total. Transfer the meat to a plate.

Pour off all but 1 tablespoon of the fat from the pot. Add the onion and garlic and cook, stirring occasionally, until the onion is softened and the garlic is golden, 3 to 5 minutes. Add the orange zest, juice, and wine and bring to a boil. Lower the heat and simmer, stirring with a wooden spoon to scrape any browned bits from the bottom of the pot, until slightly reduced.

Return the meat and any accumulated juices to the pot, cover, and place in the middle of the oven. Cook, turning the meat once, until fork-tender, 1½ to 2 hours.

Remove the pork to a cutting board, and cover loosely with foil, to keep warm. Spoon off the accumulated fat from the surface of the sauce. Use an immersion blender to puree the sauce, or transfer to a blender and puree. Add salt and pepper to taste. Slice the meat, arrange it on a serving platter, and pour the sauce over it. Serve immediately. (Alternatively, slice the meat, return it to the pot, and refrigerate overnight. Remove any solidified fat from the surface of the sauce and reheat, covered, in a 300-degree (150°C) oven until piping hot.)

tip: To make Milk-Braised Pork Loin, substitute milk for the orange juice and use the zest of a whole orange, removed in one piece with a vegetable peeler, instead of grated zest. This is a very different dish. The sauce will be a golden color, with the taste of bitter orange from the peel.

wine: A young California Cabernet will have the fruitiness to blend with the orange flavor while also cutting some of its tartness. Bottles from Cakebread Cellars and St. Francis are wonderful examples, and widely available.

8

cucina al fresco

grilling italian~style

Americans consider themselves the world's barbecue experts, but Italians were cooking over an open fire before Columbus discovered America. The Romans perfected spit-roasting and introduced some civility to outdoor dining, using linen napkins and cutlery. Today's wood-burning pizza ovens are descendents of home hearths that not only heated Italians' houses, but were used to grill meat and poultry year-round. Now Italians without wood-burning ovens can get that food at the local rosticceria—inexpensive restaurants and take-out shops specializing in grill-roasted meat and poultry, these are almost as popular as the trattoria. Most Italians don't have grills in their backyards. When they cook outdoors, they build a wood fire at the beach in the summertime, and it becomes a big social event. Even so, Italian traditional grilled foods are simple and savory, much less fussy than some of the elaborate American recipes you see today, and never slathered in sugary barbecue sauce as is the tradition here, especially in the South.

In this chapter, we hope to appeal to Americans' love of cooking outdoors by showing you some time-honored recipes and techniques for open-fire cooking that we have adapted for use with a charcoal or gas grill. We both like simple marinades. Often a bath of olive oil and wine, vinegar, or lemon juice, maybe seasoned with garlic and herbs, is the best way to prepare meat for the barbecue. The most important key to success, however, is cooking food at the proper temperature. The biggest mistake that people make is to throw the food on the grill when the fire is too hot. Anyone who has ever spent Fourth of July at a neighbor's backyard barbecue eating blackened hot dogs and hamburgers that resemble charcoal briquettes knows what we mean. To prevent this, let the fire die down to glowing embers before you even consider cooking, so that the flames never touch the food. Great grilled flavor comes from juices dripping onto the hot coals and producing smoke that rises back up to envelop the meat. The only black marks on the food should be the decorative crosshatching from the very hot bars of the grill.

Learn some patience, and you will be able to produce rosticceria-worthy items such as *bistecca alla fiorentina* (grilled Tuscan steak), grilled rabbit, mushrooms, stuffed pork chops, and even shellfish, like lobster and shrimp. In our opinion, the most difficult dish to do perfectly is a simple grilled chicken or game hen. A bird with crispy but not blackened skin that is still moist and silky on the inside is the sign of true grill mastery. This chapter's final recipe, for Cornish game hens, will show you a few tricks—e.g., choose a very small bird, and butterfly it for even cooking—for producing expertly grilled poultry, the Holy Grail of barbecueing.

mark People may be surprised that I'm more of a traditionalist when it comes to grilling than you are. Our biggest disagreement is about the heat source itself. For me, there's nothing like the romance of a real fire, made with wood or charcoal.

pino I've cooked my share of outdoor meals over a wood fire—on hunting trips, at the beach—and I much prefer the clean heat of the gas grill in my backyard.

mark You don't like to get your hands dirty. You'd rather push a button.

pino True, I'm fastidious. But it's not just the neatness and convenience. To me, charcoal has a distinct flavor that gets into whatever I'm cooking and obscures the real flavors of the food.

mark But that's what's so wonderful about grilling. If you want clean heat, use the oven. If you want

the flavor of the outdoors, build a wood fire with very dry hickory, cherry, and oak. Or use charcoal and season with wood chips.

pino Cooking over fire is romantic, but the petrochemicals in charcoal briquettes are not. I like food to taste like food, not charcoal and gasoline.

mark You know me better than that. I use natural lump hardwood charcoal, which is made by partially burning wood. It has no chemical additives, and it gives food a wonderfully smoky flavor. You can buy it at most hardware stores, including Home Depot. Last summer I did a big roof party for a customer using lump charcoal in an enormous grill. The fire was beautiful, and I was the keeper of the flame. You can't create that kind of atmosphere with gas.

pino Did you burn the building down?

mark No. I started the fire at 6:00 and didn't put the food on until 8:30—which really isn't a lot of time at all. In Texas, where they have those big pit barbecues, they get the fire going the day before and let it burn to ashes, so that what they're really cooking on is the residual heat. It's not just Italians who know how to let a fire die down, you know.

pino Well, I'm no cowboy. I don't want to gather wood and spend twenty-four hours waiting for my fire. Now gas grills come with inserts for soaked wood chips, so I can get that wood taste without spending hours preparing the fire.

mark Let me build my weekend fire. It's my right as an American male. I can take the heat. I enjoy it.

pino Stand next to my grill with its 20,000 Btus, then you'll feel the heat. What's great is how easy it is to control. I can sear a steak on high to get an incredible crust, then turn the grill to medium-low so the interior cooks to a perfect medium-rare. For delicate items like shrimp or mushrooms, I'll go as low as I can, practically turning it off, letting the hot grill rack cook the food with its residual heat. You can't control wood and charcoal like that.

mark But unpredictability is part of the fun. When you're grilling, you have to be watchful and lightning

fast. Observe where the hottest coals are. Know where the cool spot is. If a sausage causes a flare-up, move it, don't incinerate it. That's how you show your mastery.

pino Can I have the last word?

mark You usually do.

pino While you're busy mastering your fire, I can take my wife, Jessie, to an early movie or a nice, long walk, then push a button when I get home, have a glass of wine with her, and put the steak on twenty minutes later. You can't beat that.

mark You are such a suburbanite. You'll never understand the cowboy way. It's nice to have the option of gas, especially on a weeknight or if you're cooking just for yourself and maybe one other person. But when the weekend comes, there's nothing I'd rather do than tend my fire.

The following recipes will work with either a gas or charcoal grill. You choose, depending on your preference and how much time you have. A gas grill will take 15 to 20 minutes to heat up. Start a charcoal fire at least 1 hour before you want to cook; 1 hour and 15 minutes is even better. The coals should be a deep electric-red color with a lot of gray ash before you attempt to cook. Either way, judge the intensity of the heat by placing your hand 5 inches over the grilling surface: If you can keep it there for 5 seconds, then it's ready for a steak. If you can hold it there for only 2 to 3 seconds, let the fire cool down a little. With a gas grill, it's easy enough to turn down the heat. With a charcoal grill, it's a good idea to build a two-level fire, with a taller pile of coals on one side of the grill and a single layer on the other. That way, you'll have some flexibility when you cook and can move the meat around depending on how much heat you need.

Food will pick up flavors of previously cooked food from a dirty grill rack, so clean yours and oil it thoroughly before you begin. It's smart and easy to clean the rack right after you use it rather than waiting until the next time. Use a long-handled wire grill brush. The best ones have coarse wire on one side and fine wire on the other. While the grill is still hot (if you're using gas, you can turn the heat to high for a few minutes), brush the rack well to remove any bits of food. Let it cool while you eat, and then rub it with a paper towel soaked in olive oil. Now it's ready when you are to light the next fire.

Flare-ups are the bane of a barbecue chef's existence. To avoid them, let most of the liquid from your marinade drip back into the pan before you place the meat on the grill. For poultry, place it on the grill skin side up, so that the fat will melt and penetrate the meat during the initial cooking. Then flip the poultry after the fat has slowly rendered. If you place them skin side down to start, you can count on an immediate conflagration. Once you start cooking, don't turn your back on the grill, and be ready to move the food the instant you see flames.

Judging doneness can be difficult with grilled foods. Just because you see nice grill marks doesn't mean that your steak is ready. Check it the way you would judge a basketball: very rare meat won't bounce at all, medium-rare will feel like it needs a little air, and you will know you have overcooked your steak if it feels as if you can dribble it down the court. In our opinion, steak that has been cooked beyond medium-rare is too tough to eat. After you cook a few steaks and judge them this way, you'll immediately know by feeling whether or not to take yours off the grill. Unsure? Nick the underside of the steak with a knife and peek inside. Or use an instant-read thermometer: 135 degrees (57°C) is medium-rare. But remember, you'll want to take your meat off the grill before it reaches that temperature, because it will continue to cook as it rests for the recommended 10 minutes. For most steaks, 125 degrees (52°C) is sufficient.

Judge poultry by piercing it with a fork. If the juices are a little bit milky but mostly clear (an instant-read thermometer inserted into the thigh will register 165 degrees [74°C]), the meat is sufficiently cooked. Let it rest for 10 minutes before serving, and its temperature will continue to rise. Extra marinade can be used to dress the grilled food, but for reasons of food safety, make sure to bring it to a boil and cook it for a couple of minutes in a small pan over the fire before using it this way.

baby back ribs with cucumbers and frisée

ROSTICCIANA CON CETRIOLI E RICCIA

pino • I loved grilled baby back ribs as a child. They were so much fun to eat. Today when I make them for my kids, I say, "No silverware allowed. You have to put your hands on them to enjoy them." The recipe I remember called for boiling the ribs first, but I have found that these are so small that it's not necessary, and I really don't like boiled pork. When you boil it, you cook away a lot of flavor. Instead, I just get the grill nice and hot, turn down the fire (with a charcoal grill, build a two-level fire and cook the ribs over the cooler part of the grill), and then put the ribs on. I salt the tops of the racks, cook for 5 minutes, flip, and salt the other side. Total cooking time is about 30 minutes, but I keep turning them every 5 minutes. The salt keeps the ribs juicy and the constant turning helps drain off the fat. So you are left with meaty, not greasy, little ribs.

But I'm not done with them yet. I squeeze the juice from a cucumber, then make a simple frisée salad. I dress the salad, place the cut-up cooked ribs on top, and sprinkle them with the cucumber juice. The mingled tastes—the meat flavoring the salad, the juice flavoring the meat—are divine. • SERVES 6

4 medium cucumbers, peeled

2 full racks baby back ribs
(about 4 pounds/1.8 kilos total)

2¹⁄₂ teaspoons kosher salt

Freshly ground black pepper

1 head frisée, washed, dried,
and torn into 2-inch (5-cm) pieces

1 teaspoon dried oregano,
preferably Sicilian

1 teaspoon red wine vinegar

1 tablespoon (15 ml) extra-virgin
olive oil

PREHEAT A GAS GRILL to high for 20 minutes and then reduce to medium. Or, make a two-level fire if using charcoal, letting the coals burn until deep red and covered with a layer of ashes.

Use the large holes of a box grater to grate one of the cucumbers into a paper towel. Wrap the grated cucumber in the towel and squeeze the juice from it into a measuring cup. You should have ¹⁄₃ to ¹⁄₂ cup. Set aside. Thinly slice the remaining cucumbers.

Place the ribs meaty side up on the grill and sprinkle with 1 teaspoon of the salt. Grill, covered, for 5 minutes, then turn and sprinkle the other side with another teaspoon of salt. Grill, covered, for another 5 minutes, and turn again. Continue to grill, turning every 5 minutes, until you can clearly see the demarcation of white bones between red meat and the ribs are very crispy, about 30 minutes total. Transfer to a cutting board and lightly tent with aluminum foil to keep warm.

While the ribs are resting, toss the frisée, sliced cucumber, and oregano on a large deep platter or in a salad bowl. Whisk together the vinegar and the remaining ¹⁄₂ teaspoon salt in a small bowl. Add the olive oil and whisk until emulsified, 1 to 2 minutes. Pour the dressing over the salad and toss to coat.

Slice the ribs and place them on top of the salad. Sprinkle the cucumber juice over the ribs and serve immediately.

wine: This is a Florentine dish, so I suggest a Chianti from Avignonesi (in nearby Siena), one of the oldest wineries in Italy. In general, wines from Avignonesi are elegant, and their Chianti has the rich, deep flavor necessary to stand up to the ribs.

coco pazzo's grilled marinated hanger steak

BISTECCA ALLA COCO PAZZO

mark • Hanger steak is like skirt steak, but a little higher up on the animal. Almost unheard of twenty years ago, it has become popular as Americans have discovered it at French-style bistros. It's a flavorful cut, and it's a little chewy, but that doesn't bother me at all. I like to sink my teeth into a steak, and I find the more tender cuts, like filet mignon, insipid. Another reason I like this cut: it's economical. When I'm grilling for a lot of people, New York strip or rib eye is cost-prohibitive.

Hanger steak in particular benefits from marinating, which softens it up a little. The marinade I use is not very liquidy. Wet marinades tend to slide off the meat before the grill can set their flavors on the meat. Here I use a simple mixture of salt, pepper, garlic, and onion with a little tomato paste. The tomato paste adds flavor but is not so loose that it drips off the steak as the meat cooks. After the steak has marinated, I pound it a little to further tenderize it. Sometimes I place branches of herbs—rosemary, thyme, sage, or oregano—which I've dipped in water, on the grill rack. Then I lay the marinated meat over the herbs. The herbs burn, but they also burn their flavor into the meat. • SERVES 2

One 2- to 2¼-pound (about 1-kilo) hanger steak

2 teaspoons dry mustard

1 teaspoon curry powder or cumin

1 teaspoon kosher salt

½ teaspoon freshly ground black pepper

½ teaspoon crushed red pepper flakes

½ teaspoon Hungarian paprika

2 tablespoons (30 ml) soy sauce

1 tablespoon dark sesame oil

1 tablespoon balsamic vinegar

3 garlic cloves, thickly sliced

½ cup (15 grams) fresh cilantro leaves, chopped

2 scallions, white and green parts, finely chopped

3 to 4 bunches fresh rosemary, thyme, sage, and/or oregano, soaked in water (optional)

PLACE THE STEAK in a nonreactive baking dish just large enough to hold it. Whisk together the remaining ingredients except for the optional herb branches and pour over the steak. Cover and refrigerate for at least 4 hours or up to 24 hours, turning the steak occasionally in the marinade.

Preheat a gas grill to high for 20 minutes. Or, if you are using charcoal, prepare the fire and let the coals burn until deep red and covered with a layer of ashes.

Place the soaked herbs on the grill rack, if desired. Lift the steak out of the marinade, shaking off any excess, and place on the grill—on top of the herbs, if using. Grill for 7 minutes, then flip and grill on the other side for 6 to 7 minutes *more* for medium-rare. Nick the underside of the steak to check for doneness. Transfer to a cutting board, cover loosely with aluminum foil, and let rest for 5 minutes.

Slice the steak and serve.

tip: When making a marinade, combine any dry spices in advance to let the flavors meld. You can prepare them in large batches; they will hold until you add "active" ingredients like oil, vinegar, garlic, etc.

wine: A simple Cabernet from Napa, like Groth, complements this straightforward steak dish.

grilled rib-eye steak served over toasted bread with arugula

BISTECCA IN CROSTONE CON LA RUGOLA

pino · Probably one of the best breeds of cattle on the planet, the Chianina, comes from Tuscany. *Bistecca alla fiorentina*, the classic grilled Tuscan steak, is made with the T-bone or rib eye from Chianina beef. (Right now this beef isn't widely available in the United States, but the American Chianina Association, a group of committed cattle breeders, is trying to change that.) To get a dish closest in character to the authentic Tuscan steak, I choose a rib-eye steak, as thick as possible, from beef that's been aged at least ten days.

Tuscans disagree on the best way to prepare the steaks for grilling. Some marinate the meat beforehand in olive oil, rosemary, and sage. Others drizzle this mixture on as a dressing after the steaks come off the grill. I'm in the latter camp, because I think the meat gets a better crust if there's nothing between it and the grill as it cooks. When the steak is grilled just the way I like it (medium-rare), I place it over a piece of toasted crusty bread. The bread soaks up all the juices from the steak. When the steak has rested and moistened the bread, I set the bread and steak on a platter of arugula dressed with lemon juice and olive oil. It's a one-dish meal that's perfectly seasoned and in balance. I love to eat it outside, looking up at the trees and sky. Like no other dish, this one evokes entertaining in the Tuscan countryside. · SERVES 4

Two 1½-pound (680-gram) bone-in rib-eye steaks (1½ inches/3.7 cm thick), preferably aged 2 weeks

8 slices country bread

1 tablespoon kosher salt, plus more to taste

¼ cup (60 ml) extra-virgin olive oil

1 pound (454 grams) baby arugula, washed and dried

1 tablespoon (15 ml) red wine vinegar

1 teaspoon freshly ground black pepper

ONE HOUR PRIOR to cooking, remove the steaks from the refrigerator.

Preheat a gas grill to high for 20 minutes and then reduce to medium-low. Or, if you are using charcoal, prepare the fire and let the coals burn until deep red and covered with a layer of ashes.

Place the (unseasoned) steak on the grill and cook, covered, for 6 minutes on each side for medium-rare. While the steak is cooking, place the bread on the grill and toast on both sides.

Transfer the bread to a baking sheet and set a wire rack over the bread.

Place the grilled steaks on top of the rack over the bread. Pierce the meat several times, sprinkle with the salt, and drizzle with 2 tablespoons of the olive oil. Turn the steaks over, arranging them so they drip onto the bread. Cut the steak from the bone then transfer to a cutting board, and slice into thin strips.

Place the arugula in a mixing bowl, add the vinegar, and toss well. Add the remaining 2 tablespoons olive oil, tossing again. Season with salt and the pepper. Place the bread, which will now be fairly soaked with steak juices, on a serving platter and top with the steak. Drizzle with any steak juices that pool on the bottom of the platter or baking sheet. Top with the arugula salad.

wine: A super Tuscan such as Tignanello from Antinori will do the job nicely. If you don't want to spend that much, a less expensive Antinori such as Peppoli or Marchesi, or another good-quality Chianti Classico is a good option.

mixed grilled seafood

GRIGLIATA MISTA DI FRUTTI DI MARE

mark • I love eating grilled seafood in Italy in the summertime. The preparations are similar from the Veneto to Apulia, but with a regional accent usually expressed by the choice of herbs. In Liguria, you taste a lot of basil. In Tuscany, it's rosemary and sage. In the south, oregano. Imagine: You're sitting under an umbrella at a seaside café, with a colorful ceramic platter of shrimp, scallops, and calamari flavored with garlic, lemon, and oregano. You inhale the salty air and then dig in, pulling the shrimp out of their shells, getting your hands messy. When everything's gone, you dip some bread into the briny juices flavored with garlic and herbs. Not a bad way to spend your lunchtime.

    Drizzle extra-virgin olive oil over the finished dish when it comes off the grill, and as the seafood cools, the oil releases its perfume and its flavor mingles with the flavors of the seafood. • SERVES 6

12 jumbo shrimp, deveined but not peeled

8 jumbo sea scallops (about 1½ pounds/ 680 grams), side muscles removed

1 large octopus (2 to 3 pounds/1 to 1.4 kilos), cleaned, cut into strips

8 cleaned squid bodies

6 garlic cloves, crushed, plus, if using lobster, 4 cloves, cut into pieces

3 scallions, white and light green parts, chopped

1 bunch fresh oregano

2 fresh rosemary sprigs

1 teaspoon kosher salt

1 teaspoon crushed red pepper flakes, plus more if using lobster

¼ cup (60 ml) balsamic vinegar, plus more if using lobster

½ cup plus 2 tablespoons (150 ml) extra-virgin olive oil, plus more if using lobster

2 lemons, thinly sliced

Three 1-pound (454-gram) live lobsters (optional)

COMBINE THE SHRIMP, scallops, octopus, squid, crushed garlic cloves, scallions, oregano, rosemary, salt, red pepper flakes, vinegar, ½ cup of the olive oil, and half the lemon slices (gently squeezed) in a large bowl and mix well. Cover and refrigerate for at least 30 minutes, or up to 3 hours.

Preheat a gas grill to high for 20 minutes, then reduce to medium (medium-high, if using lobster). Or, if you are using charcoal, prepare the fire and let the coals burn until red and covered with a layer of ashes.

If using lobster, prepare them just before cooking: Turn each lobster on its back and split it lengthwise down the middle with a large knife (this will kill it instantly), being careful not to cut all the way through the shell. Crack the claws. Spread open the cavity and the tail (the tail will be more difficult). Remove the head sac and the intestines. Place the pieces of garlic in the lobster cavities, tails, and claws. Sprinkle with crushed red pepper, and drizzle generously with balsamic vinegar and olive oil. Place the lobster split side up on the grill, so the garlic can't fall out and grill over high heat, covered, for approximately 10 minutes, or until cooked through. Don't worry if the shells start to blacken; the meat will still be succulent and juicy. You can gently spread a lobster open to check for doneness. Transfer to a large platter and loosely cover with aluminum foil to keep warm.

Reduce the gas grill heat to medium. Or, for a charcoal grill, use indirect heat or place the seafood on the cooler part of the grill. Lift the shrimp, scallops, and octopus from the marinade, letting any excess drip back into the bowl, and place on the grill. Grill until the undersides of the shrimp turn pink and the undersides of the scallops firm slightly and turn opaque, about 3 minutes. Turn the seafood and add the squid to the grill. Continue cooking until the octopus is lightly charred and the squid—turn it once—is seared and curled, about 2 minutes longer. Transfer to the platter.

Drizzle with the remaining 2 tablespoons olive oil and garnish with the remaining lemon slices, giving them a gentle squeeze. Serve immediately.

wine: Drink a dry Sancerre here—nothing goes better with summery seafood.

tip: Always buy cleaned calamari, making sure the bodies are pristine white. Any purple or pink tinge means they're old (in which case, it's better to go for frozen).

9

the twenty~first region of italy

italian~american cooking

Mamma Mia, dammi centolire, che in America voglio andar . . .
(Mama, give me a hundred lire, I want to go to America . . .)

Between 1890 and 1920, Italian immigrants streamed into this country in large numbers, looking for work that they couldn't find in Italy. They came with big hopes and dreams, and to make themselves feel at home while they struggled to succeed, they settled together in certain neighborhoods, like Little Italy in lower Manhattan, Arthur Avenue in the Bronx, and North Beach in San Francisco, and did the best they could to re-create the familiar dishes that reminded them of where they had come from.

With one foot in the old country and one foot here, Italian-Americans developed many hybrid recipes. Some of them, like baked clams, were old dishes transformed by local ingredients that were different from what they had used in Italy. Other dishes were made with typically Italian ingredients but transformed by the American ethos of abundance (big meatballs on top of a plate of spaghetti). The best of this Italian-American food, like the best Italian food, was simply prepared using the freshest available ingredients. So appealing were Italian flavors and the Italian sense of hospitality, that restaurants opened by immigrants attracted Americans of every kind, and dishes designed to please this diverse group of customers—veal parmigiana, lobster fra diavolo—became truly American in their universal popularity.

Today Americans of every ethnic origin enjoy Italian-American food, which comforts all of us in stressful, uncertain times. We've chosen the recipes in this chapter because they are our favorites in this category, appealing to most tastes while satisfying our strict standards as chefs and restaurateurs. We can imagine an Italian-American *mamma* uttering words of encouragement ("*Mangia, mangia, bambino*") as she urges her child to eat this food. And we can also confidently urge our customers and readers to try what is here for a taste of the best of Italy's twenty-first region.

mark When I was growing up in Queens, the population was a mix of three ethnic groups: Jews, Italians, and Irish. I would go fishing with an Italian family who lived near us, and that was when I was introduced to blowfish. After we caught them, we'd clean them and bring them home to fry. That was a new taste for me, and I got curious about what else my neighbors were cooking. I'd hang around their kitchens—there would often be three generations congregated there—because I always knew they'd offer me a plate of food. I loved so much of what I tried. Now I'm a chef at an Italian restaurant. It's a typical New York story. People here show respect for each other by embracing their neighbors' food heritage. Today you see Italians in Thai restaurants and Asians who know where to get the best corned beef sandwich.

pino That melting-pot sensibility can be disorienting to the new immigrant. I came here twenty-five years ago, by plane, not boat. I had

to get a job, and I knew I wanted to go into the restaurant business, so I walked all over the city, looking for Italian restaurants with a "Help Wanted" sign in the window. But when I studied the menus, I didn't recognize most of the dishes! I finally came upon a place in Greenwich Village with Tuscan food like *cibreo* (chicken livers), *trippa* (tripe), and *ribollita* (vegetable soup) on the menu, and it was such a relief. I walked in, and they hired me on the spot.

mark And you've never really left that restaurant—you still prefer Tuscan to Italian-American cooking.

pino Well, it's what I grew up with. I admit I was at first skeptical about the fantasy most Americans have about what is Italian. But I've come to see how Americans connect with this food, and because I'm Italian, I want to give that to people. So I try to be true to my roots, choosing the best ingredients and preparing them simply, and I think

that's the way to honor this new cuisine and take it back to its roots. There is actually a lot of overlap in the recipes, especially if you compare Italian-American dishes to southern Italian ones. I'm thinking of the fresh mozzarella that's served at the simplest trattorias south of Rome, alone on a plate, no olive oil, no salt and pepper, just brought to the table with the knowledge that the product is so good it can be offered just as it is. The best old-style Italian restaurants in this country would serve the same thing.

mark I'm not so interested in making those connections. Sure, I care about quality, but authenticity just doesn't matter when I'm trying to replicate the food I ate at Angelo's on Main Street in Queens when I was a kid. Angelo knew me and my friends as little kids, and when we went in by ourselves as teenagers, he would come over and tell us to behave or he'd call our mothers. We were too embarrassed *not* to behave. Angelo was

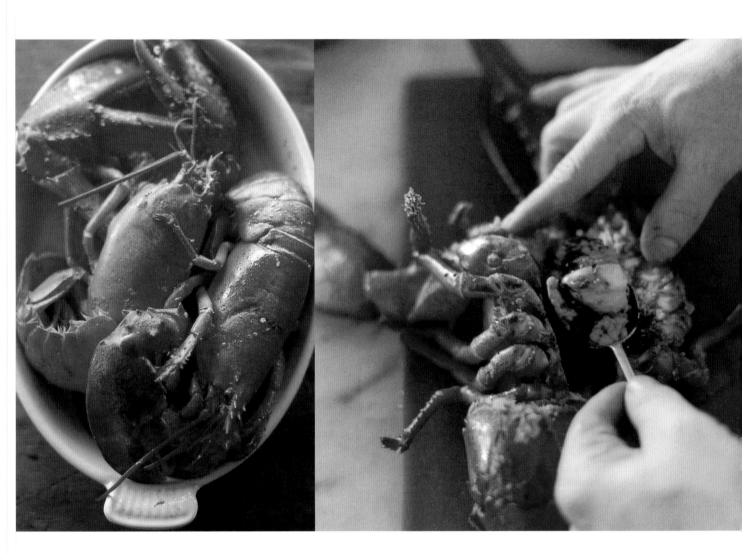

Mark makes Lobster fra Diavolo (page 231)

lobster fra diavolo

ARAGOSTA FRA DIAVOLO

mark · I remember eating lobster fra diavolo at Italian restaurants as a kid. Because it was one of the more expensive items on the menu, we'd order one for the table and everyone in the family would have a taste. Back then, lobster fra diavolo meant lobster with red sauce and a lot of crushed red pepper flakes. After I trained as a chef, that formula didn't seem so appealing. Just putting lobster pieces in tomato sauce was not much of a step up from serving the precious meat with ketchup. So I thought about how bouillabaisse is made, by using shellfish to flavor the tomato and wine sauce, and proceeded from there. The sauce is made in the pan that the lobsters have cooked in, so it takes on some of that flavor. The *tomalley* (which is the green liver) and the roe, if there is any, are added to the sauce to give the dish a bit more complexity. Finishing in the oven gives the dish complete, overall heat. · SERVES 4

Two 2-pound (908-gram) live lobsters

¼ cup (60 ml) extra-virgin olive oil

2 garlic cloves, smashed

1 dried Italian hot red pepper, split lengthwise, or ½ teaspoon crushed red pepper flakes

½ cup (120 ml) dry white wine

2 cups (480 ml) canned crushed Italian plum tomatoes, preferably San Marzano

4 anchovy fillets, chopped

2 teaspoons dried oregano, preferably Sicilian

1 tablespoon kosher salt, plus more to taste

1 pound (454 grams) spaghetti

3 tablespoons chopped fresh Italian parsley

Freshly ground black pepper

PREHEAT THE OVEN to 450 degrees (230°C).

To prepare the lobsters for cooking, turn each lobster on its back and split it lengthwise down the middle with a large knife (this will kill it instantly), being careful not to cut all the way through the shell. Crack the claws. Spread open the bodies and tails.

Place a large Dutch oven over medium heat, and when it is hot, add the olive oil. Add the garlic and stir until golden, about 2 minutes. Add the hot pepper and lobsters and cook, stirring, until the shells turn red and the lobster meat is cooked enough to be removed from the shell, about 12 minutes. Remove the lobsters from the pot and set aside.

Add the wine and tomatoes to the pot and bring to a simmer. Add the anchovies and oregano and stir well. Transfer the pot to the oven and cook until the sauce has thickened, 6 to 7 minutes. Remove from the oven.

While the sauce is cooking, fill a 10-quart stockpot with 7 quarts (6.5 liters) of water and bring to a boil over high heat. Add the salt. Add the pasta, stir, and cook until al dente.

While the pasta is cooking, remove the lobster meat from the shells: Using a kitchen towel, separate the claws from the bodies. Crack them open, and remove the meat. Split open the tails, pick out the meat, and scoop out the tomalley and any roe. Set aside.

Drain the pasta, reserving ½ cup of the pasta cooking water, and add the pasta to the pot of sauce.

Add the lobster meat, tomalley (and roe), and parsley to the sauce and simmer for 2 minutes. If the pasta looks dry, add the reserved cooking water 1 tablespoon at a time, tossing to combine between additions. Season with salt and pepper, transfer to a platter, and serve family-style.

wine: Classic southern Italian wines such as Taurasi or Salice Salentino would certainly work well with this dish, but for a real gourmet celebration, I say get a good bottle of Champagne.

Pino makes Breast of Chicken, Martini-Style (page 238)

10

sunday means dinner

We are able to disagree on so many things and yet still remain good friends because, fundamentally, we have the same priorities when it comes to food. Yes, we are chefs and restaurateurs, but cooking is not simply a job for either of us. It is what connects us with other people—customers, friends, and, especially, family. We both grew up with the tradition of Sunday dinner. Gathering around the dinner table with our families was central to our upbringing, and as fathers we are determined to pass this custom down to our children.

Like everyone else, we are so busy during the week that when we are home for dinner, we often cook just so we can eat. Everything is a rush. The kids have soccer practice and homework, and they've got to get some sleep. A rotation of quick pasta, chicken, and meat recipes gets the job done. But on the weekends we slow down. There's time for a bike ride or a movie or a romp in the snow. And when it's dinner-time on Sunday, we sit down for a leisurely meal, to celebrate our time together and to refuel for the coming week.

In this chapter, you will find the recipes that we use for bringing our families and friends together around the table on the weekends. Many are suitable for holidays when you want to feed a crowd. The Seven-Hour Roasted Fresh Ham (page 253) requires almost a whole day in the oven but very little effort on the part of the cook, beyond taking a look every hour or so. As it cooks, you'll have plenty of time to prepare the potatoes and peas that accompany it, set a nice table, and talk to your family and lucky guests. Other recipes, like the Chicken Cacciatore, Beef in Brunello, and Polenta for the Whole Family (page 260) require more work but pay off in a generous dinner to please everyone's taste. Have your friends and family help out in the kitchen with recipes like these. It's a great way to spend extra time together and makes everyone appreciate the food even more.

Also included are recipes for side dishes, so you're not just getting a main course but a full menu. Pull out your big ceramic platter and arrange your main course and accompaniments casually but beautifully. Place the platter right in the center of the table, and call everyone in for dinner.

mark I love Sunday dinner. It really brings us back to the beginning of our relationship, when we started Coco Pazzo in 1991 and we decided to serve the food family-style on the weekends. During the week, our Upper East Side customers came in all dressed up from work or for going out. On the weekends, the dress code was more relaxed, and we served the food on big platters.

pino At first people were taken aback at the lack of formality. The menu consisted of dishes that were prepared in large quantities, rather than individual portions. So we had to convince our customers to share. We even had a big communal table. Twenty years ago, that was shocking. *The New York Times* wrote that

New Yorkers would never sit down to eat with strangers. I have to laugh now that communal tables are in every trendy restaurant in the city.

mark It was definitely something new, and it took people a while to catch on. First, we only got groups of four, two couples going out for dinner together. But eventually people started bringing their kids and the grandparents.

pino The relaxed atmosphere, the reaching across the table to taste—that's what I really loved to see. From the wild days of my youth to my growing into a middle-aged man, I've left a lot behind, but no matter where I am, the moments I enjoy the most are when people gather around the table. That's

when real communication takes place, not just exchanging information, but really understanding and appreciating each other.

mark When my kids graduated from high chairs to the table, I started to think about having Sunday dinner at home instead of at the restaurant. When they were younger, I'd make spaghetti and meatballs, lasagne, the southern Italian favorites. Now that they're a little older, they like slices of rare prime rib, baked potatoes with melted cheddar cheese on top. Although I never put enough cheese on for them . . .

pino The Sunday meal is a major event in my household. When my children were little, they felt different from the rest of the kids in the

braised lamb and artichokes with oven-roasted new potatoes and spring onions

BRASATO DI AGNELLO E CARCIOFI CON PATATE E CIPOLLOTTI ARROSTO

pino • When I was a boy, my father was a medical assistant in the army. He would pack me and my brother, Riccardo, into the family Fiat 1100 and head out to the country to barter some of the extra medicine he had access to (don't ask me how it came into his possession) for some food. He'd make friends with some farmers, then exchange aspirin, vitamin C, and cough syrup for vegetables, suckling pig, and, in the springtime, baby lamb to eat at Easter or on May Day or April 25, Italy's Liberation Day. On the way out, it was medicine in the trunk. On the way back home, a baby lamb, freshly killed and skinned, but with the head still on and looking at us with its big black eyes. Somehow that sight never ruined the pleasure of eating the lamb any possible way my mother prepared it!

I make lamb for my own family always with these memories in mind. For me, it's essentially a springtime meat, so I serve it with spring vegetables—artichokes and spring onions that are its natural complement. American lamb has a less gamy, more delicate flavor than Italian lamb. My mother would marinate the leg or shoulder overnight in lemon juice, vinegar, and olive oil, with a lot of garlic and rosemary. But such strong flavors overwhelm the meat sold here, so I make a milder braise of boned lamb. • SERVES 6

FOR THE LAMB AND ARTICHOKES

2 lemons

12 small artichokes

2 tablespoons (30 ml) olive oil

4 garlic cloves, crushed

2 pounds (908 grams) boneless lamb from the shoulder or the leg, cut into ½-inch (1.3-cm) cubes

Kosher salt and freshly ground black pepper

2 cups (240 ml) dry white wine

8 oil-packed sun-dried tomatoes, drained and cut into slivers

2 tablespoons chopped fresh Italian parsley

(INGREDIENTS CONTINUE)

PREHEAT THE OVEN to 350 degrees (175°C).

TO PREPARE THE LAMB AND ARTICHOKES

Have ready a large bowl of cold water. Halve the lemons, squeeze their juice into the bowl, and then add the squeezed halves.

Remove the tough outer leaves from the artichokes. Trim away the stems, and use a sharp chef's knife to slice them thin. As you prepare the artichokes, place them in the lemon water to prevent them from turning black.

Place a 10- to 12-inch ovenproof skillet over medium heat. When it is hot, add the olive oil and garlic. Cook, stirring, until the garlic is golden brown, about 3 minutes. Add the lamb, sprinkle with salt and pepper, and cook until it loses its pink color, about 4 minutes. Drain the artichokes and add them to the pan, along with the wine and sun-dried tomatoes. Cook, stirring, for 3 minutes to evaporate some of the wine.

Cover the skillet, place in the oven, and braise for 20 minutes. Uncover the pan and braise until the lamb is fork-tender, about another 15 minutes. Remove from the oven and cover to keep warm.

(CONTINUED)

roasted yukon gold potatoes

8 to 10 large Yukon Gold potatoes, peeled and cut into 1-inch (2.5-cm) cubes

¼ cup (60 ml) extra virgin olive oil

4 garlic cloves, minced

2 yellow onions, halved lengthwise and thinly sliced

1 tablespoon kosher salt

2 fresh rosemary sprigs, leaves chopped

6 fresh thyme sprigs, leaves removed

Freshly ground black pepper to taste

PLACE A rack in the center of the oven and preheat the oven to 400 degrees (205°C).

Place all the ingredients in a large mixing bowl and mix well, then place in a baking dish.

Transfer the potatoes to the middle oven rack and roast, stirring occasionally, until they are tender and browned, 45 minutes to 1 hour. Serve immediately.

sautéed peas with mint

3 tablespoons (45 ml) extra-virgin olive oil

1 large yellow onion, minced

9 cups (1.3 kilos) fresh or thawed frozen green peas

3 cups (720 ml) Chicken Stock (page 29) or canned low-sodium organic chicken broth

3 tablespoons (42 grams) unsalted butter

½ cup plus 1 tablespoon (23 grams) finely chopped fresh mint

Kosher salt and freshly ground black pepper to taste

PLACE A 10- TO 12-INCH skillet over medium-high heat, and when it is hot, add the olive oil. Add the onion and sauté until soft and translucent, 5 to 7 minutes. Add the peas and stock, bring to a simmer, and simmer until the peas are tender, about 5 minutes.

Remove from the heat, and add the butter and mint. Season with salt and pepper to taste, and serve immediately.

11

the two meatballs go veggie

Americans are still overcoming a decades-long tradition of eating uninspiring side dishes made from canned and frozen vegetables. Rejecting "convenience" for wholesome flavor, many people have for the last twenty or so years been finding their way back to fresh, seasonal produce. Every day, it seems there are new opportunities to experience vegetables the way they were meant to be eaten: farmers' markets are opening in small towns and big cities across the country, cooperative farms are being established, and organic produce sections at the supermarket stock locally grown items. Nutritionists, environmental activists, and chefs all agree that eating more fresh vegetables, preferably in season and locally grown is a good idea. But many American cooks have little experience with vegetable dishes beyond steaming, boiling, or pouring on the salad dressing. Italians, in contrast, have a long and unbroken tradition of buying vegetables in season, cooking them in interesting ways, and placing them at the very center of their diet. Most Italians still shop for vegetables at produce shops or favorite stalls at an open food market. They not only have personal relationships with their vegetable vendors, but often know which farms their vegetables come from. Shopping for vegetables this way is a thrill, not an inconvenience, especially when produce such as artichokes or fava beans (or seasonal fruit like cherries) make their brief yearly appearance. Borrow some recipes and techniques from Italian cooking, and eating your vegetables will become a pleasure rather than a duty.

pino My mother was no different from mothers around the world, I guess, because she insisted that we eat our vegetables along with whatever meat and pasta she was serving. Like most kids, I'd rather have skipped them, but that was more out of rebelliousness than disgust. And by the time I was nine or ten, I had really come to love her vegetable dishes. She had a half-dozen delicious ways of preparing cauliflower, because that was my father's favorite. I liked her *fricassee* best, and I still make it: She blanched the cauliflower and then sautéed it with garlic, onion, and anchovies. For her *caponata,* she'd cook all of the vegetables separately before she mixed them together, so you could really taste the eggplant, tomatoes, and onions. Then she stirred in some toasted pine nuts for crunch. Definitely her vegetables were more interesting than the plain broccoli and Brussels sprouts that American kids complain about.

mark Vegetables, even Italian-style, are an acquired taste. You have to learn to enjoy them—it's a part of growing up. I still have to tell my kids, "Eat your vegetables, eat salad, eat fruit." So far, they'll eat fries and corn. In the next few years, I'm betting they'll eat asparagus. Beets are the acid test. When I get them to eat beets, I'll know they're all grown up. Once you've crossed over to beets, you've become a mature, open-minded eater.

pino Because my mother introduced so many kinds of vegetables when I was young, by the time I was eight years old, I was eating things like cardoons, which are related to artichokes. I tried to serve them to my kids once, and they utterly refused. But the next time I take them to Italy, I'll have my mother give it a try. Like me, they would never put up a fight with her, and she's gotten them to eat things that I never could.

mark I was lucky, because I grew up in the city, in a neighborhood with a lot of Italian immigrants who bought vegetables at immigrant-owned produce shops instead of at the supermarket, and that's where my mother shopped too. A lot of those vegetables were grown in New Jersey, and there was a more interesting selection than the vegetables at the supermarket, trucked in from California and Florida or stocked in cans on a shelf. We ate fresh green beans, zucchini, and Jersey tomatoes.

pino Where there were Italians, there was bound to be fresh arugula, eggplant, fresh herbs.

mark Yes, I ate all of that as a child too, but only because I was a city kid among Italians. In the suburbs in the 1950s, this was exotic stuff.

pino When I first came here and went to the supermarkets, I got depressed. It seemed like every vegetable I was used to eating fresh was canned or frozen or wrapped in cellophane. The broccoli was so gigantic it looked like an oak tree. There was some Bibb lettuce over here, some romaine over there, lots of iceberg lettuce, potatoes, onions, and oranges, but no dried or fresh beans, and only white button mushrooms piled up in boxes.

mark Alice Waters is responsible, more than anyone else, for showing chefs the beauty of locally grown vegetables. When she opened Chez Panisse in Berkeley in 1971, she served vegetables she had grown herself and began a movement among chefs.

pino The restaurant revolution was also driven by immigrants with their own high standards. The result was a huge change in the way people cook and eat at home. It's funny. When I first came to America, I was the one who was complaining about the lack of good produce. Now it is my American wife and my customers who are constantly on me to serve more vegetables, especially salads, which people seem to think are the key to good health and weight loss!

mark Once, when I was consulting for a supermarket, I noticed signs with a big number 5 all around the produce section. They were there to remind people of the USDA recommendation to eat five servings a day. Salads make that easy. My Chopped Roman Salad, with string beans, mushrooms, peppers, and three different kinds of lettuce, probably gets me most of the way there.

pino I don't need the government to tell me to eat my vegetables. If I'm going to eat my vegetables, it's not because I'm obeying a law or trying to feel virtuous. It's because I like the way they taste. I put a Caesar salad on my menu because my customers were asking for one. It had never appealed to me at other restaurants, but when I

tinkered with it, using my favorite anchovies, organic egg yolks, and just the right balance of vinegar and Worcestershire sauce, I fell in love with it. And now I eat it all the time. My mother used to make a bread salad, *panzanella,* with ripe tomatoes and sliced red onion that was so satisfying she served it as a meal.

mark You don't want to eat a salad that makes you feel like you've denied yourself. I get that. Sometimes I'm in the mood for fried potatoes or a rich, creamy gratin, and I'm not going to watch the calories or worry. You can be sure I'm going to dip those fries in mayonnaise while I'm at it. But there are ways of making healthy vegetable dishes that taste good too.

pino In the last chapter, I was the ascetic and you were the hedonist, but with vegetables, the tables are turned!

mark Yes and no. I may skimp on the egg yolks, cheese, and butter when I'm making a salad. But put bowls of Chopped Roman Salad, Raw Artichoke Salad, Farro "Panzanella," Warm Mushroom Salad, and Three-Bean Salad with Orange and Fennel in front of me, and I'll eat like there's no tomorrow.

In this chapter, you will find some of our best vegetable recipes. Along with our favorite salad recipes, some of which can be served as meals on their own, there are delicious side dishes. Most are naturally healthy, with little added fat. A few, like the Belgian Fries (page 284) and the gratins, may not get the approval of the diet police but can still be part of a balanced diet, which in our opinion includes as many vegetables, prepared as many different ways, as possible.

raw artichoke salad

INSALATA DI CARCIOFI CRUDI

pino • Tender baby artichokes can be eaten raw if they're very thinly sliced with a mandoline or other vegetable slicer. You can really taste their pure artichoke flavor this way. To prepare them for slicing, cut the sharp tips from the tops and remove the outer layer of tough leaves. If you don't have a mandoline, halve each artichoke lengthwise and slice very thin with a sharp chef's knife. They need to be soaked in a bowl of lemon juice and water to prevent discoloration. I like to grate the cheese on the large holes of a box grater so the cheese doesn't melt into the salad but stays in distinct small pieces. • SERVES 4

8 baby artichokes (1½ pounds/
680 grams), tough outer leaves
removed, tips and stems trimmed

3 lemons

1 bunch arugula, stems removed
and washed

½ teaspoon kosher salt

½ teaspoon freshly ground
black pepper

¼ cup (60 ml) extra-virgin olive oil

¼ cup (1 ounce/28 grams) shredded
Parmigiano-Reggiano cheese
(use the large holes of a box grater)

PLACE THE ARTICHOKES in a bowl and cover with cold water. Halve the lemons and squeeze the juice into the bowl. Add the squeezed rinds. Set aside to soak for 1 hour.

One at a time, remove the artichokes, pat dry with a paper towel, and use a mandoline or very sharp chef's knife to slice paper-thin. Place the slices in a bowl, add the arugula, and toss well. Add the salt, pepper, and olive oil and toss again. Divide among four salad plates, sprinkle with the Parmigiano-Reggiano, and serve immediately.

wine: The green apple flavor of the Pinot Grigio from Formentini is a good match with the sweet, slightly acidic taste of the artichokes.

chopped roman salad

INSALATA ROMANA

mark · A lot of us are on diets, but how often can you eat just lettuce? You want crunch, you want color, and you want variety, right? Chopped salad fits the bill, and if that's what you want, I'm going to give you a chopped salad that you're going to talk about for the rest of the night. I call it Roman because the dressing of red wine vinegar, garlic, and anchovies is the same one used on *puntarelle,* a classic Roman salad made with a curly variety of chicory. In addition to an appealing variety of lettuces, my salad has bottled marinated vegetables, which are a staple in pantries across Italy. Imported preservative-free baby artichokes, mushrooms, peppers, cauliflower, eggplant, and carrots marinated in olive oil are available at good Italian specialty foods stores here, and if you keep them in your own pantry, you will be able to make an exciting salad no matter what the season. · SERVES 6

FOR THE DRESSING

¼ cup (60 ml) red wine vinegar

1 garlic clove, minced

2 anchovy fillets, mashed

¾ cup (180 ml) extra-virgin olive oil

Kosher salt to taste

Pinch of freshly ground black pepper

FOR THE SALAD

1 head radicchio, halved, cored, and cut crosswise into ½-inch (1.3-cm) strips

1 endive, halved and cut into ½-inch (1.3-cm) strips

2 bunches arugula, stems removed, washed, and coarsely chopped

Two 6- or 7-ounce (165- or 196-grams) jars marinated artichoke hearts, drained and cut into ½-inch (1.3-cm) pieces

2 jarred roasted red and/or yellow bell peppers, diced

1 celery heart or 2 very tender small celery stalks from near the center of the bunch, cut into small dice

8 ounces (228 grams) green beans, trimmed and cut into 2-inch (5-cm) lengths

12 button mushrooms (6 ounces/ 168 grams), wiped clean, trimmed, and thinly sliced

TO MAKE THE DRESSING

Place all the ingredients in a small bowl and whisk well.

TO MAKE THE SALAD

Place all the ingredients in a large serving bowl. Add the dressing and toss well. Serve immediately.

tip: Add canned tuna, grilled chicken, or cooked shrimp to make this salad a main course.

wine: In the Roman spirit, serve a light Frascati with this salad.

farro "panzanella"

INSALATA DI FARRO

mark • I've won my battle with extra weight over the last fifteen years, and it's not because I've cut all carbohydrates from my diet. I could never do that. My body needs and enjoys them, and that's where I get my energy. But I've made a conscious effort to choose whole grains when I can. I came up with this recipe, which substitutes hearty whole-grain farro for the traditional cubed bread, when I was dieting. It has the same fresh flavors—from juicy tomatoes, crunchy cucumbers, and aromatic basil—as the original, but packs more nutritional punch. • SERVES 4 TO 6

1 tablespoon plus 1 teaspoon
   kosher salt

½ cup (100 grams) farro

½ (120 ml) cup extra-virgin olive oil

5 large tomatoes, diced

½ medium red onion, diced

4 scallions, white and green parts,
   thinly sliced

1 large cucumber, peeled, seeded,
   and diced

½ cup (20 grams) tightly packed fresh
   basil leaves

½ teaspoon freshly ground
   black pepper

1 tablespoon plus 1 teaspoon
   (20 ml) red wine vinegar

BRING A LARGE POT OF WATER to boil and add 1 tablespoon of the salt. Stir in the farro, lower the heat to medium-high, and simmer until tender, 55 minutes to 1 hour.

Drain well, place in a large mixing bowl, and stir in 1 tablespoon of the olive oil. Let cool to room temperature.

Add the tomatoes, onion, scallions, and cucumber to the farro and toss gently. Tear the basil leaves by hand and add to the bowl. Drizzle the salad with the vinegar and the remaining ¼ cup plus 3 tablespoons olive oil, and sprinkle with the remaining 1 teaspoon salt and the pepper. Toss again and serve.

wine: The tomatoes and herbs here pair well with a crisp and herbaceous Sauvignon Blanc. One of my favorites is from Napa Valley's Cakebread Cellars.

Pino makes Caesar Salad (page 272)

caesar salad

pino • Caesar Salad is the only name I know for this salad, and to try to translate it into Italian would be ridiculous. It was created by an Italian chef, Caesar Cardini, working in Tijuana early in the twentieth century. It became a sensation, as much for its theatrical presentation—it was assembled tableside with a dramatic cracking of the eggs—as for its powerful and appealing flavors. Early in my career here, I became curious about the dish, and over the years I've made some improvements on the basic recipe to bring out the best in the ingredients. I press my garlic at the last minute. I buy Sicilian anchovies that have been pressed and salt-cured. Available at specialty food markets and some fish markets, they're much meatier and less salty than canned anchovies. But canned Sicilian anchovies are fine if you can't find the salt-cured variety; you could even use a good anchovy paste. I try to achieve just the right balance between the vinegar and Worcestershire. The egg yolks have to be organic and very fresh. I take them out of the refrigerator just when I need them and add a couple drops of lemon juice before putting them into the salad dressing. I know people say brown eggs are no different from white, but I think yolks from brown eggs have a more defined, stronger taste than the white. To make croutons, I use soft white bread, crusts trimmed and cut into ½-inch (1.3-cm) cubes. I toast the croutons in a 350-degree (175°C) oven for 5 minutes to dry them out, then sprinkle some olive oil on them and continue to toast them until golden. This way, they crisp up faster than if tossed with olive oil before any toasting.

This is a salad that can be adapted to so many different occasions. It makes a great lunch salad with shrimp or chicken (see the variations below), and I have lately been adding steak, because the red meat stands up well to the strong flavors of the salad. I have even done it with lettuces other than romaine: endive, frisée, and *treviso*, a red chicorylike radicchio with longer leaves and more crunchiness. • SERVES 3 TO 4

2 garlic cloves, peeled

2 anchovy fillets, preferably salt-cured Sicilian anchovies, rinsed if salted and finely chopped, or 1 teaspoon anchovy paste

1 tablespoon (15 ml) red wine vinegar

2 large egg yolks

1 tablespoon (15 ml) fresh lemon juice

1 teaspoon Worcestershire sauce

2 tablespoons (30 ml) extra-virgin olive oil

2 bunches romaine lettuce (1 pound/ 450 grams), top 1 inch and bottom 2 inches trimmed off

2 tablespoons freshly grated Parmigiano-Reggiano cheese

1 cup (50 grams) ½-inch (1.3-cm) croutons (see headnote)

½ teaspoon freshly ground black pepper

USE A GARLIC PRESS to crush the garlic cloves into a large wooden or stainless steel bowl. Add the anchovies and vinegar and, using a metal spoon, crush and press together until the mixture becomes an auburn-colored liquid; it will take a couple of minutes to do a good job. Add the egg yolks, lemon juice, and Worcestershire sauce and use a spoon to break up the yolks until they blend in. Add the olive oil and mix gently but thoroughly. Add the romaine and toss well. Add 1 tablespoon of the Parmigiano-Reggiano and toss until the leaves are well coated with the cheese.

Place a few romaine leaves in the center of a large platter or on each of small individual plates. Top with another layer of leaves at a 45-degree angle, so the salad looks very attractive. Repeat one more time. Scatter the croutons on top and sprinkle with the remaining 1 tablespoon Parmigiano-Reggiano and the black pepper. Serve immediately, or refrigerate for 20 minutes and then serve chilled.

wine: Caesar needs a light wine, like Pinot Grigio. Jermann makes a good one, and there are many others out there.

shrimp caesar salad

If you want to make a Shrimp Caesar, follow the same preparation, but instead of the Worcestershire sauce, use 2 teaspoons horseradish. Grill the shrimp, slice them into pieces, and place on top of the salad.

chicken caesar salad

If you want a Chicken Caesar, replace 1 egg yolk with 1 tablespoon Dijon mustard. Grill the chicken breasts, slice, and place on top of the salad.

green beans in tomato sauce

FAGIOLINI IN UMIDO

pino • As far as I'm concerned, this is the most wonderful way to prepare fresh beans. You can use green beans, wax beans, or broad beans. I cook the beans very slowly and for a long time. I start on top of the stove, cooking the onion and celery, and then, when I add the beans and tomatoes, I put the pan in the oven and cook the beans until they've absorbed all the juices from the tomatoes and are almost dry. The beans cook very evenly and become almost caramelized in the oven. They're very good served with fish, but I often eat them alone with a piece of bread.

• SERVES 4

1 tablespoon (15 ml) olive oil

1 large yellow onion, thinly sliced

1 celery stalk, chopped

1½ pounds (680 grams) green, wax, or broad beans, or a combination, trimmed

1 teaspoon kosher salt

½ teaspoon freshly ground black pepper

1 tablespoon finely chopped fresh thyme

One 28-ounce (794-gram) can diced Italian plum tomatoes, preferably San Marzano, with their juice

PREHEAT THE OVEN to 350 degrees (175°C).

Place a 10- to 12-inch ovenproof skillet over medium heat, and when it is hot, add the olive oil. Add the onion and celery and cook until softened, 3 to 5 minutes. Add the beans and toss well. Add the salt, pepper, and thyme, tossing. Then add the tomatoes and juice. Raise the heat to high and cook for 3 minutes.

Cover, transfer the skillet to the oven, and bake for 25 minutes. Remove the cover and continue to bake until the beans are very soft and the tomato sauce is thickened, about another 15 minutes. Serve immediately.

wine: When I serve this dish by itself as a vegetarian main course, I set a piece of Caciotta Toscana (a semisoft cow's and sheep's milk cheese from Tuscany) alongside the dish and pour a Montepulciano d'Abruzzo.

potato gratin with onions and black olives

GRATIN DI PATATE CON CIPOLLE E OLIVE NERE

pino • I developed this mild-flavored gratin to accompany the Dover sole that I've always served at my restaurants. The potatoes don't compete with the delicate flavor of the fish, but the onions, black Gaeta olives, and Parmigiano-Reggiano cheese keep the dish from being boring. In fact, many customers who have tried it as a side dish later ask for just the gratin, without the fish, the next time they come in! With the salt from the olives and the cheese, I find I need to add very little, if any, salt for proper seasoning. • SERVES 4

2 pounds (908 grams) Yukon Gold potatoes, peeled and cut into 1/8-inch (0.3-cm) slices

1 cup (4 ounces/114 grams) freshly grated Parmigiano-Reggiano cheese

1 large yellow onion, thinly sliced

2 tablespoons bread crumbs (page 303) or store-bought unseasoned bread crumbs

1/2 cup (30 grams) Gaeta olives, crushed and pitted

2 1/2 cups (600 ml) heavy cream

PREHEAT THE OVEN to 400 degrees (205°C). Lightly butter a 9-by-13-inch baking dish.

Place one-third of the potatoes in the baking dish. Scatter one-third of the Parmigiano-Reggiano cheese and one-third of the onions on top of the potatoes. Sprinkle with 1 tablespoon of the bread crumbs and one-third of the olives. Repeat until all the ingredients are used up. Slowly pour the cream over everything.

Cover with aluminum foil, transfer to the oven, and bake for 40 minutes. Uncover and cook until golden brown, about an additional 20 minutes.

Remove the gratin from the oven and let rest for 10 minutes before serving.

wine: The gratin is delicious with Vernaccia, a fruity wine from Tuscany, which will also go well with fish.

leek and fennel gratin

GRATIN DI PORRI E FINOCCHIO

mark • One of the things that defines a fine-dining restaurant is a different side dish with each main course. It's easy to come up with a good variety in the spring and summer, when plenty of fresh vegetables are available, but in the winter I have to get more creative. I learned a lot of ways to prepare leeks in France, and I saw fennel prepared many ways in Italy. The two are very good together, so in the winter I combine them in this simple gratin, which I serve with my fish dishes. The two vegetables go very well with salmon in particular. There is more cream here than in a conventional gratin. Let the dish settle for a few minutes after baking, and it will set up a bit. It will still be creamy enough to provide some sauce for simply broiled or baked fish. Unlike some restaurant dishes, gratins are practical for the home cook. They can be baked early in the day and reheated, or even prepared the day before. And you can serve a gratin in the dish you bake it in, so you don't have to wash another pan. • SERVES 8

1 tablespoon (14 grams)
 unsalted butter

2 large leeks (about 1½ pounds/
 680 grams), white and light green
 parts, thoroughly washed and
 thinly sliced

2 medium fennel bulbs (about 2 pounds/
 908 grams), trimmed, tough outer
 layers removed, and cut lengthwise
 into ½-inch (1.3-cm) slices

1 teaspoon kosher salt

½ teaspoon white pepper

2 cups (480 ml) heavy cream

1 cup (4 ounces/114 grams) shredded
 Gruyère cheese

¼ cup (1 ounce/28 grams) freshly
 grated Parmigiano-Reggiano cheese

1 large egg yolk

2 garlic cloves minced

¼ cup (15 grams) bread crumbs
 (page 303) or store-bought
 unseasoned bread crumbs

PREHEAT THE OVEN to 400 degrees (205°C). Butter a 9-by-13-inch baking dish with the 1 tablespoon butter.

In a large bowl, combine the leeks, fennel, salt, and pepper. Place them in the prepared baking dish.

Place the cream, cheeses, and egg yolk in a small bowl and whisk together. Add the garlic, and pour the mixture over the leeks and fennel. Sprinkle the top with the bread crumbs.

Cover with aluminum foil, transfer to the oven, and bake for 40 minutes. Uncover and bake until the top of the gratin is lightly browned, about 20 minutes more. Remove from the oven, let rest for 10 minutes, and then serve.

wine: Ravenswood Merlot, from Sonoma County, is a light red suitable for fall vegetable dishes.

baked asparagus with parmigiano-reggiano and balsamic vinegar

ASPARAGI AL FORNO

mark • The easiest way to get people to eat their vegetables is to cover them in cheese. Here I sprinkle some Parmigiano-Reggiano on top of blanched asparagus and bake it for a few minutes to melt the cheese. A little bit of balsamic vinegar finishes off the dish. The best Italian balsamic vinegar, from Modena, where it is aged in barrels like wine for years, is fantastic on asparagus but very expensive. We use it in the restaurant (we keep it in the office and use an eyedropper), but if you're not ready to make the investment, you can vastly improve the taste of supermarket balsamic vinegar by cooking it down to a syrupy consistency, as I describe below. However, if you can, do try the real thing at least once. It is worth it. • SERVES 4

½ cup (120 ml) balsamic vinegar

1 tablespoon plus ½ teaspoon kosher salt

2 bunches (about 2 pounds/908 grams) asparagus

¼ cup (60 ml) extra-virgin olive oil

1 cup (4 ounces/114 grams) freshly grated Parmigiano-Reggiano cheese

PREHEAT THE OVEN to 350 degrees (175°C).

Place the vinegar in a small saucepan and bring to a boil over high heat. Reduce the heat and simmer, swirling the pan occasionally, until reduced by half, about 15 minutes. Set aside.

Bring a 6- to 8-quart pot of water to boil. Add 1 tablespoon of the salt and the asparagus and blanch until barely tender, about 1 minute. Drain and rinse under cold water to stop the cooking. Pat dry with paper towels.

Place the asparagus in one layer on a rimmed baking sheet. Sprinkle with the remaining ½ teaspoon salt. Drizzle with 2 tablespoons of the oil and sprinkle with the Parmigiano-Reggiano cheese.

Transfer to the oven and bake until the cheese is melted and the asparagus is hot, 5 minutes.

Use a spatula to transfer the asparagus to a platter. Drizzle with 2 tablespoons of the reduced balsamic vinegar and the remaining 2 table-spoons olive oil. Serve immediately, with the extra balsamic vinegar on the side.

wine: Serve this dish as a spring appetizer with Sonoma-Cutrer Russian River Chardonnay, its perfect match.

belgian fries

PATATINE FRITTE

mark • When I started at Fred's, I wanted to do dishes that were international, and I was happy to put these on my menu. The French give credit to the Belgians for inventing fries (they don't always show their gratitude—if a Frenchman wants to insult a Belgian, he'll call him a *pomme frite*), and I wanted to also. Authentic Belgian fries are twice-fried to get that crisp crust. I like peanut oil for frying, because it has a high smoke point, which means it can get very hot before it starts to burn. It is also flavorless, so the fries turn out crisp and with pure potato flavor. If peanut allergies are a concern, substitute pure (not extra-virgin) olive oil. We serve the fries in a paper cone and offer mayonnaise for dipping, as they do in Belgium. We also offer Sauce Américaine, which is simply mayo mixed with ketchup, because in New York, serving fries with plain mayonnaise is too much of a culture shock for some customers. • SERVES 4

6 Idaho potatoes (about 4 pounds/ 1.8 kilos)

6 cups (960 ml) peanut oil

FOR THE SAUCE AMÉRICAINE

½ cup (120 ml) mayonnaise

½ cup (120 ml) ketchup

Kosher salt

HAVE READY A LARGE BOWL of cold water and a deep-fry/candy thermometer. Line a large platter or baking sheet with several layers of paper towels. Peel the potatoes, cut into ¼-inch-thick fries, and place in the bowl of cold water.

Place the peanut oil in a 6- to 8-quart stockpot and heat it to 300 degrees over medium-high heat. Pat very dry with paper towels as many potatoes as will fit comfortably in the pot, add them to the pot, and cook until they just begin to brown, about 5 minutes. Transfer to the paper towels to drain, and repeat with the remaining potatoes, frying them in batches. Let stand for 30 minutes. (Set the oil aside.)

TO MAKE THE SAUCE

Stir together the mayonnaise and ketchup, and set aside.

Line another baking sheet with several layers of paper towels. Reheat the oil to 350 degrees (175°C). Add the potatoes, again in batches, and cook until golden brown, about 3 minutes. Do not crowd them in the pot, and gently separate them with a wooden spoon as they cook so they don't stick together. Transfer the cooked potatoes to the paper-towel-lined baking sheet and sprinkle with salt. Serve with the sauce on the side.

wine: These fries are served with beer in Belgium. If you'd like to try the combination, Stella Artois from Belgium is widely available.

12

{dessert at last}

chocolate biscotti

BISCOTTI AL CIOCCOLATO

pino • Almond biscotti, called *cantucci di Prato,* are the most popular cookie in Tuscany and the only indulgence my mother would allow us at home. On Sunday afternoons, she would let us have them with little glasses of vin santo, the dessert wine that always accompanies the cookies, and we were so happy and silly, eating the crunchy cookies and pretending to be a little drunk from the wine.

I still like almond biscotti, but my American customers prefer this variation, made with chocolate, and they have grown on me too. Serve them to your children as a snack (they are good dipped in milk) or as a light dessert, with some fresh fruit and dessert wine. • MAKES ABOUT 36 COOKIES

2 cups (10 ounces/285 grams) whole almonds

2½ cups (350 grams) all-purpose flour, plus more for rolling

½ cup (48 grams) unsweetened Dutch-process cocoa powder

2 teaspoons baking powder

Pinch of salt

10 tablespoons (1¼ sticks/140 grams) unsalted butter, softened

1½ cups (295 grams) sugar

2 large eggs

3 ounces (85 grams) semisweet chocolate, melted and cooled

2 teaspoons vanilla extract

2 teaspoons almond extract

¼ cup (60 ml) fresh lemon juice

1 large egg white, lightly beaten

PREHEAT THE OVEN to 325 degrees (165°C).

Spread the almonds on a large baking sheet and toast until fragrant, 6 to 8 minutes. Set aside to cool.

When the almonds are cool, coarsely chop them. Line another baking sheet with parchment paper.

Whisk together the flour, cocoa powder, baking powder, and salt in a medium bowl, and set aside.

Combine the butter, sugar, and eggs in the bowl of an electric mixer fitted with the paddle attachment. Mix on medium speed, scraping down the sides of the bowl, until smooth, 2 to 3 minutes. Add the melted chocolate, vanilla and almond extracts, and lemon juice and mix on medium-high speed, scraping down the sides of the bowl once or twice, for 2 minutes. Add the flour mixture, mixing until just combined; do not overmix. Stir in the almonds.

Turn the dough out onto a lightly floured work surface and divide it in half. Shape each half into a flat log about 18 inches long and 3 inches wide. Place the logs several inches apart on the prepared baking sheet. Lightly brush the logs with the egg white.

Bake for 35 minutes. Remove the baking sheet from the oven and let cool for 30 minutes.

Reheat the oven to 200 degrees (95°C).

Transfer the logs to a cutting board and cut them into 1-inch-thick slices. Lay the slices cut side down on the baking sheet, return them to the oven, and bake until crisp, about 30 minutes. Transfer the cookies to wire racks and let them cool completely. The biscotti will keep in an airtight container for 1 to 2 weeks.

wine: While vin santo is best with cantucci di Prato, with chocolate biscotti I prefer Aleatico—a sweet wine made in Puglia and on the island of Elba—or Moscato.

"ugly but good" cookies

BRUTTI MA BUONI

pino · The name of these cookies from Piedmont couldn't be more literal. The shapeless mounds with a bumpy surface aren't much to look at, but the chopped hazelnuts, almonds, and pine nuts give them great flavor and richness. They are the Piedmontese answer to Tuscan biscotti and are served the same way, as a snack at the end of a meal with a glass of sweet wine.

To toast and skin hazelnuts, place the nuts on a baking sheet and bake in a preheated 350-degree (175°C) oven until fragrant, about 10 minutes. Remove the pan from the oven, wrap the nuts in a clean kitchen towel, and let cool for 15 minutes. Then rub the nuts in the towel to remove as much of the skins as possible. · MAKES ABOUT 24 COOKIES

½ cup (70 grams) toasted and skinned hazelnuts

2½ cups (12½ ounces/410 grams) blanched whole almonds

½ cup (70 grams) pine nuts

1½ cups (295 grams) sugar

3 tablespoons all-purpose flour

1½ teaspoons cornstarch

½ teaspoon pure vanilla extract

½ teaspoon pure almond extract

4 large egg whites

Pinch of salt

PREHEAT THE OVEN to 350 degrees (175°C). Line a baking sheet with parchment paper.

Combine the hazelnuts, almonds, pine nuts, and 1½ cups of the sugar in the work bowl of a food processor and pulse several times, until the nuts are roughly chopped. Add the flour, cornstarch, and vanilla and almond extracts and pulse several more times, until well blended. Transfer to a large mixing bowl.

Combine the egg whites and salt in the bowl of an electric mixer and whisk on high until the egg whites just hold firm peaks and are still very shiny. Scrape the egg whites into the bowl with the nut mixture and gently fold together, taking care not to deflate the egg whites.

Spoon tablespoonfuls of the batter onto the prepared baking sheet, spacing them 1½ inches (about 4 cm) apart. Bake until the tops are dry, about 15 minutes.

Transfer the baking sheet to a wire rack and let the cookies cool completely. The cookies will keep in an airtight container at room temperature for up to 2 days.

wine: The combination of cookies and sweet wine is an offering of hospitality throughout Italy. In the north, they are often served with Moscato; in the south, with Aleatico.

pears in vin santo with sweet polenta

PERE AL VIN SANTO CON POLENTA DOLCE

mark · Pears are probably my favorite fruit—they're so much juicier and more complex than most apples. Here I serve them on top of sweet polenta. The earthiness of the fruit is wonderful with the crunchy, wholesome cornmeal, especially in the fall. · SERVES 6

FOR THE POLENTA

4 cups (960 ml) water

¼ teaspoon salt

1 cup (5 ounces/140 grams) yellow cornmeal

½ vanilla bean, split

Pinch of ground cinnamon

Pinch of freshly grated nutmeg

½ cup (100 grams) plus 2 tablespoons sugar

2 tablespoons (28 grams) unsalted butter

Confectioners' sugar, for dusting

FOR THE PEARS

6 large Bartlett or Comice pears, cored

3 tablespoons golden raisins

2 tablespoons chopped walnuts

6 tablespoons brown sugar

2 tablespoons (28 grams) unsalted butter, cut into small pieces

½ teaspoon ground cinnamon

1 cup (240 ml) water

1 cup (240 ml) vin santo

TO MAKE THE POLENTA

Butter a large rimmed baking sheet. Bring the water and salt to a boil in a 5- to 6-quart pot over high heat. Gradually whisk in the cornmeal in a thin stream. Stir in the vanilla bean, cinnamon, nutmeg, and sugar. Cover the pan, turn the heat to low, and cook, stirring occasionally, until the polenta is very thick and pulls away from the sides of the pan, about 40 minutes.

Stir in the butter, and spread the hot polenta in a ½-inch-thick layer on the baking sheet; discard the vanilla bean. Cool to room temperature, then cover with plastic wrap, and refrigerate until well chilled, at least 6 hours, or up to 1 day.

MAKE THE PEARS

Preheat the oven to 350 degrees (175°C). Stand the pears in an 8-inch square baking dish. Combine the raisins, walnuts, brown sugar, and butter in a small bowl. Stuff some of the mixture into each pear. Sprinkle each cavity with a little cinnamon. Pour the water and vin santo around the pears.

Bake until the pears are very soft and easily pierced through with a paring knife, about 40 minutes.

While the pears are cooking, take the polenta out of the refrigerator and use a cookie cutter to cut it into half-moon shapes. Butter another baking sheet and transfer the half-moons to the baking sheet. Dust heavily with confectioners' sugar.

Remove the baking dish from the oven, transfer the pears to a plate, and loosely tent with foil to keep warm. (Leave the oven on.)

Pour the juices into a small saucepan and bring to a boil over high heat. Reduce the heat to medium-high and cook until the sauce is thickened, about 5 minutes.

Place the baking sheet with the polenta in the oven and bake until the polenta half-moons are golden brown.

Place a few polenta half-moons on each of six dessert plates. Top each one with a pear. Drizzle with some of the warm sauce, and serve immediately.

wine: It's not necessary to use an expensive or vintage vin santo for this recipe. I recommend a good medium-priced brand such as Lungarotti or Antinori. Serve the remaining wine with the dessert.

neapolitan cheesecake

TORTA DI RICOTTA ALLA NAPOLETANA

pino · When I was little, my family would spend three or four weeks out of the year in Naples with my father's brothers and sisters. Each week of our trip, we would stay with a different aunt or uncle, and each family had its own version of this cheesecake, which was always served on Sunday.

This version has characteristic Neapolitan ingredients and flavors—raisins, lemon zest, and cinnamon. Farro adds a nutty flavor. The combination of ricotta, mascarpone, and cream cheese makes this cake much lighter than American-style cheesecakes, with a melt-in-your-mouth texture. This is the opposite of a rich, overwhelming dessert: eating a slice is more like having fruit and cheese than a piece of cake. · SERVES 8 TO 10

FOR THE FILLING

1/2 teaspoon kosher salt

1/4 cup (50 grams) farro

1/4 cup (40 grams) dried cherries

1/4 cup (40 grams) golden raisins

1/4 cup (60 ml) sweet Marsala

1 tablespoon ground cinnamon

1/2 cup (85 grams) whole-milk ricotta cheese, drained

8 ounces (228 grams) cream cheese, softened

8 ounces (228 grams) mascarpone cheese, softened

1 1/2 cups (295 grams) sugar

5 large eggs

1 tablespoon pure vanilla extract

1 tablespoon grated lemon zest

1/4 cup (60 ml) heavy cream

FOR THE DOUGH

12 tablespoons (1 1/2 sticks/168 grams) butter, softened

1/2 cup (60 grams) confectioners' sugar

1 1/2 cups (224 grams) all-purpose flour

TO MAKE THE FILLING

Bring a medium pot of water to boil. Add the salt and farro and cook until the farro is tender, about 20 minutes. Drain well and set aside to cool.

Combine the cooled farro, dried cherries, raisins, Marsala, and cinnamon in a medium bowl and let stand at room temperature for 1 hour.

TO MAKE THE DOUGH

Combine the butter and confectioners' sugar in the bowl of an electric mixer fitted with the paddle attachment and mix on medium speed, scraping down the sides of the bowl once or twice, until well combined, about 2 minutes. Add the flour and mix on low speed until combined. Turn the mixer to medium-high speed and beat until the dough is soft and smooth, about 6 minutes more. Form the dough into a ball, wrap in plastic, and refrigerate for 20 minutes.

Preheat the oven to 375 degrees (190°C). Butter the bottom and sides of a 10-inch springform pan. Wrap the outside of the pan with 2 squares of heavy-duty foil.

On a lightly floured counter, roll out the dough into an 11-inch circle. Transfer it to the prepared pan and pat it firmly into the bottom and up the sides of the pan. Place the pan in the freezer for 5 minutes to allow the dough to firm up.

Cut a 12-inch circle of parchment and place it on top of the dough. To weigh it down, cover the paper with 2 cups dried beans. Bake the crust for 7 minutes.

Remove the beans and parchment, and bake until the crust is dry and golden brown, about another 12 minutes.

TO FINISH THE FILLING

While the crust is baking, combine the ricotta, cream cheese, and mascarpone in a clean mixer bowl and mix on low with the paddle attachment, scraping down the sides of the bowl once or twice, until well combined. Add the sugar and mix for 2 minutes. Add the eggs, vanilla, lemon zest, and

heavy cream, turn the mixer to medium speed, and mix for another 2 minutes.

Bring about 4 quarts (4 liters) of water to a boil in a pot or large kettle.

Remove the springform pan from the oven and place it in a roasting pan. Lower the oven temperature to 275 degrees (135°C).

Spread half of the cheese mixture evenly into the crust. Spread half of the fruit mixture over the cheese and drizzle the liquid from the bowl over the fruit. Spread the remaining cheese mixture evenly over the fruit, and sprinkle with the remaining fruit.

Place the roasting pan in the oven and pour enough boiling water into the roasting pan to come about halfway up the sides of the springform pan. Bake for 15 minutes. Increase the heat to 300 degrees (150°C) and bake for another 15 minutes. Increase the heat to 325 degrees (165°C) and bake until the cake is set around the edges but a little loose in the middle, about 30 minutes more.

Remove the springform pan from the water bath. Carefully remove and discard the foil, and set the pan on a wire rack. Run a sharp paring knife around the inside of the pan to loosen the sides of the cake, and let cool to room temperature before removing the cake from the pan, slicing, and serving. The cheesecake is best served on the day it is made.

wine: In the spring and summer, I serve this phenomenally light, not-too-sweet cheesecake with Prosecco; a good choice is Nino Franco. In the winter, a good Merlot or Zinfandel from Oregon or the Sonoma Valley will do.

panna cotta with orange and campari sauce

PANNA COTTA AL CAMPARI

pino • *Panna cotta* translates as "cooked cream," and that's basically all this is, a very simple custardlike dessert that's thickened with gelatin rather than eggs. It is lighter than an egg custard, with a wonderful melt-in-your-mouth quality that makes it a refreshing ending to any meal. Panna cotta is popular all over northern Italy, where it is served with a variety of sauces, including a reduction of balsamic vinegar, a blackberry compote, and this sauce made of orange juice and Campari, which is my favorite. The custards will take about 6 hours to set in the refrigerator. If you are in a hurry, you can place the individual ramekins in a roasting pan filled with ice, which will help the panna cotta gel in a couple of hours. • SERVES 8

FOR THE PANNA COTTA

1 cup (240 ml) whole milk

2 envelopes unflavored gelatin

3½ cups (840 ml) heavy cream

2 cups (240 grams) confectioners' sugar

½ vanilla bean, split

FOR THE ORANGE SAUCE

2 cups (480 ml) fresh orange juice, strained

2 cups (420 grams) granulated sugar

½ cup (120 ml) Campari

TO MAKE THE PANNA COTTA

Pour ½ cup of the milk into a small bowl and sprinkle with the gelatin. Let stand until the gelatin dissolves.

Combine the remaining ½ cup milk, the heavy cream, and confectioners' sugar in a 3-quart heavy saucepan. Scrape the seeds of the vanilla bean into the pan and add the scraped bean. Heat over medium heat, whisking constantly, until the mixture just comes to a boil. Remove from the heat, add the gelatin, and whisk for 1 minute to dissolve it.

Remove and discard the vanilla bean, and pour the panna cotta into eight 4-ounce ramekins or custard cups. Refrigerate until set, at least 6 hours, or overnight.

TO MAKE THE ORANGE SAUCE

Combine the orange juice, sugar, and Campari in a small saucepan and bring to a boil over medium-high heat. Reduce the heat to medium and simmer until reduced by one-third, about 30 minutes. Let cool slightly (the sauce can be made up to 1 day in advance; refrigerate in an airtight container, and reheat in the microwave or on top of the stove).

To unmold and serve the panna cotta, fill a medium bowl with very hot tap water. One at a time, run a paring knife around each panna cotta to release it from the sides of the ramekin, then dip the bottom half of the ramekin in the water for 30 seconds. Place a small dessert plate on top of the ramekin and invert, then tap the bottom of the ramekin to unmold. Spoon some of the warm orange sauce over each panna cotta and serve immediately.

tip: Candied orange peel, available at specialty foods stores and by mail (see Resources, page 306), makes a tasty and pretty garnish.

wine: This delicately flavored dessert goes well with a light dessert wine such as chilled Moscato. Look for reasonably priced bottles from the Piedmont region.

espresso panna cotta

PANNA COTTA CON ESPRESSO

mark • Panna cotta flavored with espresso is a great way to combine coffee and dessert. Try the espresso from Illy Café (see Resources, page 306) or another Italian company for a rich coffee taste. • SERVES 8

1 cup (240 ml) whole milk

2 envelopes unflavored gelatin

4 cups (960 ml) heavy cream

1 cup (195 grams) sugar

1 cup (240 ml) brewed espresso

POUR ½ CUP OF THE MILK into a small bowl and sprinkle with the gelatin. Let stand until the gelatin dissolves.

Combine the remaining ½ cup milk, the heavy cream, and sugar in a 3-quart heavy saucepan and heat over medium heat, whisking constantly, until the mixture just comes to a boil. Remove from the heat and stir in the espresso. Add the gelatin mixture, whisking for 1 minute to dissolve it.

Pour the panna cotta into eight 4-ounce ramekins or custard cups. Refrigerate until set, at least 6 hours, or overnight.

To unmold and serve the panna cotta, fill a medium bowl with very hot tap water. One at a time, run a paring knife around each panna cotta to release it from the sides of the ramekin, then dip the bottom half of the ramekin in the water for 30 seconds. Place a small dessert plate on top of the ramekin and invert, then tap the bottom of the ramekin to unmold. Serve immediately.

wine: Rather than wine, I'd serve a liqueur that pairs well with coffee, like nocello, which is flavored with hazelnuts.

oranges with maraschino sauce

ARANCE AL MARASCHINO

mark • Here is another simple fruit dessert, wonderful in the winter, when most good fresh fruit is in limited supply but oranges are available. The maraschino liqueur, made with cherries, adds a bitter edge, tempered by the creamy ice cream and sweet, acidic oranges. • SERVES 6

¼ cup (50 grams) sugar

2 tablespoons (30 ml) water

½ cup (120 ml) maraschino liqueur

6 large navel oranges, peeled, white pith removed, and sliced into rounds

1 pint (about 500 ml) vanilla ice cream

COMBINE THE SUGAR, water, and maraschino liqueur in a small saucepan and bring to a boil over medium heat, stirring to dissolve the sugar. Boil until reduced by half, about 5 minutes. Remove from the heat and let cool slightly.

Arrange the sliced oranges on six dessert plates. Top each serving with a scoop of ice cream. Drizzle the ice cream with the warm maraschino sauce. Serve immediately.

wine: Serve tiny glasses of maraschino with this pretty dessert.

the pantry

Success in the kitchen depends just as much on skillful shopping as it does on technique. A recipe is only as good as the ingredients that go into it. And even the world's greatest chef will not be able to make dinner if the pantry is bare.

At our restaurants, we come up with daily specials inspired by the constantly changing array of fresh foods our purveyors offer us: If the vegetable supplier has beautiful baby artichokes, we'll buy some and then figure out how to prepare them. If the fishmonger is offering just-caught local striped bass, we'll take it and come up with a recipe later. We can do this because of the vast stores of ingredients we always have on hand: olive oil, vinegar, cheese, herbs and spices, dried beans, pasta, and grains. A well-stocked pantry allows us to improvise with confidence.

At home, the pantry is smaller but the idea is the same. Unless it's a special occasion or a weekend project, we don't like to plan a meal before we go to the market. Rather, we go to the market to see what looks good that day, and then come home and cook. In general, we'll need to pick up only a few items, because we know that we already have most of what we'll need—pasta, canned tomatoes, a chunk of Parmigiano-Reggiano. Ideally, we'd like you to use this book the same way. Stock your pantry with the items you use often. Then go to the market and buy what appeals to you that day. Come home, consult these recipes, and use what you've bought along with what you have to create a simple meal.

There's a security in the fact that our recipes, the ones we make week after week, year after year, use many of the same ingredients. It doesn't get boring, because the way we use those ingredients changes so dramatically with the seasons. In the summer, we might grill mushrooms, drizzle them with olive oil, and shower them with shavings of Parmigiano-Reggiano cheese. In the fall, we might make mushroom soup, flavoring it with olive oil and the cheese. These are two very different mushroom dishes, for different times of the year.

Daily shopping and cooking, using familiar flavors in constantly changing ways, is more than a routine. It is a way of living that respects nature and fulfills us creat-ively. Here is how we stock our pantry (diverging opinions included) to help us achieve a lifestyle based on shop-ping for and preparing simple and delicious food:

BREAD CRUMBS

We use bread crumbs in a variety of ways: adding them to ground meat for meatballs, topping baked clams or coating calamari with them before broiling, sprinkling them into pasta dishes to add texture and flavor. For most of these dishes, unflavored dried bread crumbs from the supermarket will do, but homemade bread crumbs are best.

To make bread crumbs, remove the crusts from leftover good white country bread, cut it into cubes, put the cubes on a baking sheet, and toast them in a 350-degree (175°C) oven, stirring occasionally, until golden, 12 to 15 minutes. Let the cubes cool on the baking sheet, then grind in a food processor until fine. Whenever you have leftover bread, make bread crumbs, and store them in a zipper-lock bag in the freezer so you will have them on hand when you need them.

We keep a couple of other types of bread crumbs in our freezer.

pino I prefer Japanese-style panko to homemade or store-bought bread crumbs on my breaded veal and chicken cutlets. They make a crunchy crust that is also very light and almost lacy.

mark Look who is straying from tradition! Matzo meal and whole matzos are similarly light and crunchy, and I use them for breading the way you use panko for a similar result.

CHEESE

The choice of cheese to grate onto pasta is as much a regional opinion as personal taste. The king of cheeses (as the Italians call it) is Parmigiano-Reggiano, a rich aged cow's milk cheese with a perfect balance of taste and texture. Use it with all savory dishes or try eating it on its own. For a less expensive but similarly flavored parmesan, try Grana Padona. Pecorino Romano is a very sharp sheep's milk cheese that will add a distinc-tive flavor to any meat sauce. For desserts (such as the famous tiramisù) the best choice is Mascarpone, a double cream cheese from cow's milk, originally from the north of Italy. It's very buttery-rich but delicate in taste with a creamy texture.

CHICKEN BROTH

Homemade chicken stock will give the best flavor in most dishes. Make a large batch and freeze it in smaller containers. What should you do if you don't have any on hand when you want to make risotto? Opinions diverge.

mark Canned low-sodium organic chicken broth—Swanson has just come out with one—will give very good results in place of homemade broth in most cases.

pino Italians use Knorr powdered bouillon in place of homemade stock, for pure chicken flavor.

CURED PORK PRODUCTS
Italy's traditional artisanal cured meats such as prosciutto, pancetta, and guanciale are a world away from the processed meats of the typical American supermarket aisle. It's worth seeking out these products as they will add their unique flavors to whatever you're eating. Our two favorites are pancetta (salt-cured pork belly) and guanciale (salt-cured pork cheeks). Both are available in specialty stores and select catalogs but in a pinch you can substitute bacon for either.

DRIED BEANS
With lentils, chickpeas, cranberry beans, fava beans, and a selection of white beans (cannellini, Great Northern, navy) in the pantry, we know we'll never go hungry. We use dried beans to make a variety of soups. For a simple meal, we also like to drizzle the cooked beans with our best olive oil, sprinkle with kosher or sea salt, and serve with a simple salad and bread.

DRIED FRUITS AND NUTS
Nuts are expensive and go rancid quickly. Store pine nuts, walnuts, almonds, and shelled unsalted pistachio nuts in airtight containers or zipper-lock bags in the freezer. Keep raisins, currants, and dried cherries moist in zipper-lock bags at room temperature.

DRIED HERBS
This is a short list, because we rely primarily on fresh herbs in our cooking. In the summer we grow our own, and during the colder months we buy the hothouse herbs that are available year-round in most supermarkets. Bay leaves and dried Sicilian oregano are the only two dried herbs we use regularly. Dried parsley and basil are tasteless; dried rosemary is unpleasantly bitter.

DRIED MUSHROOMS
Dried porcini mushrooms are a wonderful substitute for fresh ones, which are difficult to find in the United States. Keep them in an airtight container at room temperature and rehydrate in hot water before using.

DRIED PASTA
Keep on hand a variety of long cuts (spaghetti, linguine, perciatelli) and short cuts (penne, rigatoni, ziti, fusilli) so that you'll have the proper shape for any sauce you want to make. We prefer artisanal brands like Martelli and Setaro. These are made with old-fashioned machines that extrude pasta with a rough texture, which we find pleasing. But commercial brands made with the same durum wheat have the same great flavor, and are available in many more shapes than artisanal brands. Look for pasta from the Italian manufacturers De Cecco, Del Verde, Barilla, and Buitoni. For more of our thoughts on dried pasta, see chapter 3.

EXTRA-VIRGIN AND REGULAR OLIVE OILS
It would be impossible to cook Italian food without olive oil. Both of us stock three types—one regular and two extra-virgin—that cover all of our needs.

pino For frying—meatballs, artichokes, anything where I need a large quantity—I use regular olive oil. When I need a few tablespoons for sautéing and braising, I use a commercial extra-virgin olive oil like Colavita or Monini. I keep a third bottle of fine cold-pressed extra-virgin olive oil, always an artisanal brand from a small estate, to give most dishes a final drizzle. My favorite oils for this purpose tend to be from northern Tuscany and from Puglia and Sicily, but that's a matter of taste. You have to find ones you love.

mark I have a rule: If I'm going to discard it after cooking, I use regular olive oil. If I'm putting it into what I'm cooking, I use a good commercially blended extra-virgin olive oil from the supermarket. Personally, I like Monini. When I'm at the table and I want to drizzle oil over fish or meat as a garnish, I prefer a special extra-virgin oil from Tuscany or Umbria. But those are pricey. For salad dressing, I think Monini Originale is fine.

pino In general, the oils from Tuscany, Umbria, and Liguria are mild and fruity, while the southern oils are spicy. For salad, the mild northern oils are best. But if you're cooking artichokes, eggplant, or any sturdy, hearty vegetable, a spicy southern oil will add a lot of flavor. It's about using the right oil to get the right balance.

FLOUR AND OTHER GRAINS

Unbleached all-purpose flour is fine for making pasta. You can also mail-order Italian flour (see Resources, page 306) for the most authentic results. We keep stone-ground cornmeal in the pantry for polenta. It has a fuller flavor and more satisfying texture than commercial cornmeal, like Quaker, but commercial cornmeal will work fine in our recipes. Farro is another staple in our pantries. We buy it at an Italian specialty foods store or online (see Resources, page 306).

PRESERVED ITEMS

These range from flavor-boosting ingredients such as olives, anchovies, and capers to foods, like canned tuna, around which you can build a whole meal. We always have at least seven kinds of olives—three black (Niçoise, Gaeta, Moroccan) and four green (Cerignola, Sicilian, Greek, cracked) in the refrigerator. We like salt-brined capers, which should be rinsed and patted dry before using. Salt-cured fresh anchovies, which need to be filleted, are best, although flat fillets will work in our recipes. Buy only Italian tuna packed in olive oil, preferably "ventresca," which is the belly. Jars of sun-dried tomatoes packed in oil and a variety of preserved vegetables—mushrooms, artichokes, eggplant, peppers—round out this section of the pantry.

RICE

Only Italian rices, which are shorter and fatter than other short-grain rices and contain more starch, will give risotto its characteristic creamy texture. Arborio rice, grown in the Po Valley, is the most commonly available here, but there are other varieties, including Vialone Nano (from the Veneto) and Carnaroli (grown in the area between Milan and Turin), that also make excellent risotto. Try them all, and use the one you like best.

SALT

We use kosher salt in most recipes because we prefer its pure flavor to the strangely chemical flavor of iodized salt. It is the economical choice, especially for pasta, where at least two tablespoons are required to salt the water. Feel free to season your food with your favorite sea salt instead of kosher salt if you prefer.

SPICES

Along with salt, pepper, and fresh herbs, small jars of the following will allow you to season the dishes in this book: black peppercorns, crushed red pepper flakes, cumin seeds, fennel seeds, ground cinnamon, ground cumin, juniper berries, mustard seeds, saffron threads, and whole cloves. Buy whole nutmeg and grate it yourself for the best flavor. When cooking, place whole cloves and seeds in cheesecloth sachets, so you can remove them easily from your sauce or braise before serving.

TOMATOES

The supermarket carries a confusing array of tomato products, but we use just three in all of our cooking: imported canned whole San Marzano plum tomatoes, Pomi-brand pureed tomatoes in a shelf-stable carton, and imported Italian tomato paste in a tube.

VINEGAR

We use red wine vinegar and sherry wine vinegar in salad dressings; balsamic vinegar (the real thing from Modena—aged for ten to twenty-five years in oak barrels), drop by drop, as a garnish; and white wine vinegar, only rarely, for pickling and preserving.

pino I would never use balsamic vinegar the way Americans like it, over salad. I use it by the drop to brighten up risotto, or sprinkled over a bowl of strawberries as an essence.

mark The balsamic vinegar Americans pour onto salad is not what you are talking about. What's available in the supermarket consists of a very small amount of real, aged balsamic vinegar mixed with white wine vinegar. It's not the artisanal product that you use.

pino Real balsamic vinegar should be treated like your most expensive drizzling olive oil. Never cook with it. Only add it to your food just before serving. I wouldn't even put it on a salad. It's too intense.

mark Red wine vinegar is the best on salad. I also like sherry vinegar, and white wine vinegar when I don't want red wine vinegar to discolor my ingredients.

pino For me, it's red wine vinegar or lemon juice on salad, nothing else.

resources

Italian ingredients and Italian food have become so popular in America that most of the items you will need to make our recipes can be found on the shelves of any good supermarket, possibly with a trip to the butcher, cheese market, or farm stand to complete your shopping. The following online and mail-order stores stock the few ingredients you may have a hard time finding, as well as particular brands we like that you may not find locally and Italian wines that may be unavailable at your local wine shop.

A. G. FERRARI FOODS

A family-run Italian specialty foods business that has been in business for eighty years, A. G. Ferrari has thirteen stores in the San Francisco Bay Area as well as an online store. They stock Latini pasta, organic farro from Abruzzo, dried porcini, truffle paste, olive oils and vinegars, an interesting variety of imported Italian salami, organic canned San Marzano tomatoes, organic Italian pasta flour, and a small but good selection of Italian wines. Order online at www.agferrari.com or call customer service at 877-878-2783.

BUON ITALIA

This purveyor of the highest-quality Italian specialty foods is a good source for many of the ingredients we rely on: Setaro pasta; fine extra-virgin olive oil; aged balsamic vinegar; Italian cheeses such as Parmigiano-Reggiano, fresh mozzarella, and Pecorino Romano; coffee from Illy Café; prosciutto, pancetta, guanciale, salami, and mortadella; Arborio, Carnaroli, and Vialone Nano rice; tuna belly *(ventresca)* packed in olive oil and anchovies packed in salt; Sicilian oregano; and white truffle oil and white and black truffle puree. Order online at www.buonitalia.com, call 212-633-9090, or visit their retail store at 75 Ninth Avenue, New York, NY 10011.

THE CHEF'S WAREHOUSE

You can buy the same Italian cheeses, olive oils, rice, artisanal pasta, and many other products delivered to fine restaurants in the New York area every day at this website, owned by DairyLand USA, one of the country's leading wholesale specialty foods suppliers. Visit them at www.chefswarehouse.com.

D'ARTAGNAN

D'Artagnan is the place to go for game, including venison, rabbit, and wild boar. They also sell specialty poultry like Bluefoot chickens (Pino's favorite), quail, capons, and Cornish game hens; smoked meats such as guanciale and nitrite-free organic bacon; truffle oil; and an impressive selection of fresh mushrooms in season (including porcini, chanterelles, morels, and hen-of-the-woods) and reasonably priced dried porcini. Order online at www.dartagnan.com, or call to mail-order or request a catalog: 800-327-8244.

MURRAY'S CHEESE

This renowned cheese shop is where we buy best-quality Parmigiano-Reggiano, mozzarella, Pecorino Romano, and any other cheese we desire for our restaurants or to use at home. Shop the website, www.murrayscheese.com, or visit them at their two retail stores in New York: 254 Bleecker Street (212-243-3289) and Grand Central Market at 43rd Street and Lexington Avenue (212-922-1540).

SUR LA TABLE

Buy hand-cranked pasta machines and the hard-to-find chitarra for making pasta alla chitarra from this fine cookwares shop. Sur la Table also sells Illy coffee and high-quality (if expensive) organic extra-virgin olive oil from Italy. Order online at www.surlatable.com or call and order by mail: 800-243-0852.

VINO ITALIAN WINES AND SPIRITS

This New York City shop stocks hundreds of wines from every region of Italy, including dessert wines and grappas. Browse their website, www.vinosite.com, and call the store to have wine shipped. Or visit the store: Vino Italian Wines and Spirits, 121 East 27th Street (212-725-6515).

ZINGERMAN'S

This venerable specialty foods emporium has a wonderful website where you can find a great selection of Italian cheeses (including two different Pecorinos from Tuscany as well as Pecorino Romano), extra-virgin olive oils, vinegars, artisanal pasta from Martelli, Arborio rice, jars of preserved vegetables imported from Italy, *ventresca* (tuna belly), sun-dried tomatoes from Sicily, and wild Italian fennel pollen. Visit at 620 Phoenix Drive, Ann Arbor, MI, 48108; order online at www.zingermans.com; or go online to request a mail-order catalog.

acknowledgments

We would like to thank Barbara Raives for her friendship and understanding; Angela Miller, who sometimes put her clients before her goats; and Lauren Chattman, who helped us to complete this book. Ann Bramson and her entire staff at Artisan have worked tirelessly to turn our manuscript into a beautiful book.

pino · Thanks to my children and especially to my wife, for always reminding me during difficult times that my family is the backbone of my life. This project and so many others would have been impossible to imagine without their help.

mark · Thanks to the staff at Coco Pazzo and the staff at Fred's for their endless patience as I ran around the kitchen testing recipes; to Fukuko Imai for her dessert recipes; to Serine for her love, support, and understanding during those late-night recipe writing sessions; to my great kids for letting me cook during their time with Dad; to Susan for giving up her personal time, allowing me to work longer on the book.

index

Acquacotta alla Maremmana, 21
Agnello Brasato, 190
Aloi, Margarita, 91
Amaretti, Meatballs with, 59
anchovies, 272
    Caesar Salad, 272–73; illus., 270–71,
        273
Antonio's Neapolitan Lasagne, 60–61
apple(s):
    and Garfagnana Bean Soup, 26;
        illus., 27
    Green, Veal Meatballs with, 43
Aragosta fra Diavolo, 231
Arance al Maraschino, 301
Arborio rice, 131
Arrosto di Maiale all'Arancia, 197
Arrosto Toscano, 187
artichoke(s):
    Chopped Roman Salad, 268
    Jewish-Style Fried, 282
    and Lamb, Braised, with Oven-
        Roasted New Potatoes and Spring
        Onions, 251–52; illus., 250
    Raw, Salad, 267
arugula:
    Chopped Roman Salad, 268
    Fred's Autumn Salad, 275
    Grilled Rib-Eye Steak Served over
        Toasted Bread with, 208; illus.,
        209
    Raw Artichoke Salad, 267
Asparagi al Forno, 281
asparagus:
    Baked, with Parmigiano-Reggiano
        and Balsamic Vinegar, 281; illus.,
        280
    Cannelloni with Mortadella and, 117

Green and White, Risotto with, 144;
    illus., 145

Baby Back Ribs with Cucumbers and
    Frisée, 206
Barley and Farro Salad, Grilled Tuna
    with, 179
basil:
    Pesto, 33
    Vinaigrette, 164–65
bean(s):
    cranberry, 19
    Cranberry, and Sausage with
        Polenta, 195
    dried, 303
    and Farro Soup Lucca-Style, 19
    Garfagnana, and Apple Soup, 26;
        illus., 27
    green, Chopped Roman Salad,
        268
    Green, in Tomato Sauce, 276; illus.,
        277
    Ribollita, 31
    Three, Salad with Orange and
        Fennel, 283
    Worker's Farmhouse Soup, 32–33
Béchamel Sauce, 118–19
beef:
    Braciole, 226–27
    Braised, with Porcini Mushrooms,
        188–89
    in Brunello, Chicken Cacciatore,
        and Polenta for the Whole Family,
        260–61
    Coco Pazzo's Grilled Marinated
        Hanger Steak, 207

Fred's Sliced Shell Steak Salad, 211
Grilled Rib-Eye Steak Served over
    Toasted Bread with Arugula, 208;
    illus., 209
leftover pot roast, 188
Maria's Lasagne, 118–19
Mark's Mom's Meat Loaf Revisited,
    49
Meatballs with Amaretti, 59
Meatballs with Spaghetti Coco
    Pazzo, 47–48; illus., 46
Neapolitan Marriage Soup, 30
Pan-Fried Meatballs, 40, 42; illus.,
    41
Pino's Meat Loaf, 54
Prime Rib with Creamed Spinach
    and Baked Potatoes and Truffles
    or Cheese for Kids, 248–49
Rigatoni with Butcher's Sauce, 70
Stew, 260
Tuscan Pot Roast, 187; illus., 186
Belgian Fries, 284; illus., 285
Biscotti, Chocolate, 290
Biscotti al Cioccolato, 290
bistecca:
    alla Coco Pazzo, 207
    in Crostone con la Rugola, 208
Braciole di Maiale alla Griglia, 213
Brasato di Agnello e Carciofi con Patate
    e Cipollotti Arrosto, 251–52
Brasato di Manzo ai Funghi, 188–89
bread crumbs, 303
broccoli:
    Taranto-Style Cavatelli with
        Cauliflower and, 84
    Worker's Farmhouse Soup, 32–33
broth, chicken, 303

Brussels sprouts:
    Fred's Autumn Salad, 275
    Roasted, 259
    Roasted, Braised Holiday Capon with
        Sweet Potatoes and, 258–59
Brutti ma Buoni, 291
bucatini:
    illus., 69
    with Pancetta and Onion Ragu,
        73–74
Bucatini all'Amatriciana, 73–74
Budini Caldi al Cioccolato, 295
Buglione con Polenta per Tutta la
    Famiglia, 260–61
Buitoni, Allessandra, 91
Butcher's Sauce, Rigatoni with, 70

cabbage:
    Ribollita, 31
    Savoy, Lamb Shanks Braised with,
        194
    Savoy, Oven-Roasted Salmon on,
        166; illus., 167
Cacciucco, 154
Caesar Salad, 272–73; illus., 270–71,
    273
cakes:
    Neapolitan Cheesecake, 296, 298;
        illus., 297
    Warm Chocolate Pudding, 295
Calamari, Broiled, 155; illus., 156–57
Campagna, New York, 10–11
Campari and Orange Sauce, Panna
    Cotta with, 299
Cannelloni with Asparagus and
    Mortadella, 117

Capon, Holiday, Braised, with Sweet
    Potatoes and Roasted Brussels
    Sprouts, 258–59
Cappone alla Maria per le Feste, 258–59
Carciofi alla Giuida, 282
Cardini, Caesar, 272
Carre di Vitello Arrosto con Patate, Rape,
    e Pastinache, 256–57
carrot(s):
    -Orange Soup, 23; illus., 22
    and Ricotta, Fresh, Ravioli with
        Carrot and Orange Sauce, 110–11
cauliflower:
    Ragu, Grilled Chicken Livers with, 214
    Taranto-Style Cavatelli with Broccoli
        and, 84
    Worker's Farmhouse Soup,
        32–33
cavatelli:
    illus., 68
    Taranto-Style, with Cauliflower and
        Broccoli, 84
Cavatelli alla Tarantina, 84
Centolire, New York, 11, 171, 241
Cernia al Forno con Patate, 162–63
cheese, 303
    Appenzeller, 175
    Baked Asparagus with Parmigiano-
        Reggiano and Balsamic Vinegar,
        281; illus., 280
    Cheesecake, Neapolitan, 296, 298;
        illus., 297
    Fettuccini with Butter and, 108
    Fontina Val d'Aosta, 175
    Goat, Farro with Button Mushrooms,
        Cherry Tomatoes, and, 147
    Grana Padana, 57

cheese (cont.):
    Gruyère Potatoes, 257
    for Kids, Prime Rib with Creamed
        Spinach and Baked Potatoes and
        Truffles or, 248–49
    Leek and Fennel Gratin, 279
    Potato Gratin with Onions and Black
        Olives, 278
    Sheep's-Milk, Pears with Honey and,
        294
Chez Panisse, Berkeley, 265
chicken:
    Braised Holiday Capon with Sweet
        Potatoes and Roasted Brussels
        Sprouts, 258–59
    Breast, Martini-Style, 238; illus.,
        236–37, 239
    broth, 303
    Cacciatore, Beef in Brunello, and
        Polenta for the Whole Family,
        260–61
    Caesar Salad, 273
    Estelle's Soup, 28–29
    organic free-range, 241
    Parmigiana, 233
    Salt-Cured Roast alla Centolire, 241
    Scarpariello, 199
    Stock, 29
    Stuffing for, 258–59
chicken livers:
    Grilled, with Cauliflower Ragu, 214
    Tagliolini with Onion and, 115
    Tuscan Pot Roast, 187; illus., 186
chili pepper, adding to pasta water, 74
chocolate:
    Biscotti, 290
    Warm Pudding Cakes, 295
Chopped Roman Salad, 268
clams:
    Baked, Coco Pazzo, 170
    Fisherman's-Style White Risotto,
        143
    and Mussels with Green Sauce, 215
    Risotto with Shellfish, 142
    Sicilian Couscous, 159–60; illus.,
        158
    Spaghetti with Zucchini and, 85
    Tuscan Seafood Sauté, 161
Coco Pazzo, New York, 11, 23, 47, 139,
    170, 245
Coco Pazzo's Grilled Marinated Hanger
    Steak, 207

cod:
    "day boat," 175
    in Parchment, 176
    and Yukon Gold Gratin, 175; illus.,
        174
Coniglio in Vino Bianco, 198
Cookies, "Ugly but Good," 291
Costata di Maiale alla Marco, 210
Costata di Manzo al Forno con Timballo di
    Spinaci e Patate, 248–49
Cotolette alla Parmigiana, 232–33
Court Bouillon, 164–65
Couscous, Sicillian, 159–60; illus., 158
Cozze e Vongole in Salsa Verde, 215
cucumber(s):
    Baby Back Ribs with Frisée and, 206
    Steamed Halibut Fillets with Sweet
        Pepper, Basil Vinaigrette, and,
        164–65
Cumin, Jerusalem Artichoke Soup
    with, 20
cured pork products, 303–4
Cus Cus alla Siciliana, 159–60

desserts, 287–301
    Chocolate Biscotti, 290
    Espresso Panna Cotta, 301; illus., 300
    Neapolitan Cheesecake, 296, 298;
        illus., 297
    Oranges with Maraschino Sauce, 301
    Panna Cotta with Orange and
        Campari Sauce, 299
    Pears in Vin Santo with Sweet
        Polenta, 293; illus., 292
    Pears with Sheep's-Milk Cheese and
        Honey, 294
    Two Meatballs debate, 288–89
    "Ugly but Good" Cookies, 291
    Warm Chocolate Pudding Cakes,
        295
double-cooking, 28

eggplant:
    Antonio's Neapolitan Lasagne, 60–61
    Parmigiana, My Way, 234–35
    Pasta with Sausage and, 82
    Whole Wheat Pasta with Roasted
        Vegetables, 78
eggs, 93
    Fresh Pasta Dough, 94–95

Frittata with Pancetta and Onion
    Ragu, 74
Escarole, Rice with, 137
Espresso Panna Cotta, 301; illus., 300
Estelle's Chicken Soup, 28–29

Fagiolini in Umido, 276
farfalle:
    with Heirloom Tomato Sauce, 120
    illus., 102
Farfalle al Telefono, 120
farro, 132, 135; illus., 69
    and Barley Salad, Grilled Tuna with,
        179
    and Bean Soup Lucca-Style, 19
    with Button Mushrooms, Cherry
        Tomatoes, and Goat Cheese, 147
    Cooked Risotto-Style, 141; illus., 140
    Meat Loaf, 55
    "Panzanella," 269
Farro e Fagioli alla Lucchese, 19
farrotto:
    con Funghi, Pomodorini, e Formaggio,
        147
    al Pepolino, 141
Fegatini di Pollo alla Griglia con
    Cavolfiore, 214
Fellini, Federico, 91
fennel:
    and Leek Gratin, 279
    Roasted Wild Salmon with, 173
    Shrimp in Blood Orange Marinade
        with, 247
    Three-Bean Salad with Orange and,
        283
fettuccini:
    with Butter and Cheese, 108
    Carbonara, 104–5; illus., 105, 106–7
    illus., 101
fettuccini:
    al Burro e Parmigiano, 108
    alla Carbonara, 104–5
Fillabozzi, Maria, 10, 90–91, 118, 258
fish and shellfish, 147–79
    Baked Clams Coco Pazzo, 170
    Broiled Calamari, 155; illus., 156–57
    Cod and Yukon Gold Gratin, 175;
        illus., 174
    Cod in Parchment, 176
    Court Bouillon, 164–65
    Fillet of Sole Milanese, 177

Fisherman's-Style White Risotto, 143
Fish Stock, 160
Grilled Tuna with Farro and Barley
    Salad, 179
Halibut with Mushrooms, 168
Mixed Grilled Seafood, 217; illus., 216
Mussels and Clams with Green
    Sauce, 215
Octopus Baked in Its Juice with
    Warm Potato Salad, 169
Oven-Roasted Grouper with Yukon
    Gold Potatoes, 162–63
Oven-Roasted Salmon on Savoy
    Cabbage, 166; illus., 167
Pan-Seared Swordfish Steaks, 172
Risotto with Shellfish, 142
Roasted Wild Salmon with Fennel,
    173
Sicilian Couscous, 159–60; illus., 158
Sicilian Tuna Salad, 178
Spicy Shrimp Scampi, 171
Steamed Halibut Fillets with Sweet
    Pepper, Cucumber, and Basil
    Vinaigrette, 164–65
Tuscan Fish Stew, 154
Tuscan Seafood Sauté, 161
Two Meatballs debate, 151–53
Fisherman's-Style White Risotto, 143
flour, 93, 305
Fred's, New York, 28, 211, 284
Fred's Autumn Salad, 275
Fred's Sliced Shell Steak Salad, 211
Fred's Spaghetti, 112; illus., 113
Frisée, Baby Back Ribs with
    Cucumbers and, 206
Frittata all'Amatriciana, 74
Frittata with Pancetta and Onion Ragu,
    74
fruits, dried, 304
Frutti di Mare in Padella, 161
Funghi alla Griglia, 212

Gamberi in Umido con Aglio e
    Peperoncino, 171
Gamberoni al Sugo di Arance e Finocchi
    Freschi, 247
game hens:
    Butterflied, with Rosemary, 219
    Mixed Grill of Lamb, Sausage and,
        218
Game Sauce, Rigatoni with, 71

Garfagnana Bean and Apple Soup, 26;
    illus., 27
gnocchi:
    Roman-Style Baked Semolina, 124–25
    with Two Mushroom Sauces, 121–23
gnocchi:
    di Patate al Sugo di Funghi, 121–23
    alla Romana, 124–25
goat cheese:
    Farro with Button Mushrooms,
        Cherry Tomatoes, and, 147
    Fred's Autumn Salad, 275
grains, 304
Gratin di Merluzzo Patate, 175
Gratin di Patate con Cipolle e Olive Nere,
    278
Gratin di Porri di Finocchio, 279
Green Sauce, Mussels and Clams with,
    215
Grigliata Mista, 218
grilling, 201–19
    about, 202–5
    Baby Back Ribs with Cucumbers and
        Frisée, 206
    Butterflied Game Hens with
        Rosemary, 219
    Chicken Livers with Cauliflower
        Ragu, 214
    Coco Pazzo's Marinated Hanger
        Steak, 207
    flare-ups, 205
    Fred's Sliced Shell Steak Salad, 211
    Grilled Mushrooms, 212
    judging doneness, 205
    Mark's Ribs, 210
    Mixed Grill of Lamb, Game Hens,
        and Sausage, 218
    Mixed Seafood, 217; illus., 216
    Mussels and Clams with Green
        Sauce, 215
    Rib-Eye Steak Served over Toasted
        Bread with Arugula, 208; illus., 209
    Stuffed Center-Cut Pork Chops, 213
    Tuna with Farro and Barley Salad, 179
    Two Meatballs debate, 203–4
Grouper, Oven-Roasted, with Yukon
    Gold Potatoes, 162–63

halibut:
    with Mushrooms, 168
    Steamed Fillets, with Sweet Pepper,

Cucumber, and Basil Vinaigrette,
    164–65
    see also ippoglosso
Ham, Fresh, Seven-Hour Roasted, with
    Yukon Gold Potatoes and Sautéed
    Peas with Mint, 253–54; illus., 255
Hanger Steak, Coco Pazzo's Grilled
    Marinated, 207
herbs, dried, 304

Il Cantinori, New York, 10, 11
insalata:
    Autunnale alla Fred, 275
    di Carciofi Crudi, 267
    di Farro, 269
    di Funghi in Padella, 274
    Romana, 268
    di Tonno, 178
    ai Tre Fagioli, 283
Involtini di Manzo, 226–27
ippoglosso:
    ai Funghi, 168
    al Vapore con Peperoni, Cetriolo, e
        Basilico, 164–65
Italian-American cooking, 221–41
    Beef Braciole, 226–27
    Breast of Chicken, Martini-Style,
        238; illus., 236–37, 239
    Chicken Parmigiana, 233
    Eggplant Parmigiana, My Way,
        234–35
    Lobster fra Diavolo, 231; illus.,
        228–29, 230
    Two Meatballs debate, 223–25
    Veal Parmigiana, 232–33
Italian cooking:
    in changing seasons, 13
    Two Meatballs debate, 11–12

Jefferson, Thomas, 132
Jerusalem artichokes (sunchokes), 20
    Soup with Cumin, 20
Jewish-Style Fried Artichokes, 282

lamb:
    and Artichokes, Braised, with Oven-
        Roasted New Potatoes and Spring
        Onions, 251–52; illus., 250
    Braised Shoulder, 190

lamb (cont.):
  Mixed Grill of Game Hens, Sausage, and, 218
  Ragu, Pappardelle with, 109
  Shanks Braised with Savoy Cabbage, 194
lasagne:
  illus., 102
  Maria's, 118–19
  Neapolitan, Antonio's, 60–61
lasagne:
  alla Maria, 118–19
  Napoletane all'Antonio, 60–61
Leek and Fennel Gratin, 279
Le Madri, New York, 90
lentil(s):
  French le Puy, 25
  and Sausage Soup, 25
Linguine with Zucchini, Garlic, Black Olives, and Toasted Bread Crumbs, 81; illus., 80
linguine:
  Integrali all'Ortolana, 78
  con Zucchine e Pangrattato, 81
lobster(s):
  fra Diavolo, 231; illus., 228–29, 230
  Mixed Grilled Seafood, 217; illus., 216

Maccheroni con Melanzane e Salsicce, 82
mandoline, 85
Maraschino Sauce, Oranges with, 301
Maria's Lasagne, 118–19
Mark's Mom's Meat Loaf Revisited, 49
Mark's Ribs, 210
Marriage Soup, Neapolitan, 30
meat, 181–98
  Braised Beef with Porcini Mushrooms, 188–89
  Braised Lamb Shoulder, 190
  Braised Veal Gargano-Style, 191
  Braised Whole Veal Shanks with Rigatoni, 192–93; illus., 193
  Lamb Shanks Braised with Savoy Cabbage, 194
  Pork Loin with Orange Sauce, 197; illus., 196
  Rabbit Braised in White Wine and Herbs, 198
  Sausage and Cranberry Beans with Polenta, 195

Tuscan Pot Roast, 187; illus., 186
Two Meatballs debate, 182–85
meatballs, 35–61
  with Amaretti, 59
  Antonio's Neapolitan Lasagne, 60–61
  Fresh Pasta with Mushrooms and, 52; illus., 53
  Mark's method, illus., 44–45
  Neapolitan Marriage Soup, 30
  Pan-Fried, 40, 42; illus., 41
  Pino's method, illus., 50–51
  in a Quick Tomato Sauce, 42
  rolling, 48
  Sandwiches, 42
  seasoning of, 48
  with Spaghetti Coco Pazzo, 47–48; illus., 46
  Turkey, in Spicy Tomato Sauce, 57–58; illus., 56
  Two Meatballs debate, 36–39
  Veal, with Green Apple, 43
  see also polpettine
meat loaf:
  Farro, 55
  Mark's Mom's, Revisited, 49
  Pino's, 54
  see also polpettone
Melanzane al Modo Mio, 234–35
Merluzzo al Cartoccio, 176
minestra:
  Maritata, 30
  di Topinambur con il Cumino, 20
  di Zucchine e Ricotta, 24
Mixed Grilled Seafood, 217; illus., 216
Mixed Grill of Lamb, Game Hens, and Sausage, 218
Mortadella and Asparagus, Cannelloni with, 117
mushroom(s):
  Button, Cherry Tomatoes, and Goat Cheese, Farro with, 147
  Chopped Roman Salad, 268
  Cream Sauce, 123
  dried, 304
  Fred's Spaghetti, 112; illus., 113
  Fresh Pasta with Meatballs and, 52; illus., 53
  Grilled, 212
  Halibut with, 168
  Porcini, Braised Beef with, 188–89
  Rabbit Braised in White Wine and Herbs, 198

Risotto, 146
Soup from Maremma, 21
Two Sauces, Gnocchi with, 121–23
Warm Salad, 274
Wild, Sauce, 123
mussels:
  and Clams with Green Sauce, 215
  Fisherman's-Style White Risotto, 143
  Oven-Roasted Grouper with Yukon Gold Potatoes, 162–63
  Risotto with Shellfish, 142
  Sicilian Couscous, 159–60; illus., 158
  Tuscan Fish Stew, 154
  Tuscan Seafood Sauté, 161

"Naked" Ravioli with Walnuts, Sage, and Butter, 126
Neapolitan Cheesecake, 296, 298; illus., 297
Neapolitan Lasagne, Antonio's, 60–61
Neapolitan Marriage Soup, 30
nuts, 304

octopus:
  Baked in Its Juice with Warm Potato Salad, 169
  Mixed Grilled Seafood, 217; illus., 216
  Sicilian Couscous, 159–60; illus., 158
olive oils, 304
onion(s):
  and Pancetta Ragu, Bucatini with, 73–74
  Potato Gratin with Black Olives and, 278
  Spring, and New Potatoes, Oven-Roasted, Braised Lamb and Artichokes with, 251–52; illus., 250
  Tagliolini with Chicken Livers and, 115
  and Tomato Sauce, Spaghetti with, 75
orange(s):
  Blood, Marinade, Shrimp with Fennel in, 247
  and Campari Sauce, Panna Cotta with, 299
  and Carrot Sauce, Fresh Carrot and Ricotta Ravioli with, 110–11
  -Carrot Soup, 23; illus., 22

with Maraschino Sauce, 301
Sauce, Pork Loin with, 197; illus., 196
Three-Bean Salad with Fennel and, 283
Osteria Vecchio Castello, Montalcino, Italy, 124

pancetta, 74, 303–4; illus., 72
and Onion Ragu, Bucatini with, 73–74
Pan-Fried Meatballs, 40, 42; illus., 41
panna cotta:
Espresso, 301; illus., 300
with Orange and Campari Sauce, 299
Panna Cotta al Campari, 299
Panna Cotta con Espresso, 301
pantry, 302–5
bread crumbs, 303
cheese, 303
chicken broth, 303
cured pork products, 303–4
dried beans, 303
dried fruits and nuts, 304
dried herbs, 304
dried mushrooms, 304
dried pasta, 304
flour and other grains, 305
olive oils, 304
preserved items, 305
rice, 305
salt, 305
spices, 305
tomatoes, 305
vinegar, 305
pappardelle:
illus., 101
with Lamb Ragu, 109
Pappardelle al Sugo di Agnello, 109
parsnips:
Roasted Turnips and, 257
and Turnips, Roasted, Crown Roast of Veal with Gruyère Potatoes and, 256–57
pasta, dried, 63–85, 304; illus., 68–69
Antonio's Neapolitan Lasagne, 60–61
Baked Penne with Radicchio and Sausage, 76; illus., 77
Bucatini with Pancetta and Onion Ragu, 73–74
checking doneness of, 66
with Eggplant and Sausage, 82

Italian numbering system for, 83
Linguine with Zucchini, Garlic, Black Olives, and Toasted Bread Crumbs, 81; illus., 80
Meatballs with Spaghetti Coco Pazzo, 47–48; illus., 46
Penne with Veal and Sage Sauce, 83
Rigatoni with Butcher's Sauce, 70
Rigatoni with Game Sauce, 71
and sauces, 67, 88
serving, 67
Spaghetti with Clams and Zucchini, 85
Spaghetti with Onion and Tomato Sauce, 75
Taranto-Style Cavatelli with Cauliflower and Broccoli, 84
Two Meatballs debate, 65–67
Whole Wheat Pasta with Roasted Vegetables, 78
Whole Wheat Penne in a Spicy, Garlicky Tomato Sauce, 79
pasta, fresh 87–129; illus., 101, 102
approximate sizes, 100
Cannelloni with Asparagus and Mortadella, 117
cooking, 100, 103
equipment for, 92–93
Farfalle with Heirloom Tomato Sauce, 120
Fettuccine Carbonara, 104–5; illus., 105, 106–7
Fettuccine with Butter and Cheese, 108
Fred's Spaghetti, 112; illus., 113
Fresh Carrot and Ricotta Ravioli with Carrot and Orange Sauce, 110–11
Fresh Egg Pasta Dough, 94–95
getting ready, 92–93
Gnocchi with Two Mushroom Sauces, 121–23
ingredients, 93
kneading dough by hand, 92, 94–95; illus., 96–97
kneading dough with stand mixer, 92, 95
Maria's Lasagne, 118–19
with Meatballs and Mushrooms, 52; illus., 53
"Naked" Ravioli with Walnuts, Sage, and Butter, 126

Pappardelle with Lamb Ragu, 109
Ribollita-Filled Ravioli, 116
rolling and cutting dough by hand, 92, 98; illus., 99
rolling and cutting dough with hand-cranked machine, 93, 99–100; illus., 99
Roman-Style Baked Semolina Gnocchi, 124–25
and sauce, 88
Scialatielli with Roasted Peppers and Cherry Tomatoes, 127–29
serving, 120
storing, 100
Tagliolini with Chicken Livers and Onion, 115
Tagliolini with Sweet Sausage and Black Truffle, 114
Two Meatballs debate, 90–91
Pasta alla Chitarra con Polpettine ai Funghi, 52; illus., 53
Patatine Fritte, 284
pears:
with Sheep's-Milk Cheese and Honey, 294
in Vin Santo with Sweet Polenta, 293; illus., 292
peas:
Fresh Pasta with Meatballs and Mushrooms, 52; illus., 53
Sautéed, with Mint, 254; illus., 255
Sautéed, with Mint, Seven-Hour Roasted Fresh Ham with Yukon Gold Potatoes and, 253–54; illus., 255
Worker's Farmhouse Soup, 32–33
Pecorino Romano, Risotto with Sausage, Red Wine, Olives, and, 136
penne:
Baked, with Radicchio and Sausage, 76; illus., 77
farro, illus., 68
rigate (whole wheat), illus., 68
with Veal and Sage Sauce, 83
Whole Wheat, in a Spicy, Garlicky Tomato Sauce, 79
penne:
Integrali all'Arrabbiata, 79
Pasticciate, 76
con Sugo di Vitello e Salvia, 83

pennette, illus., 68
Peperoni Sauce, 129
pepper(s):
    Roasted, Scialatielli with Cherry
        Tomatoes and, 127–29
    and Sausage, 240
    Sweet, Steamed Halibut Fillets with
        Cucumber, Basil Vinaigrette, and,
        164–65
Pere al Vin Santo con Polenta Dolce,
    293
Pere con Caciotta e Miele, 294
Pesce Spada alla Pizzaiola, 172
Pesto, 33
Petto di Pollo alla Martini, 238
Petto di Pollo alla Parmigiana, 233
Pino's Meat Loaf, 54
polenta, 261
    Sausage and Cranberry Beans with,
        195
    Sweet, Pears in Vin Santo with, 293;
        illus., 292
    for the Whole Family, Chicken
        Cacciatore, and Beef in Brunello,
        260–61
Polletti Schiacciati al Rosmarino, 219
Pollini, Marta, 91
Pollo alla Scarpariello, 199
Pollo Arrosto al Sale, 241
polpettine:
    in Bianco, 40, 42
    di Carne e Mele, 43
    Sfiziose, 59
    con Spaghetti, 47–48
    di Tacchino in Salsa Piccante, 57–58
    in Umido, 42
polpettone:
    con farro, 55
    della Mamma, 49
    alla Pino, 54
Polpo al Forno con Insalata di Patate,
    169
pork:
    Baby Back Ribs with Cucumbers
        and Frisée, 206
    cured, 303–4
    Grilled Stuffed Center-Cut Chops,
        213
    Loin with Orange Sauce, 197; illus.,
        196
    Maria's Lasagne, 118–19
    Mark's Ribs, 210

Meatballs with Spaghetti Coco
    Pazzo, 47–48; illus., 46
Neapolitan Marriage Soup, 30
Seven-Hour Roasted Fresh Ham
    with Yukon Gold Potatoes and
    Sautéed Peas with Mint, 253–54;
    illus., 255
potato(es):
    Baked, and Truffles, and Prime Rib
        with Creamed Spinach or Cheese
        for Kids, 248–49
    Belgian Fries, 284; illus., 285
    Cod and Yukon Gold Gratin, 175;
        illus., 174
    Gnocchi with Two Mushroom
        Sauces, 121–23
    Gratin with Onions and Black Olives,
        278
    Gruyère, 257
    Gruyère, Crown Roast of Veal with
        Roasted Turnips and Parsnips and,
        256–57
    New, and Spring Onions, Oven-
        Roasted, Braised Lamb and
        Artichokes with, 251–52; illus., 250
    Rabbit Braised in White Wine and
        Herbs, 198
    Roasted Yukon Gold, 254; illus., 255
    Warm Salad, Octopus Baked in Its
        Juice with, 169
    Worker's Farmhouse Soup, 32–33
    Yukon Gold, Oven-Roasted Grouper
        with, 162–63
    Yukon Gold, Seven-Hour Roasted
        Fresh Ham with Sautéed Peas with
        Mint and, 253–54; illus., 255
poultry, about, 185
preserved items, 204
Prime Rib with Creamed Spinach and
    Baked Potatoes and Truffles or
    Cheese for Kids, 248–49
Prosciutto Cotto per Sette Ore con Patate
    e Piselli con Menta, 253–54

Quail, Risotto with, 138

rabbit, 185
    Braised in White Wine and Herbs,
        198
    Rigatoni with Game Sauce, 71

radicchio:
    Baked Penne with Sausage and, 76;
        illus., 77
    Chopped Roman Salad, 268
ravioli:
    Fresh Carrot and Ricotta, with Carrot
        and Orange Sauce, 110–11
    "Naked," with Walnuts, Sage, and
        Butter, 126
    Ribollita-Filled, 116
ravioli:
    di Carote al Sugo d'Arancia, 110–11
    Nudi con Noci e Salvia al Burro, 126
    con Ribollita al Pomodoro e
        Parmigiano, 116
reheating, 185
resources, 306–7
Rib-Eye Steak, Grilled, Served over
    Toasted Bread with Arugula, 208;
    illus., 209
ribollita, 31
    -Filled Ravioli, 116
Ribs, Mark's, 210
rice, 305
    Arborio, 131
    with Escarole, 137
    see also risotto
ricotta cheese, 126
    and Carrot, Fresh, Ravioli with
        Carrot and Orange Sauce, 110–11
    Neapolitan Cheesecake, 296, 298;
        illus., 297
    and Zucchini Soup, 24
rigatoni:
    Braised Whole Veal Shanks with,
        192–93; illus., 193
    with Butcher's Sauce, 70
    with Game Sauce, 71
    mezzi-rigatoni #20, illus., 69
rigatoni:
    alla Cacciatora, 71
    del Macellaio, 70
Riso con la Scarola, 137
risotto, 132–33
    Cakes, 138
    Farro Cooked in Style of, 141; illus.,
        140
    with Green and White Asparagus,
        144; illus., 145
    Mushroom, 146
    Pizza-Maker-Style, 139
    with Quail, 138

with Sausage, Red Wine, Olives, and
    Pecorino Romano, 136
with Shellfish, 142
Two Meatballs debate, 133, 135
White, Fisherman's-Style, 143
risotto:
    con Asparagi, 144; illus., 145
    ai Funghi, 146
    alla Marinara, 142
    alla Pescatora in Bianco, 143
    del Pizzaiolo, 139
    con Quaglie, 138
    con Salsiccia Ubriaca, 136
Roman Chopped Salad, 268
Roman-Style Baked Semolina Gnocchi,
    124–25
Rosemary, Butterflied Game Hens
    with, 219
Rosticciana con Cetrioli e Riccia, 206

sage:
    and Veal Sauce, Penne with, 83
    Walnuts, and Butter, "Naked" Ravioli
        with, 126
salads:
    Autumn, Fred's, 275
    Baby Back Ribs with Cucumbers
        and Frisée, 206
    Broiled Calamari, 155; illus.,
        156–57
    Caesar, 272–73; illus., 270–71,
        273
    Chopped Roman, 268
    Farro and Barley, Grilled Tuna with,
        179
    Farro "Panzanella," 269
    Fillet of Sole Milanese, 177
    Fred's Sliced Shell Steak, 211
    Raw Artichoke, 267
    Sicilian Tuna, 178
    Three-Bean, with Orange and
        Fennel, 283
    Warm Mushroom, 274
    Warm Potato, Octopus Baked in Its
        Juice with, 169
salmon:
    Oven-Roasted, on Savoy Cabbage,
        166; illus., 167
    Wild, Roasted, with Fennel, 173
salmone:
    Arrosto con Finocchi, 173

Arrosto con la Verza, 166
Salsiccia e Fagioli in Umido con Polenta,
    195
salt, 305
Salt-Cured Roast Chicken alla
    Centolire, 241
sandwiches:
    leftover Veal Parmigiana, 233
    Meatball, 42
Sapore di Mare, East Hampton, New
    York, 10, 12, 19, 90, 152, 258
Sarazin, Mark, 10
sauces:
    Américaine, 284
    Basil Vinaigrette, Steamed Halibut
        Fillets with Sweet Pepper,
        Cucumber, and, 164–65
    Béchamel, 118–19
    Blood Orange Marinade, Shrimp in,
        with Fennel, 247
    Butcher's, Rigatoni with, 70
    Carrot and Orange, Fresh Carrot and
        Ricotta Ravioli with, 110–11
    Cauliflower Ragu, Grilled Chicken
        Livers with, 214
    Court Bouillon, 164–65
    degreasing, 185
    Game, Rigatoni with, 71
    Green, Mussels and Clams with, 215
    Lamb Ragu, Pappardelle with, 109
    Maraschino, Oranges with, 301
    Meat, for Lasagna, 118–19
    Mushroom Cream, 123
    Onion and Tomato, Spaghetti with, 75
    Orange, Pork Loin with, 197; illus.,
        196
    Orange and Campari, Panna Cotta
        with, 299
    Pancetta and Onion Ragu, Bucatini
        with, 73–74
    Peperoni, 129
    Veal and Sage, Penne with, 83
    Wild Mushroom, 123
    see also tomato sauces; *specific
        recipes*
sausage, 185
    Baked Penne with Radicchio and, 76;
        illus., 77
    Cannelloni with Asparagus and
        Mortadella, 117
    and Cranberry Beans with Polenta,
        195

and Lentil Soup, 25
Meatballs with Spaghetti Coco
    Pazzo, 47–48; illus., 46
Mixed Grill of Lamb, Game Hens,
    and, 218
Pan-Fried Meatballs, 40, 42; illus.,
    41
Pasta with Eggplant and, 82
and Peppers, 240
Pino's Meat Loaf, 54
Rigatoni with Butcher's Sauce, 70
Risotto with Red Wine, Olives,
    Pecorino Romano, and, 136
Sweet, Tagliolini with Black Truffle
    and, 114
scallops:
    Fisherman's-Style White Risotto, 143
    Mixed Grilled Seafood, 217; illus.,
        216
    Sicilian Couscous, 159–60; illus., 158
    Tuscan Seafood Sauté, 161
Scampi, Spicy Shrimp, 171
Scialatielli con Peperoni e Pomodorini,
    127–29
Scialatielli with Roasted Peppers and
    Cherry Tomatoes, 127–29
semolina, 124
Seven-Hour Roasted Fresh Ham with
    Yukon Gold Potatoes and Sautéed
    Peas with Mint, 253–54; illus., 255
shellfish. *See* fish and shellfish
Shell Steak, Sliced, Fred's Salad, 211
shrimp:
    in Blood Orange Marinade with
        Fennel, 247
    Caesar Salad, 273
    Fisherman's-Style White Risotto, 143
    Mixed Grilled Seafood, 217; illus.,
        216
    Risotto with Shellfish, 142
    Sicilian Couscous, 159–60; illus., 158
    Spicy Scampi, 171
    Tuscan Seafood Sauté, 161
Sicilian Couscous, 159–60; illus., 158
Sicilian Tuna Salad, 178
Sogliola alla Milanese, 177
Sole, Fillet Milanese, 177
soups, 15–33
    Carrot-Orange, 23; illus., 22
    Chicken, Estelle's, 28–29
    Chicken Stock, 29
    Farro and Bean, Lucca-Style, 19